Ethics is a Daily Deal

Leslie E. Sekerka

Ethics is a Daily Deal

Choosing to Build Moral Strength as a Practice

 Springer

Leslie E. Sekerka
Menlo College
Pacific Grove, CA
USA

Cited Material: Credits and acknowledgements for materials cited or reproduced are noted throughout the book, as prescribed by copyright instructions.

ISBN 978-3-319-18089-2   ISBN 978-3-319-18090-8   (eBook)
DOI 10.1007/978-3-319-18090-8

Library of Congress Control Number: 2015948774

Springer Cham Heidelberg New York Dordrecht London

Printed on acid-free paper

Springer International Publishing AG Switzerland is part of Springer Science+Business Media (www.springer.com)

Acknowledgements

This book is a result of my mother insisting that it needed to be written. Mom (Lucy Sekerka) supplied infinite inspirational support. She has also been a steadfast editorial assistant, helping to ensure that drafts always continued to improve—one sentence at a time. Additional thanks go to friends and family; specifically, John Arquilla, Rick Bagozzi, Adam Bangert, Julie Carpenter, Elizabeth Gerhardt Coffee, Debbie Comer, Lindsey Godwin, William Jenkins, John Jenkins, Leonard Jenkins, Jennifer Harris Kraly, Tracey Messer, Thomas Plante, José Rosa, Sandy Sanders, Brian Sheppard, and Dana Tomasino. Each person, in their own way, has shared unique insight, wisdom, expertise, and optimism, fortifying the project's progression. Additionally, comments made by scholars in the blind peer-review process offered helpful feedback, which were used to further develop and improve the manuscript. Special thanks also go to members of the James Hervey Johnson Charitable Educational Trust. Their sponsorship of the Menlo College *Ethics in Action Research and Education Center* made continued scholarship possible. To my peers at Menlo College and Santa Clara University's Markkula Center for Applied Ethics, a heartfelt note of thanks for your sustained interest in advancing ethics as a foundational core of business. Finally, this work is dedicated to my dad, James Sekerka. He would have been proud to see this book. Then, he would have smiled and laughed.

Contents

Chapter 1
What Makes You Tick?

Learning to be an ethical person is a process that is never finalized. Human beings are malleable and have an innate ability to evolve. As adults we can choose to continue to learn, grow, and change. But deliberately or by default, we may come to rely upon our automatic reactions to guide our daily lives. Many of us are simply unaware that we have the capacity for moral deterioration or growth. Environment or context can influence our perceptions, which, in turn impact how much value we place on being ethical. Being responsible in the workplace means cultivating habits that consistently incorporate personal and organizational values into daily decisions, even when it is difficult to do so. While most people say they value goodness and have a desire to do the right thing, this does not necessarily mean they engage in behaviors that match this belief. We may truly value being honest and responsible. But without focused attention and a sustained effort, such intentions may stagnate and potentially regress, weakening the resolve to exercise and actualize the values we profess to hold.

It is possible to become more ethical at any age. That is, if you have a desire to do so and are willing to be honest with yourself about who you are. Having such a desire, however, goes beyond a simple yearning or forming an aspirational goal. It requires a sincere and persistent effort, along with practice, throughout our everyday lives. The human capacity for cognitive dexterity means that although people habituate familiar or repeated thoughts, feelings and actions, they can also choose to modify them. If we want to build routines that support moral strength, or establish new ones, it requires a personal commitment and sustained effort. It means you choose to cultivate the willingness for taking ownership of your ongoing adult moral development. Your ethical character can continue to be shaped, reinforced, and influenced by the decisions you make, each and every day. Underneath these decisions is a platform, the foundation for your ethical potential as a human being. This stage serves as the basis for becoming, acting out if you will, your best ethical self. To better understand this concept, let us consider what resides within your core character. My hope is that this book will roust the potential for greater moral strength in all of us.

© Springer International Publishing Switzerland 2016
L. E. Sekerka, *Ethics is a Daily Deal*, DOI 10.1007/978-3-319-18090-8_1

Ethics and Morality

The word "ethics" comes from both Latin *ēthicus* and Greek *ἠθικός* terms referring to the word "character" (*Oxford English Dictionary* 2013). Ethics is often used more broadly to describe the philosophy of human conduct; specifically, the determination of right and wrong behavior. "Ethics" also refers to the study of moral beliefs and the choices derived from them. This involves the examination of individual, cultural, group, and/or professional values and principles that shape the motivations for ethical or "right" action. Personal moral values are codified principles that help people establish the boundaries of ethical behavior. Having "morals" refers to excellence of character or disposition, distinguished from intellectual excellence or theological virtue. In short, to be ethical means you live the moral values you say you hold.

As an adjective, the word "moral" describes one's character and the ethical behavior associated with a person's thoughts and actions. Your morality is associated with, and relates to, that which is considered "good" or "bad." If a person is moral, they have an ability to make a distinction between right and wrong, as it pertains to the actions, desires, or character of a responsible human being. Being ethical or moral often requires the subordination of some values over others (Bagozzi et al. 2013). This effort calls for an ability to be aware and impose self-governance. Self-governance helps a person manage their temptations and control their personal desires that can intervene and distract movement toward doing the "right" thing. One way of looking at your own ethicality is as a process of thinking through your values and determining appropriate choices given the circumstances. Seeking out the ethical concerns within a situation is quite different than waiting for an issue to emerge and then addressing it.

The two terms, ethics and morals, are often used interchangeably. In business, ethics typically refers to compliance or adherence to legal requirements, whereas morality refers to exercising character or virtue, living your personal and organizational values. Taken together, ethics and morals refer to the application of right thoughts and actions that have universal acceptance as values of goodness—reflecting respect for all living things (Kinnier et al. 2000). As an independent agent, the determination of what is the best right action in any given situation is ultimately decided by you. Your personal lens or vantage point is informed and colored by what you have been exposed to and influenced by, which shapes your operational framework for how you interpret and make sense of ethical issues.

The concept of moral responsibility has been addressed and discussed among philosophers for centuries. Theorists recognize that features of moral responsibility include attitudes and emotions, their outward expression in censure or praise, and the imposition of corresponding sanctions or rewards. Historically, moral responsibility is centered on two broad interpretations. There is a merit-based view (praise or blame towards a person if he/she merits [deserves] it) and a consequentialist view (praise or blame if the action is likely to lead to a desired change in behavior). A consideration of moral responsibility in modern society (over the past 50 years) has increasingly focused on offering alternative versions of the merit-based view and questioning the assumption that there is a single unified concept (*Stanford Encyclopedia of Philosophy* 2009). In fact, the emphasis on praise and blame in organizational settings has been shown to result in a dysfunctional working environment, one that actually inhibits honest and open accounting (Anderson 2009). An examination of accountability, transparency, and stakeholder considerations has become a compelling focus of management scholars as they look at the intersection of moral responsibility and business enterprise. To support the responsibility of ethics in the workplace, research suggests we need policies and systems that reward moral strength and develop moral courage (Comer and Vega 2011).

Adult Moral Development Is a Choice

On some level, a person's ethical character is reflected by the choices they make over the course of their lifetime. Since much of our lives are spent at work (around 30 % or nearly twenty-five years), it really matters how we go about achieving our goals. We co-create the ethical identity of our organizations, but so too does the workplace influence our own ethicality. The good news is that the beauty and elegance of humanity is in our ability to continue to learn at any time, at any point in our lives. Regardless of your circumstances, no matter what you have encountered, how you were raised, the type or amount of education you have received, and whatever level of success you have mastered (or failures you have encountered), as creatures of adaptation we are all works in progress. Nevertheless, many of us tend to think that once we are adults, our moral development is complete. This is simply not true.

With every experiential encounter we add to a repertoire of takeaway lessons, core learnings from our daily observations, engagements and activities. Outcomes of our behavioral actions may affirm that being ethical or "good" is the right thing to do. But that's not always the case. Through positive and negative reinforcement, especially from people we look up to, admire, or are influenced by (both good and bad), most of us learn to do the right thing and to steer clear of trouble. But we may also learn that being unethical offers advantages. Let's face it, people cheat and engage in unethical activities because they often receive benefits from doing so.

And yet, while cheaters may experience momentary gains, over time, a lack of ethics usually costs them something in the end. This may be the erosion of personal character (or perhaps worse). Experiences of applying your best moral self, or the lack of doing so, shape the relevance of your being ethical. Said differently, the perceived value of being ethical can vary, depending upon past encounters and what is going on in your life right now. At some point, most people recognize that the choices they make ultimately shape and reflect their core identity. You can postpone looking in the mirror honestly for only so long. In the end, unethical actions catch up with you. This may not be overt, in terms of the law. But it may cost you relationships, health, and a sense of well-being and inner happiness. At the end of the day, being unethical has a toll.

Placing a value on what we care about, consciously or not, our thoughts and actions tend to prioritize and enact what is most relevant and important to us. Given the circumstances, situation and a host of other variables, some values move ahead in line (in terms of priority), while others may regress or fade. Depending upon the level of commitment or conviction we have towards a particular value, it may or may not be expressed within the choices we make throughout the day. And these choices (to favor or ignore a value) are often favorably influenced by an ability to self-regulate (Sekerka and Bagozzi 2007; Bagozzi, Sekerka, and Hill 2009). While one's background and experience set the stage for assuming responsible decision-making efforts, in some respects a choice to impose self-regulation is a central feature of a person's day-to-day ethicality.

This possibility for you to engage in moral strength remains open and available for continuous development throughout your lifespan. You have a choice to regulate your desires and fears, and to redirect your energies toward achieving a difficult ethical act—or to do otherwise. Some people ignore thinking about their ethical potential altogether. It is important to recognize that responsibility through self-regulated decision-making is at the center of your moral self. At any given moment the best in you, your ethical character, can be energized and further enhanced. Or, conversely, you may become distracted and thrown off course, aborting, abandoning or ignoring the values you say you hold. Most people have the power to determine their course of action, establishing and controlling their ethical identity—to impose or blind the capacity for self-correction—throughout their day. Are you choosing to be aware of who you are by paying attention to your choices? Do you work at exercising your ethical identity in the choices you make throughout your day? Have you made a decision to be aware of and self-correct your unethical self when you go off course?

A person's free will is expressed in the conscious awareness of the choices they make, which presumably reflect what they value most (in that moment). Whether or not you make your choices with deliberate conscious thought is influenced by your past experiences and actions as well as by what you value most in the here and now. This may be expressed as caring for friends or loved ones, being a part of a group, accomplishing a task, fulfilling a desire, or gaining money, power, or status. How you apply your values is actually a process of prioritization as you work to accomplish your daily objectives (getting up, getting to work, doing your work, running errands, etc.). We all make choices to ignore or pay attention to moral responsibility, to look for the ethical elements within a situation, and make informed mindful actions. The decision to be ethical is one that is largely within your control. Your behavior is, in a nutshell, a manifestation of votes for what you care about most. Whether you think about it consciously or not, how you approach your work and act toward coworkers reflects your moral character at work.

Reality is shaped and influenced by perceptions. Sometimes individuals package themselves according to their professional context. For example, in dealing with clients you might present yourself a bit differently than you might with peers. Similarly, we might wrap our ethical identity with astute awareness and keen sensibilities, or we might do so with more casual regard (or even disregard). Failure to address and attend to ethics, both perceived and real, can be a source of moral vulnerability. If we choose (consciously or not) to avoid, overlook, forget or ignore the importance of morality in self-management, ethical issues can easily emerge and fester. Before realizing it, you or your organization can become embroiled in a full-blown ethical crisis. Let's take for example the recall issues at Toyota and General Motors [GM]) (Piotrowski and Guyette 2010).

In March of 2015 the U.S. Justice Department investigators identified criminal wrongdoing in GM's failure to disclose a defect tied to at least 104 deaths. While the settlement was negotiated, it was expected to eclipse the $1.2 billion paid in 2014 by Toyota, a firm that concealed the unintended acceleration problems within its vehicles (Vlasic and Appozo 2014). In the Toyota case, a four-year investigation concluded that the firm intentionally hid information about safety defects from the public and made deceptive statements to protect its brand and image (Fig. 1.1). With GM's eagerness to resolve their recall investigation—a strategy different from Toyota—they received so-called cooperation credit (according to *The New York Times*, see Ivory, Protess and Vlasic 2015). This ultimately helped to reduce their penalties, which sends mixed signals to the public and other corporate leaders and their duty to make ethical decisions.

If we expect individuals to assume responsibility for the choices they make in corporate settings, people must be held personally accountable. But as described by Henning (2015), the prosecution of corporate misconduct laments that the law imposes such a high threshold to proving individual culpability for corporate decisions, it is impossible to prove criminal responsibility. So although the GM settlement points out the culpable roles played by various individuals inside the firm, none are likely to ever face criminal prosecution (some people were, however, fired). These types of moral failures in manufacturing suggest that many firms possess structures, cultures, and processes that fail to support ongoing moral development. If management and organizational members were encouraged to pause and question the choices being made, to look for potential ethical weaknesses, and were rewarded for doing so, perhaps these issues can be avoided or mitigated in the future.

Toyota and GM are not alone, as more vehicles were recalled in the United States in 2014 than ever before (new and old models combined). While the complexity of automotive vehicle manufacturing has intensified with computer-driven processes, this is no excuse for putting products on the market that may cause danger or potentially jeopardize the lives of consumers. Compounding the problem is when executives choose to withhold information from the public, when they suspect a problem. Corporate siloing and cultures that lack communication cross-functionally end up supporting limited ownership of personal responsibility. As described by Henning, GM seemed to "prize inaction and deflection" (2015).

Worse yet, we see businesses employing deceit as part of their strategic plan. Case in point, the recall of 11 million Volkswagen vehicles designed to cheat emission standards. This scandal is one of global proportion, as it caught this automobile manufacturer in an unprecedented scheme to promote clean technology while apparently doing the exact opposite. Billions of dollars in market value were

Fig. 1.1 In 2012 Toyota announced the recall of 7.43 million vehicles worldwide. Image of a Toyota Camry LE (2009) is in the public domain, courtesy of IFCAR. In the U.S., the recall affected MY 2005–2010 Yaris, Corolla, Matrix, Camry, RAV4, Highlander, Tundra and Sequoia as well as Scion xB and xD

destroyed (20% of the firm's value) when initial charges were announced by the U.S. Environmental Protection Agency in "Dieselgate" (CNN Money 2015). Volkswagen AG was forced to embark on one of the biggest recalls in European automotive history, with repair costs serving as only part of what the firm will spend to get through a corporate crisis. The company is also compensating dealers for storing cars they can't sell. They face more than 325 consumer lawsuits in the U.S., and the costs of internal investigations into the company's actions. The fines, settlements with the U.S. Environmental Protection Agency, state authorities, the Justice Department and dozens of countries in Europe forecast that the firm's costs may exceed 30 billion euros ($34 billion), according to the Center of Automotive Management in Bergisch Gladbach, Germany. This problem traces back to some point in time, a moment a few years back, when a person within management decided that cheating the system was a good idea. Despite current protestations before the U.S. Congress, it is hard to believe that executives at the firm knew nothing about it (Plungis and Katz 2015) (Fig. 1.2). Someone made a choice, a decision to move ahead with an unethical and amoral plan.

In the workplace, when management actions are perceived as less than ethical, there is a lack of moral diligence, or there is out and out unethical behavior. This sends a negative message to employees, customers, and stakeholders at large. Regardless of intent, this negativity is palpable and carries weight. Taking time to think about how your choices (or the lack thereof) may appear to others, can help you avoid getting caught up in self-deception, laziness, rationalizations or even denial about your part. It's important to look at the role you play in a decision or action, as even a small part (like looking away from or ignoring a potential ethical issue) can contribute to fledgling ethical rigor in the moment, which can snowball down the line. In the heat of business competition, multiple values, stress, and ego-laden desires can get the better of many of us, as we get engaged with the daily rigors of business. We can forget to recognize what we say and do reflect to those around us how much—or how little—we care about ethics. People listen to and

Fig. 1.2 Volkswagen AG is now embarked on one of the biggest recalls in European automotive history. Image credited to SGM/Shutterstock.com

watch one another picking up subtle cues. Regardless of your title, everyone has the potential to be a positive or negative ethical influence on others.

Those who consider themselves to be "good" often come to rely upon perceptual biases, believing they are ethical when they actually behave otherwise. The above average effect is the tendency for people to see themselves as above average on characteristics that are ambiguous and socially desirable (Myers 2002). A consistent finding in management research is that individuals tend to see themselves as more ethical than their peers, coworkers, supervisors, and others they know (Ford and Richardson 1994). And yet, many employees continue to report they feel pressured to compromise their ethical standards when performing their work (Ethics Resource Center 2011; 2012). By implication, this suggests there are organizational members who see themselves as ethical, but may not always be acting that way. Without sustained awareness and a steadfast commitment to act ethically, anyone can fall short. People can fail to live up to the best of their intentions, company codes, and/or agreed upon ethical assumptions/expectations. While the "way were raised" is an important factor in forming one's adult ethical character, it is but a stage, serving as a platform for our daily decisions.

Recall Your Childhood

As a child growing up, every experience is a first. These initial encounters are central in helping to create cognitive, affective and behavioral paths, learning what we should care about and how we ought to act in the environment we are born into. To understand what you value, you can excavate your early experiences, exposures, and surroundings to unearth your ethical core. Being from a particular culture, given the social norms established by years of tradition, shapes a personal framework for the "self." The culture bears influence on how we experience the self in the context of others, primarily as a separate or independent entity or more as an element or part of a greater collective (Hofstede 1980).

Where you grew up, your surroundings, and the history of your country, race, and ethnicity inform what you value, which contributes to forming and shaping your personal values. Were your childhood years spent in an urban area, a suburb, or maybe you were raised on a farm or ranch? Did you move around or stay in one location? How did the geographic setting and era influence your thinking, feelings, and behavior? Were certain people given more respect than others (e.g., people of a particular gender, race, or income)? Given this context, both time and place (location) in concert with those around us, we learn from our day-to-day encounters. We all come to understand what sorts of behaviors are acceptable or expected and what actions are deemed unacceptable or inappropriate. We learn what we value and what we do not, from both good and bad examples set before us. Social influences, stemming from religious or cultural traditions, further influence our early experiences and family life.

Drawing upon Bakhtinian theory, scholars have come to understand and leverage the dialogic nature of primary learning (Gardiner 1992). Researchers have applied this framework to better understand identity formation. With longitudinal studies observing child-adult play, we now know much more about how identity is initially formed. The implications of this work, generally speaking, are that ethical identity formation is a lifelong process of coauthoring, which begins in early childhood when adults join children in dramatic play. Experts in child psychology consider early play as analogous to a workshop or dress rehearsal for life, helping to prepare youngsters for the many decisions they will have to make as they grow up. Adults help children establish their ethical or moral identity through dialogic interactions as they consider multiple perspectives together during this early play period (Edmiston 2010).

Take a moment to revisit your past and reflect upon your childhood recollections. Who did you play with, what did you enjoy doing, and what are your fondest memories of play? Were examples set for you to share with others? As you grew up, were you encouraged to help others, give service, or take time to perform good deeds? Did your elders inspire you to work hard and excel or flourish in a particular subject or activity? Did faith-based traditions influence your beliefs and priorities? If you hurt someone, were you taught to be remorseful and did you apologize? Did you learn to say "please," "thank you", and "excuse me," learning to express gratitude and convey respect toward others? Our parents, neighbors, coaches, and teachers bore an influence on us in modeling how we treat the people we work with today, establishing the importance (value) of common courtesy. How we are treated by those around us when we are young can be particularly influential in forming perceptions of what we value.

A person's temperament shows up early in life. While some individuals are seemingly natural-born leaders, demonstrating relational skills early on, others may be shy, insecure, or seem different than other children. Those who are vulnerable may become the object of teasing, ridicule, exclusion, and/or bullying. Experiencing such negative encounters early on in life, being directly or indirectly ostracized, may create deep seated anger, anxiety, or resentment. Being teased can evoke deep insecurities, which can lead to reclusiveness. But negativity can also inspire resiliency, sparking determination and a desire to succeed, providing motivation to rise above trying or difficult circumstances. The personal challenges we take on in our youth serve as guideposts, potentially building our inner strength to persevere. Difficulties can also help us better understand and become aware of others, what it feels like to encounter certain challenges, which can enable us to better relate to and help support those around us (Fig. 1.3).

Developing empathy toward the concerns of others is central in becoming an ethical adult (Cojuharenco and Sguera 2014). Learning how to patiently address difficulties (Comer and Sekerka 2014) and consider the feelings of other people can fortify an inner strength and sensitivity in ethical decision-making. Such strength is needed to support moral courage in our daily adult lives—doing the right thing when an ethical challenge emerges—a circumstance that calls for moral character. But as young people, we are often tempted to engage in risky activities. The compelling lure to explore the unknown, to create a distinctive identity and separate from our parents, and/or to become accepted by a particular group is often laced with experimentation. This typically includes the use of alcohol and/or drugs, engaging in sexual activity, and stretching the moral limits, which emerge in cheating, stealing, or demonstrating other unethical choices. Taking risks for some people, at any age, is particularly enticing.

Fig. 1.3 Children learning values. Image credited to Robert Kneschke/ Shutterstock.com

The emotions we feel in the context of others, early on, also shape how we perceive ethical decision-making and moral action. Thinking about your childhood, the years you spent growing up, did you feel shame, guilt, or embarrassment when you did something wrong? Did you defy authority? Did you break the law? Did you learn from your mistakes or get away with bending the rules, fueling your desire to do so again? Did you experience pride from a job well done? Do you remember your first experiences in learning the difference between right versus wrong? What ethical incidents do you recall from your childhood and why do you think they hold particular meaning or value to you?

I can recall taking some gum by the checkout counter in the grocery store, around the age of five. When my mother asked me where I got the treat and discovered I pilfered it, she made me return it to the store manager and apologize. I felt a sense of shame and embarrassment. The experience, which was then associated with the knowledge that shoplifting is wrong and leads to dishonor, punishment, and feeling humiliated. But truthfully, I also felt a tiny bit of power and a "win." While I certainly returned the package, I believe it was minus a stick of gum. Learning to want to be ethical takes time, experiential insight is especially important. Some children need more than one experience to get the message that being unethical is not OK with others around you.

Teachable moments may have helped you begin to discern the real meaning of honesty (and dishonesty). Rather than getting into trouble, maybe you were wronged? Perhaps someone took something that belonged to you. In this case, you probably learned what it feels like to be wronged, forming an internal reminder for why we don't take things that don't belong to us. Around the age of seven, I can remember taking my brand new "Wishnik" (a troll-like doll, with long hair, popular in the 1960s) with me to the local pool one summer afternoon (Fig. 1.4). Having owned it for less than a day, it was stolen from my clothes basket. I couldn't believe it, learning with far greater impact that theft causes distress, sadness, and anger for the recipient of the crime. For me, this experience of loss brought home the wrongness of theft with much greater impact than getting caught for actually taking something (as per the chewing gum incident). For most people the feelings of shame, guilt, embarrassment and pride are social self-conscious emotions that stir right action and help deter us from unethical behavior. It was with the feeling the profound negativity of my own misfortune, due to others' unethical behavior, that elevated the lesson of being ethical. For me, the sentiments were more acute when I had been the recipient of a wrong action than being caught for wrong-doing. Think about your early experiences with theft, what brought the lesson home for you, in a memorable way?

Some children may learn to be ethical because they didn't feel like there was a choice in the matter. Others may need more convincing. But given our personalities, parenting, and/or environmental contexts, most of us eventually catch on, understanding that ethical behavior—doing the right thing—is simply the best path to take. At some point we learn that trust is essential for relationships and relationships are essential to ensure our well-being. As we grow into adolescence, and feel a need to assert our own adult identity, even with respect for authority most of

Fig. 1.4 Learning from a stolen Wishnik. Image credited to Leslie E. Sekerka; toy courtesy of Jeanne M. Pope, Alameda Point Antiques Faire

us test the limits of our own power. Despite parental forewarnings, young people often cross the line at some point, wanting to see what they can "get away" with. Again, when we do this, we garner take away lessons that shape the platform for what we value in decision-making.

The Importance of Play

In their 2009 article, Pierce and Bekoff describe the importance of understanding animal behavior, reminding us of how instinctive needs for interdependency require fair play. We all recognize that rules of right and wrong behavior underwrite human society. Prosocial acts are like support pillars, upholding and maintaining the rules of engagement in a positive way. Such behaviors include fairness, empathy, for-giveness, trust, altruism, social tolerance, integrity, and reciprocity. We have typ-ically attributed these kinds of behaviors to humans, but researchers now claim that rules that promote fairness and trust are essential for survival amongst a variety of animal species. Observing patterns of play in animals, studies show that, in many ways, these kinds of activities are similar to fair play in business.

Fig. 1.5 Animals have rules
of fair play. Image (*top*)
credited to the Good Dog
Food Store at: http://www.
gooddogfoodstore.com/2012/
07/12/good-dog-food-for-
chloe-healthy-dog-treats/.
Image (*bottom*) is in the public domain at: http://www.
pd4pic.com/dogs-play-
meadow-get-it-all.html

When animals engage in play, it's serious business. They understand and are supposed to follow mutually established rules and explicitly communicate their intentions. Painstaking analyses of videos capturing animals at play have helped researchers identify several core fundamentals of fair play interaction, stated as: be fair, ask first, be honest, follow the rules, and admit when you are wrong (for more information see Pierce and Bekoff 2009). When these rules of play are violated, fairness breaks down, and so does the business of play. For survival of the group, the goal is to prohibit cheating, which can destroy cooperation and lead to fighting (Fig. 1.5).

Growls, the showing of teeth, biting and body slamming are clues of distrust, whereas bows are signs of trust. Research shows that animals that violate this trust are often ostracized, suggesting that a violation of the rules of play is maladaptive and can disrupt the efficient functioning of the group. Among dogs, coyotes, and wolves, individuals who don't play fairly find out quickly enough that they will be ignored or avoided by other group members. And, without social bonds, loners suffer higher mortality rates than those who remain with the group. Social dynamics of animal play call for the participants to agree to the terms of engagement, which translate as: we will not try to eat one another, fight, or mate during play activity.

When there's a violation of these expectations, there are negative consequences. Those who cheat have a harder time finding future play partners.

Like animal species at play, researchers studying human child behavior believe that our early play teaches us basic lessons in morality. Pellegrini (2009) describes the fundamental rules of fairness that guide everyday play, and the egalitarian instincts in humans that appear very early on in childhood. Like other young animals, children learn in social settings that there are right and wrong ways to engage in play and that transgressions have social implications, like being ostracized.

Recall a time when you were playing Monopoly, Clue, Tag, Hide and Seek, Red Rover or some other childhood game. Children agree, often after negotiation, on the rules they intend to abide by, implicitly affirming consent not to arbitrarily change them once competition begins. I can recall times when it seemed like we spent more time on setting up the terms of engagement, then we did in actually playing the game! During play, children learn the fundamentals of reciprocal exchange (you go first; then it's my turn to go first next time), verbal contracts (no one can start before we say "1-2-3 go"), and the social consequences of failing to play by the rules (you cheat, we won't play with you anymore). These lessons—particularly about fairness —are also the foundation of fairness among adults.

As adults we also constantly negotiate with others about matters of give and take, and we rely daily on verbal contracts in the workplace and other social settings. Presumably we follow a myriad socially constructed rules of fairness, at work, every day (clean up your area when you're through, respect one another, do not interrupt, etc.). But how we perceive fairness is culturally constructed as well; based upon norms that vary with the social and economic structure of a given group, context, or cultural setting.

To understand this better, researchers studied children's behavior from three different cultures, which reflected very different ideas about what it means to be fair (Schäfer et al. 2015). Whereas children from a modern Western society distributed the spoils of a joint enterprise precisely in proportion to productivity, those from a gerontocratic pastoralist society in Africa did not take merit into account at all. Children from a hunter-gatherer egalitarian culture, a different region of Africa, distributed the spoils more equally than did the other two cultures, with merit playing only a limited role. The results of their study suggest that some basic notions of distributive justice are not necessarily universal amongst humans, rather culturally constructed behavioral norms. While the nuances of determining fairness likely vary, given cultural norms, some basic rules around unethical conduct for both animals and humans present striking parallels.

The larger and more developed pre-frontal cortex in humans gives us the capacity to be self-aware. As a result, we can impose critical self-reflection, which distinguishes our so-called morality from that of other animals. But the fact that we are more developed in some regards, does not mean animals lack morality. Nor does it mean we humans are more ethical, just or fair than other species. Moreover, in the twenty-first century scientists like Damasio (*Descartes' Error: Emotion, Reason, and the Human Brain*), Gazzaniga (*The Ethical Brain*), Haidt

(The Righteous Mind: Why Good People are Divided by Politics and Religion), and Wegner *(The Illusion of Conscious Will)*, underscore how human morality is more emotional and less rationally driven then we originally believed. It might even be said that human development may not be particularly beneficial to our health and survival, in that our instinctive nature to play fair and honor group membership may now be trumped by values of self-interest.

Parents as Teachers

As children, we are exposed to and gradually adopt certain values. We watch and emulate the behavior of others, particular those close to us. Some people, especially those who grow up experiencing oppressive and harsh circumstances, may have learned that they do not want to be like the adults who were around them when they were young. Such realities can motivate a person's desire to do better, be different, or to break away from unacceptable or harsh conditions. Rising above one's environmental realities, however, is tough. There may be no precedent or example to follow. Indeed, the decision to foster a desire to do better and/or break away from a negative example is an admirable ability.

Parents are our teachers from day one. In reflecting on your own life, perhaps you can recall a time when your parents or a respected adult told you that being honest was an important aspect of building relationships and living a good life. For example, in finding something of value, like a wallet or phone, you were encouraged to return it to its rightful owner. If you got caught lying, you were reprimanded. In situations where there was an inequity, maybe you observed your elders stand up for what they believed in, or saw them defend the rights of others. Parents often share stories with their children about the challenges or predicaments they faced, when they were young. Hopefully, parents assume their role by demonstrating good or appropriate ways of thinking and acting. They may also try to help their children learn from their own mistakes.

I can recall my dad telling my sister and me about how he broke some school windows as a prank. He then had to work to pay off the debt for the damage he had caused. Dad laughingly shared with us, that as a teenager, he learned to tell himself when some action seemed like a really good idea to him, to do just the opposite. He talked about how his mother, my grandmother, worked very hard to keep the family afloat during the depression. Despite hard times she and my grandfather were generous, sharing with neighbors and helping out others when they were able to do so. Whenever my dad, grandpa, and I went fishing, we would always take some of the catch to our neighbors. This sense of community was passed on to me. My mother shared stories with us about her childhood. She talked about the importance of getting an education and how much she valued learning. Living in the country, a rural setting, she described how getting to the bookmobile was a meaningful and significant experience for her. She maintained the importance of knowing your family history, emphatic about valuing one's personal heritage. Today, we still discuss the adventures of our great great grandfather, among other relatives, and how they influenced and shaped who we are today.

Adults in the family serve as our earliest role models in life. Parents and mentors guide and shape what we learn to see as important—what is of value—and to know right from wrong. Ideally, a platform for one's ethical character is encouraged, developed, and reinforced by one's entire family. You might recall how your mom or dad imposed rules like a curfew, expected your homework to be completed each night, and held you accountable for your actions. Or perhaps you had the freedom to make decisions for yourself and dealt with the consequences accordingly, as they unfolded. As we grow older, we often adopt values that center on helping us connect and work with others. The skills we learn early on in play, give us the foundation for how to form relationships and offer cooperation—essential competencies for establishing long-term well-being. Ties with family and friends provide the social bonding and a sense of belongingness that we all crave as human beings. For some, however, sheer survival may become the primary focus of one's childhood. This perspective often gives rise to values associated with self-defense, especially when a young person is left to fend for himself without nurturing relationships and positive role models.

Many of us also learn values in route to personal or group achievement. This may involve competition, which can escalate a focus on winning and potentially encourage risk-taking behaviors as a means to get ahead of what we perceive as "winner take all." Regardless of how we were raised, or the values we were exposed to, most of us can recall a moment when we chose to test the lines of authority, went beyond ascribed convention, or flat out broke the rules in an effort to get ahead (acquire or achieve something we wanted for ourselves). Understanding and managing the potentially selfish nature within our human core is central toward becoming an adult and continuing to grow as an ethical person.

How we navigate our way in the world is observed early on, as we learn by watching our parents. When adults display mature or immature behavior in front of their children, it sets the stage for more of the same. The picture (below) conveys a father and son caring for their residential backyard; here we see a demonstration of duty and commitment to accomplishing one's chores i.e., a work ethic (Fig. 1.6). With his father's encouragement and support, at the age of two, this lad emulates these actions. Conversely, I recently observed two adult women in theater nearly come to blows in front of a child over a petty dispute. After the altercation had been seemingly put to a halt by an usher (the incident was at a performance event), after stepping away, one of the women returned to the area and actually started hurling mothballs at the other individual, right in front of the child. While it was disgusting to see an adult be so ridiculously immature, what disturbed me more was that this example was being set forth for the child to model (in this case, the woman's granddaughter). The little girl watched and laughed, enjoying the scene as if it were a reality entertainment show on prime time television. This kind of behavior is much of what we see on today's so-called "reality TV": people behaving badly. Children are shaped by what they consume visually and experientially.

Fig. 1.6 Children emulate
adult behavior. Image credited
to Adam and Oliver Bangert

From the moment we are born, every encounter we experience collides with our personality. Given how we perceive and apply incoming data from the world around us, our character, identity, and the "self" emerges. As we make decisions to engage in particular ways or act without thinking things through, we build a compendium of evidence that reflects our character. What we value and what is most important to you, shows up not in your words but in your daily actions. Unfortunately, in our adult lives, by choice, default and/or environmental distractions, many of us tend to learn to react to situations without deliberate thought. When it comes to the ethics of our lives, many of us do not learn to place focused attention on why we are doing what we're doing, before we react. As a result, we can inadvertently devalue the importance of considering the needs of others and we may overlook the longer-term implications of our actions. Regardless of whether we apply focused intent or are driven by unconsciously propelled motives, our actions continue to bear a mark on who we are (or continue to become) as adults. Actions create precedent, which, in turn, influence habituated behaviors. We are what we repeatedly do. Typically, the need to belong and the desire to fulfill short-term self-interests are core drivers for our behavior throughout much of our lives. The former is often more about a *need* to be appreciated and accepted by others—the latter about getting what we *want* for ourselves. Immediacy often takes priority, with the long-term potential consequences of our actions rarely at the top of the list of our primary concerns.

As our ethical or moral identity takes shape, daily thoughts and behaviors reflect what is valued by us (and those around us). Character continues to be shaped by our everyday choices as we strive to get what we need and want. Along this path, we spend energy and effort to prevent loss. Loss aversion refers to people's tendency to prefer avoiding the discomfort of losses over the joy of acquiring gains. Some studies suggest that psychologically, negative experiences of loss are twice as powerful as positive experiences of gain (Tversky and Kahneman 1991). Taking this idea forward, valuing the ability to forgo what we want and letting go of what we do not need runs contrary to the vast majority of the incoming information we take in each day, seemingly from every corner of society. Modernity is all about creating the perception of need, inspiring new wants and desires. Business is inherently about building and fulfilling these demands, real or perceived, often overriding needs that may have already been addressed (continually creating new ones). If you think about it, every time you surf the web or watch television you realize you need something—an article of clothing, access to a show or program, a new mattress, juicer, garden hose, or a pill for depression or some other malady. Working to satisfy personal self-interest in a Western consumer-oriented society has become so widespread, it now drives much of the emerging global culture and the worldwide economy.

The values we were exposed to as children are learned adaptations, which can continue to be influenced by our environment. Complementing our beliefs are our personal traits, which are endogenous characteristics. Traits such as being tenacious, competitive, and willing to take risk are often deemed desirable in business. Such attributes are often associated with drive, which, in turn, can translate into achieving performance. But when these characteristics carry an association with greater ethical risk, they can leave a person and the organization they represent, open to ethical vulnerability, where moral lapses can then become more likely to occur. This suggests that some people may have to pay more attention to the ethics embedded within their choices and behaviors than others.

If, for example, you are highly competitive, enjoy taking risk, and are driven to win the game, deal, or point, you might need to learn to pause and cross-check your motives. Getting honest with yourself means looking at where you apply your core values—really—as you are motivated to win, achieve, score, and succeed. In other words, business men and women can learn to value the act of inner corrective balancing (at any age). While cognitive mapping may already be in place, adults can learn, grow, and change, if they have a desire to do so. Making a conscious effort to impose self-monitoring can help ensure that your decisions and actions are in ethical alignment with your presumed ethical identity. Of course, external influences, particularly those in the workplace, may support or deter us from ongoing learning and a desire to be ethical at work.

While firms do not always measure how performance goals are achieved, it is actually in how employees go about accomplishing their goals that builds a healthy cornerstone of being ethical in business. When hard-driving performance pressures employees to set the curve, beat quota, hit the numbers and make target goals, and this focus is coupled with diminished self-regulation, positive values like honesty, dedication, and commitment to ethics can be trumped by risk-taking behaviors (Gailliot et al. 2012). Just because you profess personal and organizational values does not make them genuine or activated on a daily basis. In business, "Did you make the numbers?" is typically asked more often than "How did you make your numbers?" Applying tenaciousness, confidence, and competitiveness toward *how* you achieve a goal is just as important as achieving it. But with short-term quarterly demands imposing a relentless need to show profits, many in business view ethics as a regulatory limitation, a constraint or impediment to success, rather than as a means to support principled performance. Whereas character traits and values are influenced by personality and upbringing, a lifetime of experiences, decisions and actions continue to shape a person's ethical identity. Where you work and who you work with and for—both the type of business you're in and the organizational context—influence what values and characteristics are relevant to you in any given moment. Values most salient at any particular time, in the certain situation or circumstance, and the behavior by you and those around you, can ultimately influence what values you choose to use and apply in your work. This is why framing ethics "as a daily deal" is so important; it is important to make a conscious decision to pay attention to doing the right thing each and every day.

You Are Not a Cookie

The good news is that human development is unlike a recipe that at some point is complete. *You are not a cookie!* We are not mixed, molded, baked, and suddenly done. Our interpretations, thoughts, and actions remain open for us to manage throughout the span of our lives.

Learning to be ethical is neither a one-time task nor an effort reserved for particular problems, issues, or challenges. While upbringing and education certainly influence how you think about and apply your values, your background is no assurance of ethical behavior. Of course, these elements are important factors in helping you to become aware of what is unethical. As an evolving sentient being you have the capacity to make decisions about who you want to be in the world on a daily basis. Following the law does not mean you are necessarily being ethical (Fig. 1.7).

A lot of people in business forget to think about the fact that this requires ongoing attention, making an effort to look for how, when and where individual and corporate values can be applied. Regardless of where you are in your life today, most people have the ability to change, if they have a desire to do so.

Solomon (1993) explains that moral selfhood is associated with an ability to develop, change, and respond to events and criticisms around us. If you have the willingness to be honest about who you are, you can choose to grow, and move towards becoming a more consistent ethical person. Just like how a firm develops its statement of purpose, you need to decide who you want to be in the world (Plante 2004).What is your purpose? What is your vision? What is your mission statement? Do you want to be an ethical person in business? Do you consistently take pride in doing the right thing, regardless of contextual influences? Waking up to the reality of who you truly are by seeing if your actions match your perceptions of self is an essential starting point. From there, the notion of building congruency between your real (actual) and ideal (best) self is the *sine qua non* of personal development (Boyatzis 1998). Your character is defined, in part, by the thousands of choices you make each day and how you choose to address or ignore the ethical elements within them. When desires and character defects compete with doing the right thing, your ability to be honest can become hindered or even blocked. Being

Fig. 1.7 Are you an
executive cookie? Image
credited to Gilles
DeCruyenaere/Shutterstock.
com

ethical or unethical doesn't happen by accident. It takes a sustained desire to care
about, be aware of, and make decisions with ethical mindfulness. This means doing
the right thing, even if this action does not necessarily offer any apparent
advantages.

In organizational settings, if we want to learn about a person, we typically
examine their job history and track record. We look to see what experience they
have, consider input from references, and review their education and past performance. We might scout for indications of capability and commitment. And yet,
when we think about someone else's ethical identity, we tend to assume that this
aspect of character is based upon how they were raised (Thompson 2009). It is
difficult, if not impossible, to determine a person's ethicality and if they have a
genuine desire to be ethical, by reading a resume (even if they tell the truth about
their experiences).[1] While upbringing and past actions shape character, moral
identity continues to remain fluid in adulthood. If we want to hire ethical people for
our organizations, we need to look at and see how they apply their character
strengths on an everyday basis.

---

[1] For example, Yahoo! Inc. Chief Executive Scott Thompson resigned from the digital media
company in 2012 after a shareholder called attention to his misrepresentation of college credentials
on his resume. See: http://articles.latimes.com/2012/may/14/business/la-fi-yahoo-thompson-
resigns-20120514.

Understanding your own moral (ethical) identity (Aquino and Reed 2002; Shao et al. 2008) means learning about your best or virtuous self and working to enable the character strengths that this identity represents. This sense of self (Stryker and Serpe 1994) stems from a variety of attributes that serve as guides to thoughts and actions. Although very few people see themselves as unethical or "bad," the importance or centrality of being ethical or "good" varies considerably among most people. For some, ethics, morality, character, and their virtue strengths are cast peripherally. In so doing, this can relegate ethics into a blind spot (rendering ethical values as potentially less important than others, like earning, spending or saving money). Most of us naturally value short-term gratification over long-term potential benefits. Recall the saying, "A bird in the hand is worth two in the bush?" But when immediacy takes priority, congruence between who we think we are, may be disconnected with our actual behavior. Some people have learned to make their character strengths or virtues a central focal point for their lived or realized identity. Traits, like being empathetic, describe who they are, which, in turn, is closely related to how they choose to behave on an everyday basis.

Contemporary theory on character tends to be more granular than the construct of ethical (moral) identity. Specific elements of character or virtue strength are often used to depict an individual's moral or ethical identity. This distinction has been clearly articulated in the Values in Action (VIA) research, a classification of character strengths developed within the domain of positive psychology (Peterson and Seligman 2004). A person's ethical identity or their moral self has become the basis for understanding moral agency (Shao et al. 2008). Character strengths support one's capability to act in morally responsible ways. To help shape ethical performance in the workplace, organizational members need to consider what promotes the development and use of personal character, the internal sponsors of moral agency. When virtues are central to the identity of selfhood, they can bolster a willingness to engage in moral action and then serve as navigational aids when moving to address an ethical challenge, problem, or issue. The role of the self in moral functioning has gained considerable theoretical and empirical attention over the past 25 years (Jennings et al. 2014). Although this work has advanced our understanding of moral thought and behavior, there has also been a lack of clarity as to the nature and functioning of the moral self.

Two perspectives of identity, character and social-cognitive, are key in advancing our understanding of the construct of "self." These frameworks help us to be aware of factors that support the desire and ability to exercise character strengths. In deconstructing moral identity, Blasi (1983, 1984, 2005) offers a model of the self. This theory is useful in understanding moral agency, commitment, self-efficacy, and determination, when it comes to a person acting upon their moral beliefs and values. When one's definition of self is centered on being ethical, the person is often compelled to act in a manner consistent with this construal (Blasi 1984). Dimensions of your ethical identity include facets like having respect for others and a sense of responsibility and/or duty. But the value of such characteristics can be influenced by your everyday social relations (e.g., interactions with management and co-workers on the job).

Professional Identity

As we all know, many of our relational interactions occur in the workplace. Social learning also evolves within our professional community of practice, creating ethical codes and schemas that people are likely to draw upon when they face an ethical issue (Verbos et al. 2007). Without a congruent personal and professional ethical self-schema, a person may not take notice of the ethical aspects of their professional identity. Ethical standards within the professions are often socially constructed, shaped by members of the group and society at large (Matherne et al. 2006). Our roles, whether at home or at work, are associated with specific and enduring scripts for how we are expected to behave and act toward others in a given setting (Gergen 1997). Professions typically convey a dedication and expertise to a particular field (e.g., accountant, physician, attorney, or professor). But regardless of the type of job you perform, anything from plumbing to programming, teaching to managing, or selling to designing, what we do for a living is a series of daily decisions and actions that not only influence what we do, but continue to shape who we are, and who we are becoming.

A once narrow path to professional development has become broader over the years, with many roles now interrelated, cross-pollinated, or even fused. For example, when I last saw my physician, she was responsible for not only making a diagnosis and prescribing the appropriate medications, but she also managed the entire medical record-tracking process (inputting insurance codes, preparing letters, etc.). I am able to contact my physician directly, 24/7, through my healthcare provider's online system. Using this IT interface, patients can procure test results, renew prescriptions, make appointments, and ask questions of their healthcare providers. Clearly, the physician's role has changed over the years, largely due to advancements in technology and our ability to easily access, use, and share information. With broad-sweeping access to data, insights emerge from multiple perspectives, prompting a ubiquitous capability for knowledge transfer.

How you look for, listen to, and share information is a statement about your ethicality. It says to others, directly or indirectly, "This is what I care about at this moment. This is what is most important to me." And, the way you treat information, especially personal data, reflects the degree to which you consider privacy an ethical issue—protecting information (yours or other people's) as a form of honesty, courtesy or respect. The kinds of information we share, especially when we first meet someone, is typically where we are from or currently reside and what we do for a living. Americans often introduce themselves by their job titles, rather than by offering insights about their families, friends, and personal interests. People I have met in other countries seem to have less focus on their profession or work life as the definitive force behind their identity. Work—more specifically, the "work ethic"—is embedded within the zeitgeist of the American culture.

Perhaps this is why it is almost second nature for Westerners to present themselves in terms of what they do for a living. Part of our overall identity is our ethicality. As stated, this can continue to be shaped and defined by our day to day workplace experiences (Verbos et al. 2007; Romani and Szkudlarek 2014). In years past, and to some extent today, being a member of a particular profession and/or organization was held in high esteem. Upholding the ethics of that identity was of real value at the individual, group, and employer levels. Honor, duty, and respect were associated with one's job. This premise is somewhat dubious in today's business world.

For those of us engaged in business enterprise, there is a sense of urgency regarding the lack of ethics in our organizational settings. A way to tackle this issue is to be responsible and take charge of our own actions. Are you paying attention to how your behaviors match your presumed identity? Does what you say match what you actually do? Are you actively seeking out the ethical elements of your everyday decisions and actions? Do you strive to do more than avoid unethical action; rather seeking out where to engage in acts of moral strength? Determining how ethical you want to be is an ongoing effort that must be addressed and practiced daily if you want to claim to be genuinely ethical. Are you living up to your character potential? Do you activate your best ethical self as a conscious effort? Do you have a desire to maintain and build your moral strength? To help you address these questions and concerns, we consider reality, perceptions, and what it means to be your best self.

Takeaway Points

1. You are what you repeatedly do; daily habits are a reflection of your ethical and moral identity.
2. Values are formed in childhood but remain fluid, and can continue to evolve over a lifetime.
3. Your professional identity, including moral strength, is open for ongoing growth and development.

Reflection Questions

Recall moments of your childhood, incidents when you demonstrated character strength or weakness. How do you leverage these strengths and mitigate character weaknesses in your everyday work life today?

References

Anderson, J. (2009). Illusions of accountability. *Administrative Theory & Praxis,31*(3), 322–339.
Aquino, K., & Reed, A, I. I. (2002). The self-importance of moral identity. *Journal of Personality and Social Psychology, 83*, 1423–1440.
Blasi, A. (1983). Moral cognition and moral action: A theoretical perspective. *Developmental Review, 2*, 178–210.

Blasi, A. (1984). Moral identity: Its role in moral functioning. In W. M. Kurtines & J. L. Gewirtz (Eds.), *Morality, moral behavior, and moral development*, pp. 128–139. New York: John Wiley & Sons.

Blasi, A. (2005). Moral character: A psychological approach. In D. K. Lapsley & F. C. Power (Eds.), *Character psychology and character education* (pp. 67–100). Notre Dame, IN: University of Notre Dame Press.

Bagozzi, R. P., Sekerka, L. E., & Hill, V. (2009). Hierarchical motive structures and their role in moral choices of managers. *Journal of Business Ethics, 90*(4), 461–486.

Bagozzi, R. P., Sekerka, L. E., Hill, V., & Seguera, F. (2013). The role of moral values in instigating morally responsible behavior. *Journal of Applied Behavior Sciences, 49*(1), 69–94.

Boyatzis, R. E. (1998). Self-directed change and learning as a necessary meta-competency for success and effectiveness in the 21st century. In Sims, R. and Veres, J. (Eds.), *Keys to employee success in the coming decades*, pp. 15–32. Westport, CT: Greenwood Publishing Group.

CNN Money, London. (September 22, 2015). Volkswagen scandal widens. Accessed September 22, 2015. http://money.cnn.com/2015/09/22/news/vw-recall-diesel/.

Cojuharenco, I., & Sguera, F. (2014). When empathic concern and perspective taking matter for ethical judgment: The role of time hurriedness. *Journal of Business Ethics*, 1–9.

Comer, D., & Sekerka, L. E. (2014). Taking time for patience: Recognizing, respecting, and reclaiming an undervalued virtue. *Journal of Management Development, 33*(1), 6–23.

Edmiston, B. (2010). Playing with children, answering with our lives: A Bakhtinian approach to coauthoring ethical identities in early childhood. *British Journal of Educational Studies, 58*(2), 197–211.

Ethics Resource Center. (2011, 2012). *National business ethics survey*. Arlington, VA: ERC.

Ford, R. C., & Richardson, W. D. (1994). Ethical decision-making: A review of the empirical literature. *Journal of Business Ethics, 13*, 205–221.

Gailliot, M. T., Gitter, S. A., Baker, M. D., & Baumeister, R. F. (2012). Breaking the rules: Low trait or state self-control increases social norm violations. *Psychology, 3*(12), 1074–1083.

Gardiner, M. (1992). Dialogics of critique: M. M. Bakhtin and the theory of ideology. NY: Routledge.

Gergen, K. J. (1997). *Realities and relationships: Soundings in social construction*. Cambridge, MA: Harvard University Press.

Henning, P. J. (September 21, 2015). Many messages in the G.M. settlement, *The New York Times*. Accessed on September 22, 2015, http://www.nytimes.com/2015/09/22/business/dealbook/many-messages-in-the-gm-settlement.html

Hofstede, G. (1980). *Culture's consequences: International differences in work-related values*. Thousand Oaks, CA: Sage.

Ivory, D., Protess, B., & Vlasic, B. (May 22, 2015). G.M. Inquiry said to find criminal wrongdoing, *The New York Times*. Retrieved May 26, 2015, from http://www.nytimes.com/2015/05/23/business/gm-inquiry-said-to-find-criminal-wrongdoing.html?_r=0.

Jennings, P. L., Mitchell, M. S., & Hannah, S. T. (2014). The moral self: A review and integration of the literature. *Journal of Organizational Behavior*. doi: 10.1002/job.1919.

Kinnier, R. G., Kernes, K. L., & Dautheribes, G. M. (2000). A short list of universal values. *Counseling and Values, 45*, 4–16.

Matherne, B. P., Grove, S., Forlani, V., & Janney, J. J. (2006). Walk the talk: Developing personal ethical agency through a business partnership program. *Journal of Management Education, 30* (1), 106–134.

Myers, D. G. (2002). *Social psychology* (7th ed.). New York: McGraw Hill.

Pellegrini, A. (2009). *The role of play in human development*. New York: Oxford University Press.

Peterson, C., & Seligman, M. E. P. (2004). *Character strengths and virtues*. NY: Oxford University Press.

Pierce, J., & Bekoff, M. (2009). Moral in tooth and claw. *The Chronicle Review*. Retrieved July 7, 2015, from http://chronicle.com/article/Moral-in-ToothClaw/48800/.

Piotrowski, C., & Guyette, R. W., Jr. (2010). Toyota recall crisis: Public attitudes on leadership and ethics. *Organization Development Journal, 28*(2), 89–97.

Plante, T. G. (2004). *Do the right thing: Living ethically in an unethical world*. Oakland, CA: New Harbinger Publications.

Plungis, J. & Katz, A. (2015). VW's emissions retrofit may be among costliest recalls ever. Bloomberg.com News, http://www.bloomberg.com/news/articles/2015-10-22/vw-s-emissions-retrofit-may-be-among-costliest-recalls-ever. Accessed on November 11, 2015.

Romani, L., & Szkudlarek, B. (2014). The struggles of the interculturalists: Professional ethical identity and early stages of codes of ethics development. *Journal of Business Ethics, 119*, 173–191.

Schäfer, M., Haun, D. B. M, & Tomasello, M. (2015). Fair is not fair everywhere. *Psychological Science*, published online before print June 26, 2015. doi: 10.1177/0956797615586188.

Sekerka, L. E., & Bagozzi, R. P. (2007). Moral courage in the workplace: Moving to and from the desire and decision to act. *Business Ethics: A European Review, 16*(2), 132–142.

Shao, R., Aquino, K., & Freeman, D. (2008). Beyond moral reasoning: A review of moral identity research and its implications for business ethics. *Business Ethics Quarterly, 18*(4), 513–540.

Stryker, S., & Serpe, R. T. (1994). Identity salience and psychological centrality: Equivalent, overlapping, or complementary concepts? *Social Psychology Quarterly, 57*, 16–35.

Solomon, R. (1993). *Ethics and excellence: Cooperation and integrity in business*. New York: Oxford University Press.

Thompson, R. A. (2009). Early foundations: Conscience and the development of moral character. In D. Narvaez & D. Lapsley (Eds.), *Personality, identity, and character: Explorations in moral psychology* (pp. 159–184). New York: Cambridge University Press.

Tverksy, A., & Kahneman, D. (1991). Loss aversion in riskless choice: A reference-dependent model. *The Quarterly Journal of Economics, 106*(4), 1039–1061.

Verbos, A. K., Gerard, J. A., Forshey, P. R., Harding, C. S., & Miller, J. S. (2007). The positive ethical organization: Enacting a living code of ethics and ethical organizational identity. *Journal of Business Ethics, 76*(1), 17–33.

Vlasic, B. & Apuzzo, M. (March 19, 2014). Toyota is fined $1.2 billion for concealing safety defects. *The New York Times*. Retrieved July 16, 2015, from http://www.nytimes.com/2014/03/20/business/toyota-reaches-1-2-billion-settlement-in-criminal-inquiry.html?_r=0.

Chapter 2
You Are What You Do

Are you at home or perhaps on the road? Maybe you are in an airplane? Are you reading online, in a library, or listening to this book as you jog or drive down the street? Regardless of your location, the chances are that other people are not far off. We share this planet and co-create its successes or failures. As philosophers and scientists observe theoretically and empirically, our lives are socially constructed (Gergen 1997). How we behave is experienced by others, which generates collective meaning as we go about living our lives. We all have a hand in shaping this world, one day at a time.

A lack of ethical awareness and commitment to being morally sound can inadvertently contribute to moral hypocrisy. When there's a mismatch between who we think we are and what we actually do, it suggests a lack ethical alignment. The notion of living one's best ethical self is designed to foster goal setting and striving, to advance adult personal growth and development (Roberts et al. 2005). It is not intended to help you visualize or create an appreciative view that is left unattended. It is essential that we learn to want to make a sincere and forthright attempt at honestly knowing where our strengths and limitations reside. If you want to be ethical, you must first get honest with yourself about your motives and intentions. When you engage in a particular course of action, make a decision, or choose to behave in a particular way, you need to be truthful with yourself about the nature of your goal. In making ethical decisions, it is important to ask yourself, "Why am I choosing this particular action? Is it to get ahead, get my way, or to gain power over others? Is it to garner favor or to win? Or is it to be useful, be of service, or to empower others? What are my motives?"

The ethical character of our organizations and communities is forged in the context of others as we exercise our values. Being relational creatures, we offer a contribution to the world as we are simultaneously shaped by it. How we engage with one another is an essential element of our survival and growth. This affirms the importance of continuing to advance one's best ethical self, learning to manage your ethical identity in the context of others. We depend upon one another to live and thrive. When other people meet, engage, or work with you, who do they see?

© Springer International Publishing Switzerland 2016
L. E. Sekerka, *Ethics is a Daily Deal*, DOI 10.1007/978-3-319-18090-8_2

Connecting Ethically

According to Robert Putnam, the fabric of a connected culture is represented by a type of social capital (Putnam 2000). His research describes how relational connectedness builds and enhances community strength. Thanks to the Internet, we are more connected to one another, now more than ever before. But these connections may lack quality. The forces of smartphones and Facebook continue to bring friends, users, and consumers into new and emerging communities. Communications taking place via technological platforms are often in an abbreviated form, while simultaneously taking time away from face-to-face interaction. Ironically, many of us are so busy relating to others virtually, we may not take the time to be present with those around us. An employee at AT&T shared with me that to get his colleague's attention at work, he had to send him a text, and the individual was standing right next to him. The text read "Look up!" Have you ever gone to dinner, class, or some event, and the people around you are so entrenched in dialogue with others online that it feels like they're somewhere else?

You might consider the following, make a concerted effort to look up from your computer or device and say hello, thank you, and smile to the people you encounter throughout your day. Do you make eye contact with those in need? Do you offer a handshake or hug willingly? Being ethical is about taking time for those around you. It is interesting that one of Oprah Winfrey's recent campaigns sought to prompt her fans to "just say hello." She describes how we all seek and need validation. Referencing the numerous guests she welcomed over the years to her program, "I started to see that pattern. And what I realized is that everybody is looking for the same thing. No matter if it's a politician or Beyoncé…we're all looking to know, did you see me, did you hear me, and did what I say mean anything to you? So just saying hello is a way of validating even a stranger" (Kurtz 2014, np) (Fig. 2.1).

Fig. 2.1 Do you recognize and acknowledge those around you? Image credited to Rawpixel/Shutterstock.com

Validation of others can be an opportunity to exercise your moral strength. For example, if a store clerk or attendant is having a rough experience with the equipment, technology, or other customers, do you react in frustration or reassure them it's OK, as you patiently wait your turn? When the cable, phone, or health insurance company sends you a bill that is wrong (for the third month in a row), do you get angry or strive to remain calm as you work things out with the service agent? If someone is doing something thoughtful, kind, or with a positive attitude, do you take time to explicitly acknowledge them and their efforts? Are your ethical values expressed by respecting others' space? Affirming the value of people and the planet can also be expressed by taking care of the natural environment and local community. Do you sort your garbage? Do you take bags to the store with you? Do you pick up stray trash on the ground (items you didn't toss), placing them in a wastepaper container? Do you support local business in your community? Do you help out at your local hospital, charity, community center, or youth club? Do you know your neighbors?

It's difficult to think locally sometimes, when we live in a world of virtual communication and global enterprise. It's exciting to have our citizenship broadened to the global community. But being a good citizen starts at home. In the West, citizenship typically means obeying the laws, taking care of one's family, maintaining your home, investing in education, and voting. Today we're also asked to be global citizens. Understanding one's responsibility on the local and global level is sometimes challenging and can potentially be overwhelming. How you present yourself, locally and globally, virtually or in person, is the way in which other people experience your ethical identity. Interactions fuel associations and judgments, as those observing you consider what your actions reveal about you. It takes time to make a conscious effort to be ethical.

Faster Is Better?

The human brain works to maximize efficiency. Nudging the preference for quick over slow, we are prone to take cognitive shortcuts (Kahneman 2011). Add to that, the notion that bad is often stronger than good, and we see how it becomes easier to jump to a focus on differences rather than similarities. Fueled by ego and fanned by arrogance, our natural tendency to impose personal self-bias can escalate our thoughts into extreme binary oppositions. Given that our brains naturally make sense of incoming information by use of categorizations, we tend to organize new input based on prior experiences, applying prior means of sense-making to file and understand incoming new material. This instinctive process, trying to make sense of the world we live in, can inadvertently create extreme distances between views. In the United States, for example, you can get into some heated debate very quickly based on liberal and conservative typologies. It seems obvious there are likely good, honest, and ethical people in both camps. And yet, within our daily communications with family, friends, and colleagues (at the lunch or dinner table) we can see

how differences can unintentionally become distorted, leading to grossly disrespectful or inappropriate inferences, rendering unethical thoughts, comments,
and/or actions.

For example, a colleague of mine became distressed about a conversation he had
with a lifelong acquaintance. He was quite literally distraught and disgusted by how
his friend, a well-educated man whom he regarded as a learned associate, had
become quite radical, using extremist terms like "fascist" to describe a political
administration and their policies. In restraining himself from an over-heated dia-
tribe, he pulled back from the situation. Rather than reacting with equal opposition,
which he said he was tempted to do, he chose instead to reflect on how that person
may have come to develop such an extreme stance. For most people, in the heat of
the moment, it seems easier to just react to what we disagree with, rather than to
listen and seeking to understand. This becomes especially difficult when the parties
engaged may not be interested in listening to or considering any other view but their
own. And it's particularly disconcerting when their view seems hurtful, short-
sighted, or potentially harmful to others. Words create the world we live in.

Moral responsibility is about creating inclusivity rather than exclusivity. Applied
ethics is working to get along with others. It is reflected in your willingness to give
respect, offer patience, and, if in disagreement, model empathy and compassion.
Perhaps the way to understand views apart from our own is to appreciate the
goodness in everyone. People typically get angry, resentful, and afraid when they
perceive their rights are challenged, threatened, or they are being undervalued.
People want to ensure what belongs to them is not taken and that they do not get left
with less then what they think is their fair share. Extend yourself. Think about how
others might feel and what leads them to value what is important to them. Broaden
your understanding toward a completely different view. You might ask, "What has
happened that might cause this person to feel this way?"

The pursuit of ethical growth is a form of art, one that is profoundly human. We
are limited only to the extent that our imagination and/or faith are constrained.
Coupled with a sense of responsibility and an acceptance of our own fallibility, we
need to continue to embrace tolerance in route to learning. Encouraged by wise
people who preceded us, we must acknowledge that we might be wrong. When we
forget this fact, we can begin to believe we know only one truth and that the ends
justify the means.

Perception as a Stage

Goffman (1959) wrote about how the perception of the self was a staging area for
one's character. This unseen, less formal, and privately constructed world is where
perceptions and prior experiences are called upon "behind the scenes" to help
people interpret information and make distinctions about themselves and others.
This metaphor begs the question: What masks do you wear? Is your moral identity
genuine? Are you authentic in your business presence (Figs. 2.2 and 2.3)?

Fig. 2.2 What masks do you
wear? Image courtesy of
freeimages.com

Today we have an entirely new stage for identity, via virtual communication and
the ethical self we portray using social media. When you respond, blog, share
information with others, and present yourself to the world online, is this your ethical
identity? Are your actions congruent with your best ethical self? How you act in
person, is it consistently ethical? The roles you portray in all areas of your life—
virtual, home, family, work—are they consistent with your values? Understanding
is no small feat; it's complicated. With motivations that fuel competing desires for
autonomy, power, security, and relational care, we can draw upon different value
sets, given the current or pressing circumstance.

Mental schemas help each person make sense of what they see and feel, helping
to create how they experience the world. As an individual takes this information in
and engages with others, internal subjective cues contribute to perceptions, while
simultaneously posing an influence upon and shaping the reality for other people as
well. Our perceptions are continuously interlaced with the people who are around
us. Generally, tacit cues are beliefs we draw upon from what we already know. But
a personalized framework for how we see ourselves, a person's ethical identity, is
constantly evolving as we participate in ongoing social interactions. Therefore, your
character and ethicality is forged in the context of others.

This is based on the assumption that how life experiences are perceived, interpreted, and understood depends upon your thoughts and feelings in a particular
place, context and moment in time. Continually influenced by basic needs, we see
how our lives are continuously shaped and can move in different directions, given
our attention or focus on seeking autonomy and change, care and empathy, power
and competition, and/or security and stability. Movement toward personal growth,
relationships, competition, or having a desire to stay in place may stay the same or
shift. Additionally, the fluidity of self may be more robust in some people than in
others.

We come to each moment with a unique view, shaped through our experiences,
which we use to interpret the present reality. We face the day with particular needs
and goals, given our current life space (based on health, family needs, work

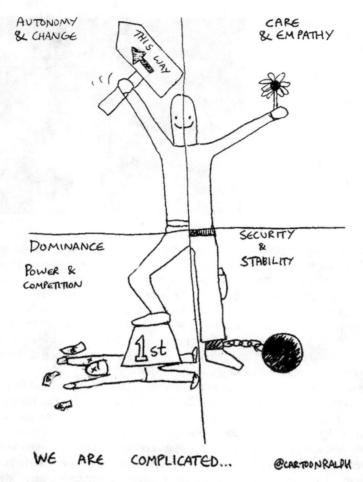

AUTONOMY & CHANGE

THIS WAY

CARE & EMPATHY

DOMINANCE

POWER & COMPETITION

SECURITY & STABILITY

1st

WE ARE COMPLICATED...   @CARTOONRALPH

Fig. 2.3 The complicated self. Image credited to CartoonRalph

deadlines, etc.). Through head and heart, incorporating cognitive, emotional, and spiritual processes, we make sense of life on a day by day basis.

We shape the plot of our lives by how we see and react to the world around us. Everyone shares and narrates their own storyline in a world of other living beings, all doing the same thing. People may or may not be aware that they are the authors of their own text. Regardless, we are all cast members in a living play, simultaneously assuming a role in our own and other peoples' narratives. While the human life is experienced as your own personal creation, if you can rise above your individual lens, there are other splendid vantage points. Here, you are no longer the sole filmmaker, but an actor cast in the broader show. Perception from this grander view is achieved by thinking more holistically (i.e., where you are no longer at the center of everything).

The world is created by our own perceptions. Investments, the stock market, and currency itself are all viable because of the consensual beliefs that these things have value. What if we started to take more time and energy, striving to value others around us? What if we gave more time to consider others' perspectives, exercising empathy, thinking about what might be important to them? Given the situation, take time to consider the needs of others. Ask yourself, what would I be thinking or feeling if I were in their shoes? What would be important to me if I were looking at the world from their eyes? Given this information, what might that person need to support their well-being? How might I work to better understand the needs of others? To help you address these concerns, you can assume a view of the situation as if you're in a helicopter, getting up above yourself and garnering a broader picture of the grander scheme. While we each are tainted by our own lens even when we strive to be empathetic, efforts to look at the big picture, as it pertains to ethics, can help us see we are a part of a shared production, rather than the lead character in a one man/woman show.

Paradoxically, we are all cast as actors in this large unfolding event, as a solo and collective life-experience on earth. We share a common role and fate as we navigate our time here, together. Such a generalized observation has variances in interpretation, given one's religious and spiritual beliefs. And yet, we are the same in the sense that we share a common platform. A personal sense of ethics comes not only from feeling compassion for others; it is also in thinking about the broader view and assuming a more holistic approach to business life. Ownership of personal responsibility stems from loyalty, which comes from respect between employees and their employers. This respect emerges by working together to achieve a common goal, one that strives to achieve goodness. As stated by His Holiness the

Fig. 2.4 His Holiness the Dalai Lama believes compassion and business go hand in hand. Image courtesy of His Holiness the Dalai Lama and photographer Tenzin Choejor

Dalai Lama, "The future is open. When there is intention to do good, there is no remorse" (2014). Hearing him speak at the Markkula Center for Applied Ethics at Santa Clara University in 2014, I was moved by his jovial nature and sincere belief that business and compassion are not mutually exclusive. When joined together, work and caring for others helps us evolve as spiritual beings (Fig. 2.4).

The Stories We Tell

Regardless of how complex or mundane the issue, we use stories to help us understand, move on, and even to inspire greatness. We tell ourselves stories to live (Didion 2006). Some writers weave tales of moral disintegration, driven by social fragmentation. Other stories give us the means to cope. Narratives help us deal with life's challenges, providing examples of how to make sense of our circumstances. In the West, our values have been bolstered by stories that reinforce a belief in success, achievement, and self-confidence. Horatio Alger, Jr. is the author of a fictitious character who conveys the American myth that opportunity is available to all. In his stories he affirms the ideal of individual potential. While this allegory bears some truth, in that the ideology is based on self-efficacy, many Westerners believe that anyone can be successful with hard work and determination. On some level this perception helps shape the reality of industrious success, reinforced by spirit of capitalism and democracy (Fig. 2.5).

Fig. 2.5 Horatio Alger, Jr., the acclaimed novelist who told tales of children escaping poverty and his book "Ragged Dick". Images are in the public domain. *Ragged Dick* is a story by Horatio Alger, Jr., serialized in *Student and Schoolmate* in 1867, released as a novel in May 1868 by A.K. Loring. It was the first in a six volume *Ragged Dick Series*, becoming the author's all-time bestseller. The tale follows a poor chap's rise to middle class respectability in nineteenth century New York City. Scholars have criticized its simplistic fantasy-approach toward class assimilation. Stamp reproduced from the United States Postal Service Stamp Gallery: http://usstampgallery. com/view.php?id=e22cd461c068aea5dff1c3462214880d76b3e39c

Alger's writing describes the adventures of impoverished boys moving from "rags to respectability" through "pluck and luck." The tales emerged as a genre, as widespread urbanization followed the Civil War, reflecting the rise of industrialism. The stories made heroes of impoverished boys who displayed uncommon courage and moral fortitude. Struggling against all odds, they worked to achieve wealth and acclaim. These rags-to-riches vignettes became popular, guiding many to believe in America as the land of opportunity. The majority of the lads in his stories experienced accidental good fortune that ushered their success. Rather than achieving riches because of hard work, sacrifice and determination, fame was an outcome derived from a sheer twist in fate. Frank Courtney's break in *The World Before Him* (1880) is a typical plot line.[1] Young Frank grabs his fortune by sheer luck. And yet, perceiving your potential with assuredness and self-confidence and a belief in the possibility of greatness helps to create that reality.

Between the late 1860s and Alger's death in 1899, Alger published more than 100 of these formulaic novelettes. As an author he paradoxically established his own fortune by simply pursuing his craft, ardently telling and retelling these mini-tales of success. Perhaps what is most relevant in the stories that relates to the ethic of hard work, is that success is not only the gift of luck, but found in an ability to have hope and to keep trying, despite failure. To believe in the potential for success, by putting yourself out there and being resilient, you have a greater chance for positive outcomes to emerge (Balaram 2008). When imagination and preparation meet opportunity, luck has a chance to thrive, contributing to more creativity and invention. So engrained is this myth in America, we see its representation in modern day culture, with an abundant focus on innovation and entrepreneurship.

Perhaps we can learn from our ancestors, many of whom were driven to discover a new way of life, one that supposedly offered freedom of choice (Fig. 2.6). In the United States, our forefathers endured horrific hardships brought on by war, hunger, mistreatment, disease, loss and death. But regardless of their circumstances, of those who survived, many carried with them an enduring hope for a better future. Americans have descendants from all over the world. Many of these people arrived with modest means and faced harsh and unforgiving circumstances. But they carried with them a faith, a belief in the notion of opportunity for themselves and their children. This entrepreneurial spirit is not solely based on the idea of wealth creation, but it is also about the potential for advancement. The social ideal of the "American Dream" means the ability to seek prosperity, which includes access to education. With education, people had the hope of viable options, the ability to choose what you might do for a living. Hard work and determination were valued, regardless of one's profession. These qualities helped to further define a "work ethic," which was a value of steadfast commitment to doing a job right and doing it well. The moral virtue of diligence was valued in its own right. Work was considered admirable. A person's work ethic stood for something of value.

---

[1]See http://historymatters.gmu.edu/d/4997/.

Fig. 2.6 Ancestors create our family narrative. Images (*top left*) courtesy of the Lang family, (*top right*) courtesy of the Sekerka family, (*lower left*) the Jenkins family; (*lower right*) the Metropolitan Museum of Art, The Horace W. Goldsmith Foundation Gift through Joyce and Robert Menschel

We know that having a belief in our own abilities is a powerful force in achieving success (Coffee et al. 2009). Research suggests when opportunities for development are precluded, self-efficacy is often compromised and performance can suffer. Studies in the area of resiliency reflect the importance of rebounding from failure, reaffirming a belief in self, and continuing to seek self-enhancement (Gillian and Rothstein 2010). A belief in the self is central in motivating action and in helping people recover from difficulties. Our images of who we think we are and who we think we can become, both real and perceived, shape what we experience and how we experience it. Recognizing the symbolic and socially-constructed nature of the human universe, scholars embrace the notion that positive images help create positive action (Cooperrider 1990). A recent empirical study conducted in the field revealed evidence for moral contagion as a result of other people's good deeds and moral self-licensing through one's own good deeds (Hofmann et al. 2014). This work also affirmed the integrated nature of happiness and a sense of purpose with acts of morality in everyday life (both ethical and unethical).

When a positive backdrop is missing, when those around you are unethical and/or you find yourself in hard times, then what? Toward advancing the notion of resiliency as a primary element of driving success in very difficult times, the story of Mario Capecchi merits consideration. As described by Balaram (2008), Capecchi is known for his Nobel Prize-winning work in Physiology and Medicine in the field of gene targeting. At a speech he delivered in 1996, accepting the Kyoto Prize, he shared his beliefs that abrasive juxtaposition of unique sets of life experiences help produce a form of creative inner strength, far too complex to pre-orchestrate.

He noted that his success grew from the antithesis of a nurturing environment, which most of us want to believe is conducive toward fostering a thoughtful, creative, and successful adult. Born in 1937 in Italy, at a time when Fascism and Communism were looming, he was a child of a single mother. As an artist and member of a Nazi opposition group, she was arrested and sent to Dachau in early 1941. He was taken in and looked after by a peasant family, but when the money ran out, Capecchi, as a child of 4½, was left on his own. He states, "I headed south, sometimes living in the streets, sometimes joining gangs of other homeless children, sometimes living in orphanages and most of the time being hungry. My recollections of those 4 years are vivid but not continuous, rather like a series of snapshots. Some of them are brutal beyond description, others more palatable" (p. 1546). The Capecchi story included miracles beyond belief, with his mother surviving liberation and finding him on his ninth birthday. Emigration to America was a turning point for him. In Capecchi's words, "I was expecting to see roads paved with gold in America. I found much more: an opportunity." In looking back at his early years Capecchi says he marvels at the resilience of a child. He goes on to add that the genetic and environmental factors contributing to talent are far too complex for us to predict. In the absence of such wisdom, we must provide children with ample opportunity to pursue their passions and dreams.

Our internal frameworks, how we make sense of our circumstances, are constantly helping us determine and navigate what is, and what can be. We rely and depend upon cognitive back-staging and feedback loops to shape the meaning of

our life experiences. But our ability to imagine, considering what principled performance might look like in the face of unethicality, is where we can arouse the
creative energies to help make it so, at the very least in our own choices. Such
willingness can continue to mold our perceptions of reality and the ethical elements
we perceive. Because of the plasticity of the brain and the ability to select and direct
our own thoughts, people can choose to alter how they see and shape their lives.
But you need to be aware of this capacity and choose to use it. Calling back the
rugged resiliency of our childhood and the strength found in goodness, we can all
strive to edify a desire to do what is right, honest, and ethical. And we can do so at
any moment, throughout our adult lives.

Choosing to Be Your Best

By becoming more aware of who you are in the world, thinking about how your
ethical identity is reflected in thought, word and deed, you can begin to see if your
inner and outer selves are congruent. You can learn where gaps might reside and if
you have areas of ethical weakness or hypocrisy. Your extended self is who others
see, perceive, and experience as you go about your day-to-day activities. Whether
you make a deliberate effort to present yourself in a certain way or embrace the
world without forethought, you will be perceived by others in varying ways. Do
you make an effort to manage who you are in the world? Do you consider how you
are perceived? Is being ethical something you value? This is a real choice that you
will make; construed with deliberate care or by de facto i.e., ignoring the decision
or being indifferent, a decision made through apathy.

Each person has the potential to be their best or worst—on any given day. Based on
your temperament, experiences, and the situation or context, you may or may not
choose to be ethical. The durability of your character can be strengthened or weakened
over time. We can be detoured from being our best ethical self. But we are also capable
of strengthening our capacity. As human beings, we are malleable. If you want to be
ethical you have to put your mind to it and, with focused intent, recommit to this goal
on regular basis. Much like a good marriage, being ethical takes work and involves a
daily renewal, recommitting to the shared goal. It is not just a one-time "I do" and
you're good to go. Rather, it is a goal that one works to achieve on a daily basis.

Over time, you can build paths for effectiveness and avoid the areas known to
impose ethical risk. You build precedents for ethical action by being ethical.
Positive anticipatory views can be an amazing resource for garnering confidence
and resolve. Mustering the courage to act, believing you are of good character, can
give rise to self-efficacy and optimism that can support your ability to proceed with
right action. Rather than creating false projections of your ethicality, you can own
your space on the planet honestly. As Helen Keller once said, "The world is moved
not only by the mighty shoves of the heroes, but also by the aggregate of the tiny
pushes of each honest worker." The tiny pushes you make include observation of
and critical reflection on your own behavior (Fig. 2.7).

Fig. 2.7 Helen Keller in 1904 at the age of 24. Image in the public domain

We spend a lot of time judging others, which leaves the practice of personal critical introspection wanting. It takes effort to allocate resources toward personal growth. But learning to take a time out as a regular practice has value. Considering the importance of incorporating a reflective pause in their day, a business student reading about moral competencies commented, "Be it an ethical situation, a tragedy or a thought-provoking experience, time simply enables the pieces of what can seem like shattered glass to come together and ensure an adequate reflection." When you wake up each morning as a person with character strengths and weaknesses, you have the opportunity to leverage your strong suits, like gratitude, curiosity, and determination. You can choose to develop your areas that lack strength, such as patience and compassion. You might also remind yourself where your areas of ethical weakness reside, identifying places or circumstances where you become tempted to engage in unethical behaviors, and choose to address them proactively (e.g., if you have a propensity to speed on the highway, you leave earlier and allow yourself more time).

Teaching yourself to be mindful means paying attention to where you are vulnerable; situations where you tend to give way to temptation. Observing who you are now, based on your past actions, is important. But it is also essential to recognize that you are never done with the process of becoming. Each day presents a new opportunity to engage in life ethically, to be more effective at your ability to engage in moral action. Given the dynamics of human development, we are never done with the process of becoming more ethical. Evolutionarily speaking, our perceptual biases enable us to overcome our fears and to participate in cooperative activities.

By definition, all reflection, learning about the self, is a retrospective effort. Self-awareness is an internal process constantly in the mode of playing catch-up.

Fig. 2.8 Obama Awards
Nobel Prize to Kahneman.
Image credited to Rena
Schild/Shutterstock.com

And, as described by Nobel laureate Daniel Kahneman, the way we remember things is not particularly accurate (Fig. 2.8). We recall bits and pieces, and assign positivity or negativity to the experience based on what we consider "highlights" of the event or experience. We cast these peaks and endings in a particular way, which goes on to influence our future experiential perceptions. Our personal memories about the self and others serve as reference points for interpreting new experiences. Because the process of memory is skewed and not particularly accurate, our knowledge remains fluid and relatively illusive.

Dr. Jacob Bronowski, a Polish-born British mathematician who wrote a number of highly-regarded books on science, insisted that human error is inextricably bound up with pursuit of new knowledge. He claimed this requires not just calculation but thoughtful insight, an interpretation and a personal act of judgment, for which we are all responsible. The emphasis on the moral responsibility of knowledge was an essential message in all of his works, and an underlying point shared on his acclaimed television program "The Ascent of Man" (BBC 1973). As described by Critchley (2014), Bronowski explained that the acquisition of understanding entails a responsibility for the integrity of who we are as ethical beings. Knowledge and information that passes between us can only be exchanged "within a play of tolerance."

In working to explain Werner Heisenberg's uncertainty principle,[2] Bronowski insisted that the idea was a misnomer, giving the impression that we are always uncertain. He believed this was incorrect, claiming that knowledge is, in fact,

---

[2]Heisenberg described an electron as a particle that yields limited information; its speed and position are confined by the tolerance of Max Planck's quantum, the basic element of matter.

precise. But he went on to say that precision itself is confined within a certain *toleration* of uncertainty. Bronowski thought the uncertainty principle should therefore be called the *principle of tolerance*. Pursuing knowledge means accepting this rampant uncertainty. Heisenberg's principle has the consequence that no physical events can ultimately be described with absolute certainty or with zero tolerance. As such, the nagging paradox is that the more we know, the less certain we can be.

Similarly, your own truth, who you are, is but a snapshot. It is a picture of you in a particular circumstance, time, and place—a moment. We must embrace one another's truths with tolerance. Perceptions are going to be different based on a host of factors, including experience, what you recall, what is happening, and how you are feeling in that moment. The malleability of our perceptions is a gift that comes with a duty to be morally responsible. Because human character, individually and collectively, is consistently in the making, it is essential that we regard our moral development as an ongoing task. If this mission is undertaken with rigorous honesty, self-awareness and empathy, it can continue to be worthwhile, productive, and fulfilling (Fig. 2.9).

Using your innate reflective capacity in concert with feedback from others can help you strengthen your character. Metaphorically, you are a fragment of a larger symmetry, shaped in the context of others, while also influencing those around you. To consider your strengths and weaknesses, it is important to understand who and what you are. This is an effort in sustained mindfulness. The very act of imposing ongoing self-awareness toward ethical awareness, growth and achievement, is a choice to work at being your best self. When broaching business ethics as a platform for human aspiration, a vision of seeing a more ethical world can become realized in a manageable and steadfast manner. A society where people, commerce, and the natural environment effectively co-exist without harm, and continue to evolve in a cooperative way, assumes we each take responsibility for ethics on a personal level. In a democracy we have a right to choose to be a part of co-creating a shared future, one that is just and strives to build individual and collective moral strength. Are we expecting others to do this for us, or are we shouldering our share of the chores, acting as adults to help ensure an ethical social structure for our children's children?

Fig. 2.9 Getting honest with yourself. Image credited to Niels Hariot/Shutterstock.com

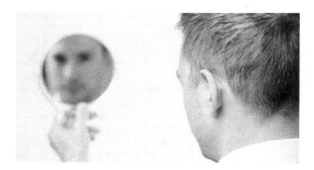

If we hope to achieve cohesive connections, cooperation, and trust in organizational life, we must begin by looking at and understanding ourselves. Do you care about being ethical? Do you want to build your moral strength? What do you want to achieve in life? What are your motives for accomplishing your goals? How do your actions reflect your values? Are you willing to work at strengthening your character as a realizable area for personal growth? Continue to think about these questions as we consider how being more attentive will help you answer them more honestly.

Takeaway Points

1. The ethical character of our organizations and communities is forged in the context of others. We are a prism, reflecting what we truly care about by what we do each day.
2. Consider how your perceptions and reactions shape your reality.
3. Motivations can impose competing values, which may conflict or vie for priority.
4. Being ethical takes personal commitment, fortitude and endurance. Reflect on how you strive to use your personal abilities to become successful in business, ethically.

Reflection Questions

How do you exercise taking responsibility for ethics in your workplace? Do you raise ideas about how to be more proactive in how you go about achieving your organization's goals with moral strength? Do you identify areas of ethical risk, bringing them forward prior to problematic circumstances?

References

Alger, H. [1880] (1966). The world before him (originally serialized in *Golden Days*). In W. Coyle (Ed.), *Popular American fiction series* (pp. 249–252). New York: The Odyssey Press (H. Alger, Jr., Adrift in New York and the world before him).

Balaram, P. (2008). Resilience and imagination. *Current Science, 94*(12), 1545–1546.

BBC. (1973). *The ascent of man* (television series). Retrieved March 26, 2014 from http://www.bbc.co.uk/programmes/b00wms4m.

Coffee, P. R., Haslam, T., & Alexander, S. (2009). Bouncing back from failure: The interactive impact of perceived controllability and stability on self-efficacy beliefs and future task performance. *Journal of Sports Sciences, 27*(11), 1117–1124.

Cooperrider, D. L. (1990). Positive image, positive action: The affirmative basis of organizing. Appreciative management and leadership: In D. L. Cooperrider (Ed.), *The power of positive thought and action in organizations* (91–125). San Francisco, Champaign: Jossey-Bass, Stipes Publishing.

Critchley, S. (2014, February 2). The dangers of certainty: A lesson from Auschwitz. *The Stone.* Retrieved February 24, 2014 from http://opinionator.blogs.nytimes.com/2014/02/02/the-dangers-of-certainty/.

Didion, J. (2006). *Tell ourselves stories in order to live: Collected nonfiction.* New York: Knopf Doubleday Publishing.

Gergen, K. J. (1997). *Realities and relationships: Soundings in social construction.* Cambridge: Harvard University Press. (First Harvard University Press paperback edition).

Gillian, A., & Rothstein, M. G. (Eds.) (2010). Resilience and leadership: The self-management of failure. In M. G. Rothstein & R. J. Burke (Eds.), *Self-management and leadership development* (pp. 361–394). Northampton: Edward Elgar Publishing.

Goffman, E. (1959). *The presentation of self in everyday life.* Garden City: Doubleday.

His Holiness the Dalai Lama. (2014, February 24). *His Holiness The Dalai Lama at Santa Clara University: Incorporating ethics and compassion into business life. A conversation between his Holiness the Dalia Lam and academic and business leaders.* Santa Clara: Santa Clara University.

Hofmann, W., Wisneski, D. C., Brandt, M. J., & Skitka, L. J. (2014). Morality in everyday life. *Science, 345*(6202): 1340–1343.

Kahneman, D. (2011). *Thinking, fast and slow.* New York: Farrar, Strauss, & Giroux.

Kurtz, J. (2014, February 19). Oprah Winfrey urges people to "Just Say Hello. Retrieved February 24, 2014 from http://piersmorgan.blogs.cnn.com/2014/02/19/oprah-winfrey-urges-people-to-just-say-hello-every-human-being-is-looking-for-one-thing-and-that-is-to-be-validated-to-be-seen-and-to-be-heard/?hpt=pm_t1.

Putnam, R. D. (2000). *Bowling alone: The collapse and revival of American community.* New York: Simon & Schuster.

Roberts, L. Morgan, Dutton, J. E., Spreitzer, G., Heaphy, E., & Quinn, R. (2005). Composing the reflected best-self portrait: Building pathways to becoming extraordinary in work organizations. *Academy of Management Review, 30*, 712–736.

Chapter 3
Power from Within

Arguably, there is a moral element to every decision you make. You may not be aware of it or see it initially, but ethics are a part of every action, which is always preceded by choice. Take something as benign as whether or not to hit the snooze button on your morning alarm clock. Should you get up or enjoy an extra 30 min of sleep? This is a fairly simple decision. Perhaps the best idea is to hit the button and get more rest. Indeed, taking care of your health is important. Being responsible for duties at home and work require a good night's sleep. That said, perhaps an even healthier choice might be to get up and eat some breakfast. Taking this one step further, what about your family? Do your children or partner need your time and attention? Perhaps a few moments in meditation or prayer would set the day off right? Does the dog need to be walked? Maybe extra time could be used to help a friend or colleague? Perhaps sleeping in may inadvertently cause you to run late, thus increasing your chances of speeding on the way to work and being less attentive on the roadways.

On the face of it, these sorts of daily choices may not be viewed as moral challenges. But consider what can happen when people do not care about the health and well-being of others on a daily basis. Eventually, seemingly benign choices, when consistently ignored, can become major moral issues. What happens when people do not consider the long-term implications of their self-focused narcissism? Without developing a sustained pattern of mindful consideration, neglect of the ethical self and others can become a crucible for breeding complex social issues that affect us all. Some of these issues can be amended, others are irreversible (e.g., the loss of life due to poor working conditions and lack of safety).

Of course, it is unrealistic and ridiculous to expect that every decision requires a thorough deliberation, especially when you are just waking up! But this simple scenario shows how there are ethical facets with moral implications to even the most rudimentary of decisions, from the moment we awake. It is important for every individual to spend more time thinking about the potential outcomes that his or her actions have on others, possessing some ability to shape and influence reality, given the choices we make. Whether you consciously think about it or not, decisions are choices that express what you value most in any given moment. Most of our decisions hold potentialities that have an implicit or explicit relationship to the livelihood of others. Our moment-to-moment circumstances provide us with an

© Springer International Publishing Switzerland 2016
L. E. Sekerka, *Ethics is a Daily Deal*, DOI 10.1007/978-3-319-18090-8_3

ongoing stream of opportunity to demonstrate our ethical character—or, to choose to do otherwise. Because our present actions reinforce the potential for similar future actions, we continue to mold and reinforce—shape and develop—our character. In so doing, we create who we are and the world around us by the decisions we make every day of our lives.

Similarities and Differences

Schwartz's work on universal human values has become a baseline reference for helping us understand that basic shared values bind our human existence together. However, these same values can also separate us, driving us apart. Although it is accepted that there are values and self-evident truths we all share (Schwartz 1992, 2006, 2012; Figs. 3.1 and 3.2), we must come to terms with determining the rightness or wrongness of our own actions. In so doing, we begin to see how these values can conflict, both within ourselves and in working with others.

For example, as a business person I may have a combination of values that focus largely on self-direction, achievement and power, yet I hold a sincere respect for others. If a strategic decision at work calls for a consideration of stakeholder concerns, given the amount of resources involved, my benevolence for these issues may moderate my level of commitment to the welfare of others. While appreciation and tolerance may be among my personal values, in business, I am also responsible to ensure the success of the firm, attending to shareholder demands for profit. Given a short-term view of achievement, my commitment to compassion may wane. Variances show up in the strength and application of our values. In some circumstances, we may see the issue as "black and white," which suggests there is a clear

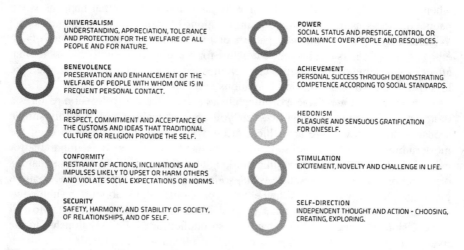

Fig. 3.1 Universal value clusters. Figure credited to Schwartz (2006)/Creative Commons 2015

Fig. 3.2 Schwartz's value circumplex. Figure credited to Schwartz (1992)/Creative Commons 2015

path to right or wrong. In fact, most issues are gray, or at least they bear shades of gray. In other words, determining the appropriate right action can be vague, unclear, or vary depending upon the person, situation, and context (Treviño 1986). People see things very differently; what may be crystal clear to one person may be ambiguous to another. Furthermore, individuals are not necessarily consistent in how they see things, or for that matter, in how and when they apply their own values.

I can recall being a part of a study group, managers engaging in an applied ethics workshop. In reviewing the assigned case, the team was given a few hours to resolve it as a collective effort. After reading through the material, one participant declared, "The answer is clear!" He outlined his solution with specificity and ardent resolve, followed by announcing how pleased he was to have the afternoon off, since the case was done. "There's no need for any discussion or deliberation on this issue," he exclaimed. While his framework for ethical decision-making may have served him well, and for that matter may have led to a "right" solution to the case, it was not particularly helpful in this situation. We were assigned to tackle the ethical issue with others, people representing a variety of disciplines. What seemed clear to him was not so obvious to his peers, nor did everyone agree with his solution. Binary declarations of what is right or wrong may be useful as a basic guideline in certain circumstances in a given context. But rigid frameworks may also short-circuit collaborative discourse.

With 12 million square miles (7.68 billion acres) of arable land on the planet's surface, if we shared this proportionately, we would each get about an acre. With planetary changes from natural and manmade influences, available land mass continues to be depleted, with losses at 1 % annually. Land degradation and conversion of cropland for non-food production including biofuels, cotton, and others are major threats that could reduce the available cropland by 8–20 % by 2050 (GRID-Arendal, UNEP (2014)). According to the United States Census Bureau and the world population clock, an estimated number of people on the planet as of June 2, 2015 is 7,247,300.[1] Population around the world varies by country, with China and India leading the way by a huge margin, followed by the United States, Indonesia, Brazil, and Pakistan. This number grows by approximately 212,522 people daily. In 2011 we hit the 7 billion mark. As our planet earth and humanity evolves, we can readily observe change, eminent for each and every one of us. Everything is in an ongoing state of change. Because of this continuous phase of motion, our life is one of enduring developmental potential.

Dialogue around ethical issues is conducive for creative thinking, embracing multiple perspectives, and to establish agreement, confidence and buy-in (Sekerka 2009; Gentile 2014). Black-and-white thinking can sometimes foster an overly simplistic packaging of ethics. Rule-based codes of ethics do not guide the full complexity of living and evolving ethically in working with others, particularly in today's arena of diverse workgroups and stakeholder partnerships (people representing different organizations, generations, industries, countries, cultures, etc.) (Fig. 3.3). Given the population increases around the world, it's quite clear that both the Asian and Indian cultures will continue to influence and shape the global economy. How ethics is perceived in business has to be understood from multiple perspectives. It must be communicated in ways that people can relate to, given what's important to them and what they value. For example, while everyone might say they care about ethics, how this is perceived and enacted as a value, can vary by cultural interpretation (cf. Marar Yacobian and Sekerka 2014)

---

[1]See https://www.census.gov/popclock/.

Fig. 3.3 Countries ranked by
population (2015).
Information provided by the
United States Census Bureau,
International Data Base at:
http://www.census.gov/
population/international/data/
idb/informationGateway.php

Rank	Country	Population
1	China	1,361,512,535
2	India	1,251,695,584
3	United States	321,362,789
4	Indonesia	255,993,674
5	Brazil	204,259,812
6	Pakistan	199,085,847
7	Nigeria	181,562,056
8	Bangladesh	168,957,745
9	Russia	142,423,773
10	Japan	126,919,659

Habits Predict Your Future

In light of this realization, you have the potential to construct a revised and improved ethical self—a better you—on an ongoing basis. But leveraging this opportunity requires an awareness of your capacity and having a desire to cultivate and exercise it. Understanding who you are is to honestly study your inner motives and to see how they are associated with past, present and potential future actions. Daily habits and intentions are great predictors of future behaviors (Danner et al. 2008). For example, we know that cheating today predicts cheating tomorrow. The reproducibility and persistence over time of dishonest behavior highlights the danger of disregarding any unethical act, no matter how small it may appear to be. Teixeria (2013) examined university students' level of cheating, with robust dataset of 7000 participants representing 21 countries. The study findings showed how variations in cheating were similar to the corruption levels in their country of origin. Of course, different countries around the world are represented by cultures that reflect different levels of tolerance toward corruption. But this study made a point of underscoring how levels of cheating start early and forecast a future of such behavior (Teixeira 2013). Point being, if a country is high in corruption today, unless there is some sort of explicit intervention, future leaders are likely to continue in the same vein. Taking a stand against corruption means the global business community needs to make it less attractive to those currently benefitting from it. The reality, however, is that in some countries and industries corruption is so engrained it is viewed more as a practice than an anomaly. This does not bode well for ethical action in business; that is, unless people value and demand it.

Research by Transparency International (2013) placed Denmark as #1 with a high score reflecting the least amount of corruption, with New Zealand and Finland close behind (Fig. 3.4). Afghanistan, North Korea, and Somalia were at the bottom

of the list, found to be the most corrupt countries in the world. The USA followed Australia, Canada, Germany, and the United Kingdom, amongst others, ranked at a relatively unimpressive #19. Given today's economy is interdependent, there is a world of opportunity and an ocean full of ethical dilemmas set before us. When there is little concurrence among business and government leaders about what is fair, just, and honest in business practice, ensuring that values are upheld is especially challenging. But facing this "tall order," moral strength can be a market differentiator, appealing to talent and consumers alike (Jennings 2014).

While current research by the Josephson Institute of Ethics reported a decrease in student cheating in America, the numbers still reflect that more than half of high school students admit to having cheated (2012). Depending upon the methodology, reports of cheating in high school, college, and medical school vary widely (from 3 to 80 %), given the definition used in the study and whether or not elements of cheating are stated or merely implied when participants take part in the research. For example, some scholars explicitly state what they mean by cheating (e.g., cheating on an exam, engaging in underage drinking, sharing homework answers, paying someone to write your term paper, having sex with a person known to be coupled with someone else, etc.). Other studies are designed in such a way that the researchers let the participants determine what cheating means to them, and then they proceed with the inquiry using their own self-declared implicit definition.

With consideration of context, people admitting to having cheated, say on an exam, vary from 39.3 % (when both perception of detection and severity of punishment are low) to 3.4 % (when both perceptions of detection and severity of punishment are high) (LaSalle 2009). Regardless of how you define cheating, or alter the context in which it occurs, an emerging pattern of such behavior reflects a lack of ethics, a pattern likely to continue unless we encourage awareness and education, and build up the social and personal value of the moral self. What you do, including those seemingly little "one-time" deceptions, tells the world what is most important to you, and these actions reveal your ethical identity. People may say they care about ethics, but it's often conditional (e.g., "I care about ethics when I'm paid to care").

For example, in January of 2015, a Malaysian defense contractor pleaded guilty in a corruption scandal of epic proportions. Having admitted he bribed scores of U.S. Navy officials with $500,000 in cash, hundreds of thousands of dollars in prostitute sex, and lavish hotel stays, the list of luxury items went on and on (spa treatments, Cuban cigars, Kobe beef, Spanish suckling pigs and an array of other luxury goods) (Whitlock 2015). Leonard Glenn Francis, a businessman charmed a generation of Navy officers to accept bribes while resupplying their ships in Asia. He admitted in a U.S. federal court that he led a decade-long corruption scheme involving his Singapore-based firm, Glenn Defense Marine Asia. The biggest corruption case in the Navy's history, Francis admitted he bilked the U.S. government and military out of tens of millions of dollars by overcharging for food, fuel and basic services. Five current and former Navy officials have now pleaded guilty. But prosecutors have advanced their investigation and expect to charge many others. What happened here? Military officers are typically ethical people, committing to duty, honor, and service to their country. In many cases, it seems that power and exaggerated pride (hubris) can contribute to sense of entitlement, a belief that the rules are for other people (leaders can operate by a different set of rules/norms). It appears that leaders can get blinded by greed and lack of focused attention toward sustaining their own moral strength.

Writer and ethics commentator Bruce Weinstein highlights that the lack of ethics surrounds us today, as bankers, athletes, and government officials are caught cheating, which gives way to the rationale, "If these people can get away with it, why shouldn't I?" (Weinstein 2009). When questionable performance issues hit the news headlines, it makes the game a little less fair and a little more dishonest. While this sort of cheating is sometimes viewed as trivial by diehard fans, in reality it creates an unequal playing field. If everyone cheats, ultimately no one gains in the long run. Business enterprise, in sports or any other industry, is transactional and based on cooperation, trust, and reciprocity. One approach to address the tendency to cheat is to encourage people to think about what we owe ourselves and others, to honor and support people who play by the rules, and to make an effort to lead with ethics as a personal choice. But doing this means you have to be aware of your values, sustain this awareness, and continue to apply them on an ongoing basis.

Larry Hinman, Professor of Philosophy and Director of the Values Institute at the University of San Diego, explains that ethics is about helping people learn what they have in common with humanity. As described in an article by Weinstein (2009), Hinman believes that the ethical concerns of today are not so much about how well we can live within our group, but more about how our group can live well with other groups throughout the world. He encourages us to spend more time listening to what other people have to say about their values, rather than making assumptions. The more common ground we can establish with others, seeking to find the similarities as opposed to elevating the differences, the better our chances of building a stronger global society. Ethical guidance is also needed and, unfortunately, many adults are not setting good examples.

A way to see whether or not your values are dormant or active is by thinking about how you respond to simple situational encounters, issues we all face regularly. Consider these questions and answer them as honestly as you can:

- Do you keep your word, even when it's not convenient?
- Does a handshake mean something to you?
- Do you consistently complete tasks in a timely manner?
- Do you let others do tasks for you, menial or less rewarding jobs you would rather avoid?
- Do you stay open to other people's views, listening before drawing conclusions?
- If you mistakenly receive a higher pay amount or commission rate do you report the error?
- Are you truthful with your doctor about how much you drink and smoke?
- If you are accidentally undercharged for a product or service, do you report it?
- Do you cut people off when driving?
- Do you gossip, talking negatively about other people behind their backs?
- Do you arrive late or unprepared to meetings?
- Do you copy or share music or movies illegally?
- Do you tell white lies, embellish stories, or exaggerate situations to gain attention or build up your self-esteem?
- Do you claim to have "not received" something that you did, to feign an inability to act?
- Do you pay people back when you borrow money, no matter how small or large the sum?
- Do you admit when you are wrong and then take corrective action to right matters?
- Do you own your full share of the bill, when dining out with others?
- If you damage a car in the parking lot, do you leave a note?
- Are you courteous and patient with coworkers and other people you encounter throughout the day?
- Do you apologize when you hurt someone's feelings, create an inconvenience, or cause harm?

Doing the next right thing means being aware of how your thinking and behavior (or the lack thereof) influences others and their needs. To be ethical, each person has to continually work at being mindful of the ethical elements embedded in their everyday activities.

What Are Your Motives?

An easy reminder is to always "check your motives" before you act. Ask yourself, "What is my real reason behind my acting or not acting this way?" A personal examination of your genuine motives helps to illuminate your real intent (to win, be ahead, succeed, not lose, be late, etc.). It can be difficult to be aware of your motives unless you work at it. And you have to be brutally honest with yourself, as self-deception in this regard can be harmful to you and other people over time. Perhaps even more challenging is to self-correct your response-action plan, if you fine that temptation is pulling you toward a self-serving goal that may cause you to supersede your ethical values. Everyone has to figure out where their natural tendencies and temptations reside and then manage and direct their energies toward enacting the core values they profess to hold. When values compete, for example, "I care about being a good person but with a few ethical shortcuts I can make an extra buck," see if your character strengths can hold their own. It takes practice to embolden your ethical will. Your ethicality is revealed in the little things you do day in and day out. What do your daily actions say about what you truly value? Have you ever "gotten real" with yourself, and changed the course of direction, recognizing that your will was selfish and uncaring?

Current research in psychology shows that authenticity is linked to a sense of morality. When asked to describe how they behave (with or without authenticity), researchers found that when people focus on their inauthentic experiences, they tend to feel more immoral and impure than when they reflect on their authentic experiences. Such feelings of immorality are associated with an increased desire to cleanse the self and to engage in moral compensatory behaviors. In other words, being disingenuous makes you feel dirty. When people were given the opportunity to cleanse themselves the relationship between inauthenticity and moral compensatory behavior was eliminated. Gino et al. (2015), the authors of this work, indicate that the findings provide initial evidence to show a link between authenticity and morality.

Excellence of character stems from habituated effort, rather than simply from human nature. Aristotle (1999) offers a way for us to become habituated in virtue, by performing virtuous acts (1105a25b3). In comparing art and virtue acquisition, he suggests that the former is primarily a matter of internalizing procedural principles and producing a product that embodies this knowledge (e.g., a business). Conversely, virtue is not about learning procedures, but about having reliable motives, expressed in selected actions, which come to have meaning and value. To be virtuous is to act virtuously. A person can gain a better understanding of ethics by getting into the habit of thinking about and exercising their character strengths. To become aware of the circumstances where specific virtues can be applied—to form the right emotional responses and decisions for action—is to possess virtue. This generally evolves over time with focused attention and practice. Arguably, the pleasure of being ethical often emerges as you get better at it. By acting ethically you can develop an appreciation and skill for it, further endorsing the strength and stability of your character. And, when you become known as a person who is consistently ethical, people are less likely to come to you with business ideas, schemes, and/or processes that fall below the moral line.

Recapping, we know that identifying the ethical elements embedded in our everyday decision-making is a practice that requires conscious effort (juxtaposed to sole reliance upon automatic responses). Living your values needs to be framed 'less' as assumed element of your character and 'more' as a sustained habit of choice, built up through deliberate exercise. To sustain the standards and beliefs you claim to hold, you have to put them to work. In so doing, you not only affirm your ethical identity, but you also influence how you experience life and how others experience their lives as well. But this "so-called" practice is easier said than done. Applying values to daily duties and one's lifestyle typically requires focused intent, effort, and persistence. This means learning how to generate a sustained willingness to think about and address decisions with ethical awareness and refueling a desire to do the right thing on an ongoing basis (Sekerka and Bagozzi 2007). With a multitude of distractions that vie for your attention every hour of the day, enacting your best ethical self requires an ongoing commitment to ensuring your ethicality. Being an indefatigable moral agent does not mean you are a caped crusader. Rather, it is about sustaining a self-directed willingness to do your ethical best in the situations you encounter. While moral agents in the workplace might be considered superheroes, strength in being ethical comes from moral mindfulness and striving to be your best ethical self (Fig. 3.5).

For the Great Generation, those who went through the Great Depression and World War II, great suffering and hardship also meant learning how to come together to survive. Realizing that everyone had to do their part, reminders were everywhere, asking to citizens to give what they could spare, share, be fair, and rally as a country (Fig. 3.6).

After the war, massive industrialization and a robust consumer-driven economy shaped society to become the marketers dream. Today, we all face a succession of wants and desires that present competing alternatives by the moment. Duties and lures alike demand our time, attention, and consideration on the Internet, cell phone, and other various technology-driven devices. Surrounded by a sea of options, we can easily be distracted or dissuaded from focusing on the ethical features of the present moment. Scholars (Bauman and Donskis 2013) suggest that moral blindness permeates our society. This blindness actually dulls our senses and prevents us from being ethically aware. In this state, people frame situations and others' needs outside the boundaries of their own moral obligation. Referred to as *adiaphora*, this

Fig. 3.5 Moral agents may be considered superheroes, but they're actually you and me. Image credited to Rawpixel/Shutterstock.com

Fig. 3.6 A poster from the 1940s "Rationing means a fair share for all of us". Issued by the U.S. Office of Price Administration (established in 1941), this poster was used to help manage rationing. It appeals to women's desire to be a good American, encouraged to sympathize with the woman who has nothing, and to find the woman who takes more than her share objectionable. The image below illustrates how women, and shopkeepers should behave; each woman is being a good housewife, but by taking her share she is being a responsible citizen and allowing every other American housewife the same opportunity. Image courtesy of the Victorian & Albert Museum, gift of the American Friends of the V&A; Gift to the American Friends by Leslie, Judith and Gabri Schreyer and Alice Schreyer Batko

indifference to the world contributes to a kind of moral numbness. When relevance is dictated by ratings and returns, when people are preoccupied with the latest fad, gadget, and gossip, and information comes at us continuously at a hurried pace, the ubiquitous nature of these distractions pose a risk to our ability to be consciously mindful.

It is obvious that today's information-age environment is not conducive to encouraging ethical awareness. Rather, it is more likely to endorse distraction from our striving to be attentive! Even with the best intentions to be aware of the moral elements of a circumstance, a belief in "mindfulness" and valuing ethics can inadvertently fall by the wayside. Distraction is often complemented by deeper cultural attitudes associated with business and personal success (demands for ratings and returns, performance expectations, etc.). While achieving success is not usually considered a distraction, we can unintentionally redirect our focus on other values (sense of belonging, money, status, power, etc.) and potentially away from ethical mindfulness.

Dependencies on all-consuming communication tools—cell phone usage, texting, and other virtual activities have, in many ways, become a social expectation. Technological devices can inadvertently draw our attention away from ethical awareness, critical for sustaining morally responsible behavior in the workplace. Responding to an incoming message is so compelling to some people that they text while driving at high speeds. Typing "LOL" while driving is not funny—it costs lives. A study conducted by the Center for Disease Control analyzed 2011 data on distracted driving, including talking on a cell phone or reading or sending texts or emails while behind the wheel (CDC 2013). Findings showed that 69 % of drivers in the United States aged 18–64 reported that they had talked on their cell phone while driving within the previous 30 days. In the United States, statistics reflect that, on average, 9 people are killed and 1,060 people are injured in crashes every day, from accidents that involve a distracted driver (NHTSA 2013).

In addition to the continual pull of life's distractions, it is hard to sustain a desire to pursue ethical action when we perceive that those around us do not value or affirm it. Many of us feel cheated and frustrated by the behavior of others. On a large scale, the collapse of the financial market in 2008 reflected the involvement of many who regularly engaged in dicey, unethical, and unseemly practices. Taxpayers paid the bill for the misdeeds of business leaders, subsidizing massive bailouts and taking major personal losses, with the value of their own pensions, investments, and homes markedly decreased. Since that period, we continue to see prices rise and packages shrink. Meanwhile, profits are soaring once again. With the mercurial nature of the stock market combined with rewarding risky decision-making on Wall Street, most of us are left wondering not "if", but "when" the next recession will occur.

Rewarding Bad Behavior

While the regulators are doing their best to rein in flagrant practices (e.g., bankers trading for their own accounts), not much has changed in the financial services industry. Many of us still pay into a retirement system that lets high-frequency traders gamble with other people's money. With stupidity, greed, arrogance, and corruption fueling an elite system that is "rigged" (Lewis 2014; Patterson 2013), we are bound to see another market collapse. When bad behavior is rewarded, as it was in 2008, we can certainly expect more of it. Activities like high-frequency trading may not violate the rules on permissible stock trading, but that does not make it right, ethical, or just (Henning 2014). As described in *The New York Times*, "The tactic smells to high heaven, creating an unlevel playing field that costs investors money" (Nocera 2014) (Fig. 3.7).

Fig. 3.7 People ignoring creditors, regulators, or the law isn't new. Satirical print entitled "Too Deep for the Knowing Ones, or How to Cheat the Bailifs'." The debtor is being pushed in a barrel towards the gates of Sadler's Wells whilst the bailiffs stand unaware outside a public house. Etched by Isaac Cruikshank ca. 1790. Harry Beard Collection. Image courtesy of the V&A Collection

Such concerns seem to relate to a gradual reduction in the value of assuming personal responsibility. It is hard to care about being ethical when we see others lacking in moral fortitude; worse yet, role-models engaging in business with limited scruples. If we expect moral strength to come from those around us, rather than from ourselves, we may inadvertently fuel a cycle of reacting and redirecting accountability away from the "self." Developing a habit of letting others shape our personal norms of morality suggests you are willing to give away your power of influence. In so doing, a bit of your personal freedom is lost when you choose to look away, ignore, or direct your attentions away from what is ethical. If you stop paying attention to your ethical identity and its development, you are allowing others to impose their will upon your power of choice, you are, in essence, handing over your responsibility to another person and letting them choose for you.

Ironically, when stepping aside from moral responsibility regresses into a lack of ethical attention and engagement, such distancing can, over time, create the illusion that we have little or no ability to change the world we live in. Apathy can set in, along with a sense of entitlement. In America, it can often seem as though the very rich and big-moneyed operations (e.g., Political Action Committees) hold enormous power in shaping the future of the country. Each person is responsible for helping to reclaim systemic balance, which includes personal awareness and involvement in civic duties. It seems remarkable to me that so many people are seemingly willing to be manipulated by others. When we assume others are leading us ethically, we usher in an external authority, to dictate what is right for us. Thus, your personal code of ethics is then determined by external sponsors, individuals, groups, and/or entities, all of whom have their own agenda. In turning over our power, casually, blindly, or lazily, we run the risk of no longer caring. This becomes a dysfunctional systemic social issue, one that is made blatantly obvious, over and over again. A recent article in *The Washington Post* put to its readers that perhaps a little corruption no longer matters to voters, noting that officials seem to win despite ethical and campaign finance challenges as elements of their resumes (Krieger 2014). Do you find this disturbing?

The broader question is: Do you give away your responsibility to uphold the ethical foundations of society? Do you assume the associated duties that accompany the rights to freedom in a democracy, free to make decisions and aspire to achieve your moral potential? Perhaps we might all take heed, looking for how, where, why, and when we play a role in creating the current norms, a platform where business and government often tell us what we should value or need to have (e.g., Nike shoes, national health care). Perhaps even more disconcerting, is examining what we often simply disregard or ignore. How might we encourage and build moral responsibility under these emerging social circumstances?

Buying into the System

If you are wondering why there is degradation in the value of responsibility, it may be because we spend a great deal of time and energy focusing on unethical activity rather than on the development of moral strength. We do not seem to be paying attention to how to elevate the best within us, our potential to be virtuous. Is being responsible—a person of ethical character— important to you? If you want to see a world where business operates ethically, you have to start with the business of knowing and becoming your best ethical self. Paying attention, waking up to the ethical aspects of our daily lives, offers a platform to strengthen individual ethical identity, moving to advance our collective moral fortitude.

You have the ability to choose if you want to be responsible or not. You can decide to focus on or away from an issue and the ethicality of your course of action. But with a natural propensity to be self-centered and often distracted with our own agendas, many of us have lost the value of paying attention to the ethics embedded within our daily decisions. In so doing, personal desires can take the lead and inadvertently work to dull our ethical senses. A life focused on personal achievement may inadvertently distract us. This may serve to mitigate the level of concern we would hope to apply toward others (i.e., thoughtful consideration), such as care and empathy. This has potentially contributed to a lessening of how we see, embrace, and value the notion of assuming responsibility.

The price for a depletion in or lack of responsibility is reflected in a deterioration of ethics in our culture (Callahan 2004). In getting into a habit of just reacting to the news and others, we can begin to think about wrongdoing as something that happens *out there*. We examine events as incidents that occur outside our realm of responsibility, that which is external to us. Combined with a natural proclivity to see ourselves in a favorable light, we tend to point fingers and assign blame (implicitly and/or explicitly). This frames ethics, or the lack thereof, as an external force. By directing ethicality away from personal attribution, we look outwardly to a focal point; then with a critical eye we often work to determine and assign fault.

Fig. 3.8 Who stole the
people's money? Image
credited to Thomas Nast,
Harper's Weekly, August 19,
(1871) is in the public domain

People typically resolve ethical incongruities by looking outside themselves to see who is responsible for the mishap or transgression. Working to ensure that we are not the source of the problem provides a way to rationalize our way out of duty, we assign fault or culpability externally. As a result, many people develop patterns of assigning responsibility outwardly (Fig. 3.8).

A spoof on this type of blame game was captured in 1871, when newspapers exposed a series of corruption scandals. Thomas Nast's memorable caricature of the Tweed Ring illustrates the thieves in a circle all pointing outwards. In their attribution of blame to anyone but themselves, the perpetrators deflect responsibility elsewhere. This shows up in cases where management works to identify a "scapegoat." When firms experience an ethical issue they often leap to assign blame, point fingers, and charge someone with causality. Show me an ethical conflagration at a company and I'll find the person (or people) who have been "labeled" as the cause of the problem. Interestingly, the human tendency to assign fault outwardly may not be so obvious. It is important to pay attention to this propensity because it can have a debilitating effect on our own ethicality.

Consider your role as a consumer. After World War II, many Americans were lulled into believing they need the latest fashion or gadget. But we also expect and want products and services at affordable prices. We all experience the ongoing stream of marketing coming at us from every direction, 24/7. This type of culture creates new and ongoing demand for goods by encouraging trendy, cutting-edge products or by building in obsolescence. Most of us are aware that these goods are often produced using cheap labor, where working conditions are substandard to Western regulatory demands. Of course, many firms choose to make business decisions that employ off-shore labor, striving to increase demand for their products (as a result of cost efficiencies, mass availability, etc.). At some point, however, someone ends up paying for these shortcuts. But the burden often lands on those with less power, money, and voice (e.g., the working poor). As timeless adages portend—"You get what you pay for," "There is no such thing as a free lunch," and "If it's too good to be true, it probably is"—there are always costs. Whether they are short- or long-term, explicit or implicit, strategic operations based on cutting corners tax our collective well-being.

In the case of cheap apparel, hidden costs are often shouldered by employees who produce these goods earning very low wages, in conditions that are often unacceptable (according to Western standards). The lives of garment workers employed in China, Indonesia, Africa, Bangladesh and other nations (largely lesser developed countries) are often put at risk. Human health and well-being may be put in jeopardy in order to stock stores with inexpensive retail merchandise. This occurs across the industry spectrum, including apparel and a host of other retail products. In the agriculture sector, migrant workers are often expected to endure hazardous conditions to earn a living (e.g., tobacco pickers in the United States) (Planet Matters and More 2011). The underlying costs for the lack of social responsibility are not something we, as consumers, readily think about when we buy our clothes, food, household goods, and the various items that we regularly consume.

There are alternatives—management and consumers do have options. People can choose to garner their resources ethically. Businesses and consumers alike can work to hold suppliers and purveyors of goods and services accountable, holding them to a higher standard of ethics by guiding, directing, or even withholding demand. We all have an ability to choose what we consume, as representatives of our organizations and families. We can strive to become more informed, making an effort to buy items produced by companies that work to inculcate supply chain ethics. Or we can choose to ignore how the products we buy are created and delivered. Pure and simple, business enterprise and the business of being a consumer are both about making choices. But far from being clean or simple is the ability to make ethical decisions when you work for an industry or people who care very little about being moral. That said, everyone who participates in the Western consumer-driven society has the ability to vote with their wallet. From the producers and merchants to the buyers themselves, we all have an opportunity to consider the ethical elements of commerce and how our role in it contributes to its moral strength—or the lack thereof.

Where you spend your time and money says a lot about who you are and what you truly value. The lack of ethics in industry is a consumer problem, as well as a management concern. Ethics in business means you are willing to assume responsibility for principled performance. It means working to understand how choices and actions influence short- and long-term operations, and how decisions support or detract from the ethics of your enterprise. Consumers may inadvertently perpetuate certain business practices, buying into (literally and figuratively) a system that is often buoyed by unethical activities. Few of us take the time to consider who pays the hidden costs of cutting ethical corners. We rarely think about the workers who embody what we buy and the environment that shoulders our throw-away society.

For example, in Bangladesh 3.6 million garment workers are employed in a $20 billion industry (Alam 2013). These people are surrounded by government corruption and are often desperate for jobs; they engage in an industry that is often indifferent to human rights. People in Bangladesh earn some of the lowest wages in the world at $38 a month, all too often in conditions that are unsafe (Johnson 2013).

Fig. 3.9 Burned sweatshop garment factory after fire disaster. Image credited to Baloncici/
Shutterstock.com

The fire that broke out in a Bangladeshi clothing factory in 2013 took over a thousand lives (Hussein 2013). At the time, employees were reportedly creating garments to be sold in Wal-Mart stores (Fig. 3.9).

When you wear clothing produced in substandard conditions, you implicitly choose to agree with the processes that manufacture the items. On some level, you are an accomplice to the firm's decisions if you "buy into" them (i.e., by purchasing something from them). Ignorance or lack of knowledge is no longer an excuse today. We know too much. But by the same token, unless a firm centers its identity, strategy, and performance metrics on human and social responsibility, it is difficult for consumers and suppliers to consistently and accurately become informed and to subsequently make prudent and ethical choices (Kleyn et al. 2012). Nevertheless, we need to try. Have you made an attempt to understand what practices and processes are associated with the products you buy?

Of course, there are people who need a job, any job, regardless of the working conditions (Kristoff 2009). Despite substandard, unfair, or even unsafe working conditions, some people feel that it may be worth the risk, in order to feed their families. An argument is also made that perhaps offering discounted prices gives some people the ability to afford clothing for their families who might not otherwise be able to do so. These arguments have some validity. But they can also be excuses, pretexts that divert us from developing our own moral awareness. Without careful consideration, such leveraged relativism can unintentionally support our own selfishness. Some scholars go so far as to say that it is unreasonable to place full responsibility and/or blame on management, given their systemic constraints, limited resources, and increasing demands (Kleist 2013). Business ethicists have argued that the corporation as a moral agent is actually a misnomer. Given business is a collective responsibility (Sverdlik 1987) means accountability and obligation need to be fully distributed (Cowton 2011).

It's Impolite to Point

It is easy to point fingers, blame others, or to turn our head when considering the role we play in the ethics of business. In any industry, people need to be held accountable when they choose to operate unethically. But whether or not an organization and its members are moral, we are all involved and bear some level of responsibility for the ethics of business. Corrective measures can be a challenge, because people rarely want to fix things they did not break. Researchers in social psychology and relational dynamics observe that when people assign attribution for their issues outside of themselves, they are likely to also assign accountability externally. In other words, if I am not to blame for the problem, I am not responsible for resolving it (Mitchell 1998). This is faulty reasoning. Our power stems from within. Change requires a modification to how we frame, interpret, and respond to life. How we react to daily life shapes what we experience.

Where you spend your time and money is a statement about your ethical character. If we shirk off ethics as someone else's duty or problem, we really need to ask ourselves, "Who is minding the store?" By ignoring the matter, we are, in some respects, putting our own wants above the needs of others. It is important to get into a habit of asking yourself, "What role do I play in the ethics of this situation?" This may be more obvious when it comes to our consumer behaviors. Think about these questions:

- Do you seek out information about what goes into creating the products, services, and entertainment you buy?
- Are you willing to reject products manufactured or delivered in ways that are harmful to people, other sentient beings, and the natural environment?
- Do you consciously look to see if your values are aligned with what you buy?
- Do you make an effort to learn about the companies you frequently do business with, seeing if their social and environmental stance fits your own beliefs?
- Do you challenge companies that make unsupported claims?
- Do you strive to work with and for organizations that demonstrate respect for others and the planet?

If you are in the habit of disregarding these types of questions, you may be extricating yourself from the responsibility of being ethical. In so doing, you may, over time, deplete your capacity for moral strength in other areas. Without regularly practicing ethical awareness, reflection, and action, you cannot assume moral strength will be there when you need it. Like any other skill, if you do not use it, its strength is likely to be limited or diminished.

Not My Problem

It is important to see the role you play in shaping the broader ethicality of society, individually and holistically. Understanding that there are ethical elements to every decision, you can begin to see how your everyday choices can, over time, reflect your lived ethical identity. Not paying attention to the ethics within your decisions, or simply ignoring their existence, does not remove or absolve your duty to attend to them. But let us assume you have a willingness to be responsible. You are deciding whether or not to take on a new project, knowing that the workload is already heavy. An ethical element of this decision might be to consider how the assumption of this resolve may stretch your resources, potentially driving your costs up, a monetary or taxing toll that either you or your firm must absorb. What do you do when you are inconvenienced, denied something, or your performance is impacted by decisions to be more ethical? What do you do when you realize that you are connected to the production of goods and services that are not up to what you would consider an appropriate ethical standard of quality? Are you willing to own the ethical elements of your choices?

If you are willing to pursue this notion, one way to examine or challenge your ethical durability is to seek out and examine how you may unintentionally support unethical practices without even realizing it. How might the absence of mindful actions, or simply the presence of apathy or disinterest, serve to enable or fortify a lack of ethicality? With the daily streams of information that highlight the moral degradation of our society, some people have become numb to imposing an internal cross-check. And, in business, when ethics is determined and shaped by adherence to government regulation, there is little impetus for goal setting and striving. Perhaps this is why we see officials sentenced, consumers fleeced, heroes stripped of their titles, incentives that prompt illegal shortcutting, and compliance directors being relieved of their duties.

A glaring example where we can create a demonstrative change in our culture is to strive to attain ethics within the industry of sport. With an omnipresent passion for sporting events, athletic competition is loved worldwide. Fans are adamantly committed to particular players, teams, and annual competitions with a kind of fervor that is, in many cases, unparalleled. Either as participants or observers, young and old alike form a sort of camaraderie, making connections and bonding with others, as they root for, bet on, or play in their game of choice. At any given time we see some sort of playoff or championship going on (e.g. Final Four, Stanley Cup, World Series, Olympic events). This year, the entire Google planet seems to have embraced the fight for attaining the World Cup, as football (soccer) players compete for the coveted title of world champions (for weeks the Google search engine page brought attention to these games during the playoffs). Seeking ethics in sport and in the industry itself seems, at times, almost futile. Because there is so much money involved, ensuring morality from the players, managers, and organizations that own and/or operate the teams can almost seem out of reach. But consumers of sport hold the power of refusal...refusing to attend or watch the games.

Criminal activity has become so rampant within organizations like the Fédération Internationale de Football Association (FIFA), soccer's global governing body, leaders are blatantly arrogant and seemingly able to operate above the law. Alexandra Wrage, a governance consultant who unsuccessfully attempted to help overhaul FIFA's methods, famously labeled the organization "byzantine and impenetrable." But in May of 2015 Swiss authorities arrested several top soccer officials and extradited them to the United States on federal corruption charges (as reported in *The New York Times*, Apuzzo et al. 2015). As leaders of FIFA gathered for their annual meeting, law enforcement arrived unannounced at the Baur au Lac hotel, an elegant five-star property overlooking the Alps. The charges allege widespread corruption in FIFA over the past two decades, involving bids for World Cups as well as marketing and broadcast deals. This includes wire fraud, racketeering and money laundering. According to case prosecutors, FIFA's Secretary General Jerome Valcke is linked with a $10 million payment set to a former FIFA Vice President Jack Warner, in exchange for a positive vote on South Africa's bid for the 2010 World Cup.

Just days after the arrests, Sepp Blatter, the President of FIFA stepped down. Blatter stated that, "We need deep-rooted structural change," suggesting a reshaping of the powerful executive committee and the importance of imposing term limits. This was a bit ironic, given his lengthy presence as FIFA's leader (17 years). FIFA is a multibillion-dollar organization governing the world's most popular sport and has been plagued by accusations of bribery for decades, with Blatter at the helm for 17 years. In 2004, FIFA released its first code of ethics, prior to which the organization had no ethics rules whatsoever (Borden 2015).[2] Critics of FIFA point to the lack of transparency regarding executive salaries and resource allocations for an organization that has sustained revenues reaching nearly $6 billion between 2011 and 2014. Policy decisions are known to have been made without debate or explanation, and a small group of officials—the executive committee—operates with authoritative power. FIFA has long operated with little oversight and even less transparency (Fig. 3.10).

What if leaders and the organizations they represent, like FIFA, received inordinate pressure from fans to change their behavior? The public can always express their dismay towards corruption by refusing to purchase tickets. In so doing, people have a say in the ethical practices of sport. If leagues or teams show a decline in revenue, the demonstrative ineffectiveness of leadership would be obvious, and management would be "forced out." But with the present leadership, declaring that corrupt practices will continue regardless of who is at the helm, coupled with fans remaining unwilling to impose personal constraint (using their purchasing power as a tool to demand ethics in sport), there is no motivation or incentive for anything to change. The arrogance and hubris driving the current modality of operation is simply left unbridled. Unless sports enthusiasts (consumers of sport) exercise their desire for ethics and step up to the plate to demand its presence, there can be no

[2]For a timeline of Blatter's "rise and fall" see: http://www.nytimes.com/interactive/2015/05/27/sports/soccer/28fifa-timeline.html#/#time376_11017.

Fig. 3.10 Sepp Blatter, President of FIFA, forced to resign in wake of corruption charges. Image credited to Rnoid/Shutterstock.com. Blatter is awarding the Adidas Golden Glove to Mammarella of Italy in FIFA Futsal World Cup in Bangkok, Thailand, November, 2012

Fig. 3.11 Alex Rodriguez "A-Rod" is suspended. Image credited to Mary A. Lupo/ Shutterstock.com

expectation for ethical performance in the years to come. If nothing changes in term of demand, nothing will change (Fig. 3.11).

Stories about ethical issues in finance run right alongside news of the latest stars to fall from baseball glory. Many of us are sports enthusiasts. Ryan Braun, the Milwaukee Brewers winner of the National League's Most Valuable Player award, and Alex Rodriguez (A-Rod), a slugger from the New York Yankees, are among several of the latest names to hit the nightly news. Braun was suspended for the remainder of his 2013 season. Rodriguez received an unprecedented punishment: a suspension until the end of his next year's season (2014). Major League Baseball's sweeping investigations continue to address the sad mix of athleticism and performance-enhancing drugs (Eder 2013).

In 2014, football player Ray Rice found his behavior on video go viral. An elevator surveillance camera captured him literally punching his girlfriend and

Fig. 3.12 Ray Rice prior to
his domestic abuse scandal.
Image credited to Ovidiu
Hrubaru/Shutterstock.com

knocking her out. While his contract with the Raven's was subsequently terminated, the way the National Football League (NFL) managed the case and others raised additional ethical concerns. The NFL's policy states that "All persons associated with the NFL are required to avoid conduct detrimental to the integrity of and public confidence in the National Football League." The Rice case brought forward the concern that how, when and where the policy is enforced lacks consistency and rigor (Fig. 3.12).

The NFL Commissioner, Roger Goodell, apologized publicly for the way he went about handling this case, and subsequently announced sweeping changes to the league's Personal Conduct Policy. He explained that violations regarding assault, battery, domestic violence or sexual assault that involves physical force would be subject to a suspension without pay of six games for a first offense. A second offense would result in banishment from the NFL for at least 1 year. Goodell announced that a former FBI agent was now conducting an investigation to determine "what the NFL knew and when they knew it" about the Ray Rice videos. Regardless of the findings, clearly there was a policy, but how and when the league chooses to enforce it was negotiable. Inconsistent policy enforcement by the NFL has been and continues to be an ethical concern. For example, San Francisco 49ers defensive end Ray McDonald was allowed to play in the season opener after he was arrested on domestic violence charges, after the new "standardized penalties" were announced. As Linda Ellerbee used to say, "And so it goes."

If you enjoy sports, at what point are you willing to say, "Hey, that's not right. This is not the way sports ought to be played." Do you ever consider how watching the games on television and buying tickets endorse the current system, the way that the games are currently managed, rewarded, and played? If you say, "This is not my problem," you are essentially denying the fact that you buy into the current system and endorse it with every game you watch. Advertisers count on you, the audience, being there. If fans started to demand rigorous ethics in sports and withheld their viewing or attendance until change emerged, you can be rest assured the motivation for industry change would percolate expeditiously.

While the sports industry has no shortage of cases that demonstrate a lack of moral strength, evidence for the lack of ethics in business is often exemplified by the financial sector. Even after the crash of Wall Street in 2008 and the bail-out imposed by the United States government, insider trading continues to be touted as a sustained and current wrongdoing that is "on a scale without known precedence" (McCoy and Mullaney 2013). Continuing to be investigated by the United States Security and Exchange Commission and under their sustained spotlight, are firms like SAC Capital Advisors (for more information see the United States Department of Justice 2013). Traders at this firm aggressively and unethically bought and sold stocks around market-moving events (e.g., announcements of quarterly earnings or big merger and acquisition events). The company's success between 2006 and 2007 brought the organization's CEO, Steven Cohen, personal earnings exceeding $900 million annually. As a case in point, when government is the core regulator of business ethics, it cannot be properly and/or fully pursued. There will never be enough funding to ensure that all of the rules are followed and wrong-doing is caught and punished. As a result, we must all be mindful that business ethics, on some level, rests on our own shoulders.

When you think about doing business with or investing in a company, do you consider the ethical soundness of the firm? Do you take the time to look at the company's mission, purpose, and record of accountability to determine the strength of their ethicality?

The Negativity Bias

Stories about falling from grace seem to capture our interest and attention. You may wonder, "What does this have to do with me and my ethicality?" Negativity often takes precedence in our lives, as we strive to make sense of it. We take in a steady diet of information about corporate malfeasance and personal ineptitude. Over time, we come to expect illicit activities and bad news. Negative information seems to grab our attention and then it is leveraged to sustain our interest; many of us even crave bad news. In part, the success of reporting human failure is driven by the reality that bad is stronger than good (Baumeister et al. 2001). As humans, we are all wired to prepare for impending threat. Evolutionarily speaking, our bodies and minds are primed to pay attention to what is wrong, bad, or potentially hazardous.

This propensity, termed the "negativity bias," is a natural proclivity, designed to help ensure our survival (Vaish et al. 2008). But the media plays off this tendency, leading with negative images, news feeds, talk shows, and spurring controversial blogs. Whether it is about a person, corporation, or a larger economic or global issue, when we hear what is broken or dysfunctional, we're compelled to listen to it. With all of the information coming at us 24/7, through a plethora of technological devices, filtering information of value takes a concerted conscious effort.

When you hear about these issues, it is unlikely that you are moved to assume responsibility, or engage in corrective action—quite the opposite, actually. Negative stories give us something to react to. Taking in all of these problems, we seek to make sense of this information, working to identify the source or origin of the issue. Rarely do we see causality stemming from within ourselves. We might ask, "Who is responsible for this outrage?" We are inclined to look outwardly to determine the external causality of the event. Perhaps we focus on the system, industry, management, or a particular person. Typically, people want to find fault and punish those who are to blame. Regardless of the level or kind of impropriety, someone usually gets fingered as the causal agent or scapegoat and takes the fall. Sometimes those who blow the whistle or are trying to bring an issue forward are also caught up in the wake of the turmoil, becoming enveloped in the crossfire and negative muck and mire.

As with the alarm clock example, you may choose to press the snooze button and sleep through the ethical elements of your life. You may pass on the opportunity to apply your values to your consumer choices. Perhaps you are saving your strength to attend to ethics in other ways. Maybe you want to address a circumstance where you can apply your values in a more effective manner to achieve greater impact. But such a decision requires a conscious awareness and a determination to direct your energies toward right action, in the right way and at the right time. If you sincerely do not care about anyone but yourself, then it is unlikely that you care about your ethical character. Being ethical requires a sustained effort, in all areas of your life, which necessitates supporting an ongoing desire to achieve goodness. This decision, to want to be ethical, must come from within. Ethics is not confined to a certain circumstance. Nor is ethics a matter of convenience or suddenly applicable when the problem has been assigned to us. The opportunity to "do the right thing" resides in all aspects of our lives, calling for our deliberate attention and care at work, home, and while at play.

Take some time to think about what you truly value. If it's your family, think through how your choices may eventually affect them, down the line. What are the long-term implications of your actions, especially if everyone chose to behave in this same way? What principles are important to you—standards that you live by— values you believe define you? Are these beliefs exercised in your professional role? What about the decisions you make outside of work (e.g., as a consumer)? While answering all of these questions may seem to be a rather daunting assignment, if you have but a modicum of desire, you can leverage your capacity for adult moral development. Because ethics is not a one-time decision, you have ample opportunity to work on the strength of your commitment in the choices you make every day—throughout your day.

Takeaway Points

1. Identify specific personal and organizational values that are important to you. Look at how these values may compete against or complement a desire to be ethical.
2. Consider how "ethics" is embedded within all of your decisions (its presence or the lack thereof).
3. We tend to think about ethics when there's an immediate problem, focusing on correcting unethical behavior, rather than building moral strength. Look for ways to demonstrate your character strengths on a daily basis, creating a lifestyle where ethical issues may be prevented from occurring.
4. Think before you take action. Look at how you may rationalize your decisions after you have already taken action.
5. If you find that someone else is at fault for an ethical concern, consider you part in situation. What can you do to assist, help correct or resolve the issue?

Reflection Questions

Think about your current goals at work. Articulate how you will go about achieving these goals ethically. Do your performance evaluations examine both what you achieve and how you go about achieving them? What can you do as a leader within your organization to promote ethical strength as an element of measured performance criteria?

References

Aristotle [350BC]. (1999). *Nicomachean ethics*. T. Irwin (Trans.) Indianapolis, IN: Hackett. Publishing Co.

Alam, J. (2013). Bangladesh factory collapse death toll hits 1,034. *Associated Press*. Retrieved March 4, 2014, from http://bigstory.ap.org/article/bangladesh-factory-collapse-death-toll-912.

Apuzzo, M., Schmidt, M. S., Rashbaum, W. K., Borden, S. (May 22, 2015). FIFA officials arrested on corruption charges; face extradition to U.S., *The New York Times*. Retrieved May 26, 2015, from http://www.nytimes.com/2015/05/27/sports/soccer/fifa-officials-face-corruption-charges-in-us.html?emc=edit_na_20150526&nlid=67225337&_r=0.

Bauman, A., & Donskis, L. (2013). *Moral blindness. The loss of sensitivity in liquid modernity*. Palden, MA: Polity Press.

Baumeister, R. F., Bratslavsky, E., Finkenauer, C., & Vahs, K. D. (2001). Bad is stronger than good. *Review of General Psychology, 5*(4), 323–370.

Borden, S. (June 2, 2015). Sepp Blatter to resign as FIFA president, *The New York Times*. Retrieved June 2, 2015, from http://www.nytimes.com/2015/06/03/sports/soccer/sepp-blatter-to-resign-as-fifa-president.html?hp&action=click&pgtype=Homepage&module=a-lede-package-region&region=top-news&WT.nav=top-news.

Callahan, D. (2004). *The cheating culture: Why more Americans are doing wrong to get ahead.* New York: Harcourt Books.

Centers for Disease Control and Prevention (2013). *Injury prevention & control: Motor vehicle safety: Distracted driving.* Retrieved August 11, 2013, from http://www.cdc.gov/motorvehiclesafety/distracted_driving/.

Cowton, C. J. (2011). The moral status of the corporation, collective responsibility and the distribution of blame. In A. Tencati and F. Perrini (Eds.), *Business ethics and corporate sustainability*: 18–28. Northampton, MA: Edward Elgar Publishing.

Danner, U. N., Aarts, H., & de Vries, N. K. (2008). **Habit** vs. intention in the prediction of future behavior: The role of frequency, context stability and mental accessibility of past behavior. *British Journal of Social Psychology, 47*(2), 245–265.

Eder, S. (2013, July 22). Doping tarnishes baseball again as Brewers' Braun is suspended. *The New York Times.* Retrieved March 21, 2014, from http://www.nytimes.com/2013/07/23/sports/baseball/ryan-braun-suspended-for-doping.html?pagewanted=all.

Gentile, M. C. (2014). Giving voice to values in the workplace: A practical approach to building moral competence. In L. E. Sekerka (Ed.), *Ethics training in action:An examination of issues, techniques and development* (pp. 167–182). Charlotte, NC: Information Age Publishing.

Gino, F., Kouchaki, M., & Galinsky, A. D. (2015). The moral virtue of authenticity: How inauthenticity produces feelings of immorality and impurity *Psychological Science* 0956797615575277, published online May 11, 2015.

GRID-Arendal, United Nations Environment Programme (UNEP). (2014). *Impacts on environmental degradation on yield and area.* Retrieved April 10, 2014 from http://www.grida.no/publications/rr/food-crisis/page/3566.aspx.

Henning, P. (2014, April 7). High-frequency trading falls in the cracks of criminal law, *The New York Times.* Retrieved April 7, 2014, from http://dealbook.nytimes.com/2014/04/07/high-frequency-trading-falls-in-the-cracks-of-criminal-laws/?_php=true&_type=blogs&emc=edit_dlbkpm_&nl=business&nlid=67225337&_r=0.

Hussein, S. (2013). Six months after Bangladeshi factory collapse, workers remain in peril Special for CNN. Retrieved February 1, 2014, from http://www.cnn.com/2013/10/24/opinion/bangladesh-garment-workers/.

Jennings, M. (2014). The tall order of tackling relativism in ethics training for international firms. In L. E. Sekerka (Ed.) *Ethics training in action: An examination of issues, techniques, and development.* Charlotte, NC: Information Age Publishing.

Johnson, K. (2013). Brands risk image in varying Bangladesh building collapse responses. *Associated Press.* Retrieved March 14, 2104, from http://www.concordmonitor.com/news/6060086-95/brands-risk-image-in-varying-bangladesh-building-collapse-responses.

Josephson Institute of Ethics, (2012). *The ethics of American youth: Honesty and integrity.* Retrieved June 19, 2014, from http://charactercounts.org/programs/reportcard/2012/installment_report-card_honesty-integrity.html.

Kleyn, N., Abratt, R., Chipp, K., & Goldman, M. (2012). Strong corporate ethical identity: Key findings from suppliers. *The California Management Review, 54*(3), 61–76.

Kleist, C. (2013). Using Sartre's critique of dialectical reason for managerial decision- making. *Journal of Business Ethics, 112*(2), 341–352.

Krieger, (2014, March 21). Should a little corruption matter to voters? *The Washington Post.* Retrieved April 11, 2014, from http://www.washingtonpost.com/opinions/should-a-little-corruption-matter-to-voters/2014/03/21/181f057c-aeb8-11e3-96dc-d6ea14c099f9_story.html.

Kristoff, N. D. (2009, January 14). Where sweatshops are a dream. *The New York Times.* Retrieved March 21, 2014, from http://www.nytimes.com/2009/01/15/opinion/15kristof.html.

LaSalle, R. E. (2009). The perception of detection, severity of punishment and the probability of cheating. *Journal of Forensic Studies in Accounting & Business, 1*(2), 93–112.

Marar Yacobian, M. & Sekerka, L. E. 2014. Business ethics and intercultural management Education: a consideration of the Middle Eastern perspective. Journal of Business Ethics Education, *11*, 157–178.

Lewis, M. (2014). *Flash boys: A Wall Street revolt.* NY: W. W. Norton & Co.

McCoy, K. & Mullaney, T. (2013, July 25). Hedge fund SAC Capital indicted. *USA Today.* Retrieved March 21, 2014, from http://www.usatoday.com/story/money/business/2013/07/25/sac-capital-indictment-insider-trading/2582331/.

Mitchell, C. E. (1998). If I am not to blame, does that mean I don't have to be responsible? Possible effect of a systems approach on personal accountability within families. *Family Therapy, 25*(3), 227–230.

Nast, T. (1871, August 19). Who stole the people's money? (illustration). *Harper's Weekly.* Retrieved March 21, 2014, from http://www.nytimes.com/learning/general/onthisday/harp/0819.html.

National Highway Traffic Safety Administration. (2013). *What is distracted driving?: Key facts and statistics.* Retrieved March 11, 2013, from http://www.distraction.gov/content/get-the-facts/facts-and-statistics.html.

Nocera, J. (2014, April 4). Michael Lewis's crusade, *The New York Times*, The Opinion Pages. Retrieved April 7, 2014, from http://www.nytimes.com/2014/04/05/opinion/nocera-michael-lewiss-crusade.html.

Patterson, S. (2013). *Dark Pools: The Rise of the Machine Traders and the Rigging of the U.S. Stock Market.* NY: Crown Business.

Planet Matters and More (2011). *Migrant farm workers and unfair labor practices.* Retrieved August 10, 2013, from http://www.planetmattersandmore.com/sustainable-agriculture-2/migrant-farm-workers-and-unfair-labor-practices/.

Schwartz, S. H. (1992). Universals in the content and structure of values: theoretical advances and empirical tests in 20 countries. In M. P. Zanna (Ed.), *Advances in Experimental Social Psychology, 25* (pp. 1–65). Orlando, FL: Academic Press.

Schwartz, S. H. (2006). Basic human values: Theory, measurement, and applications. *Revue française de sociologie, 47*(4), 249–288.

Schwartz, S. H. (2012). An Overview of the Schwartz Theory of Basic Values. *Online Readings in Psychology and Culture, 2*(1). See http://dx.doi.org/10.9707/2307-0919.1116.

Sekerka, L. E. (2009). Organizational ethics education and training: A review of best practices and their application. *International Journal of Training and Development, 13*(2), 77–95.

Sekerka, L. E., & Bagozzi, R. P. (2007). Moral courage in the workplace: Moving to and from the desire and decision to act. *Business Ethics: A European Review, 16*(2), 132–142.

Sverdlik, S. (1987). Collective responsibility. *Philosophical Studies, 51*(1), 61–76.

Teixeira, A. A. C. (2013). Sanding the wheels of growth: Cheating by economics and business students and 'real world' corruption. *Journal of Academic Ethics, 11*(4), 269–274.

Transparency International (2013). *Corruption perceptions index 2013.* Retrieved June 19, 2014, from http://cpi.transparency.org/cpi2013/results/.

Treviño, L. K. (1986). Ethical decision making in organizations: A person-situation interactionist model. *Academy of Management Review, 11*(3), 601–617.

United States Department of Justice (2013). United States v. S.A.C. Capital Advisors, L. P., et al., 13 Cr. 541 (LTS); United States v. S.A.C. Capital Advisors, L. P., et al., 13 Civ. 5182 (RJS). Retrieved March, 2014, from http://www.nytimes.com/interactive/2012/11/21/business/dealbook/20121121insider-document.html?nl=business&emc=edit_dlbkpm_20130725.

Vaish, A., Grossmann, T., & Woodward, A. (2008). Not all emotions are created equal: The negativity bias in social-emotional development. *Psychological Bulletin, 134*(3), 383–403.

Weinstein, A. (2009). *Ethics in the classroom: What you need to know.* Retrieved June 19, 2014, from http://www.education.com/magazine/article/cheating-ethics/?page=2.

Whitlock, C. (2015). Defense contractor pleads guilty in massive bribery case. *The Washington Post.* Retrieved January 16, 2015, from http://www.washingtonpost.com/world/national-security/navy-captain-enters-guilty-plea-in-massive-bribery-case/2015/01/15/b09688ba-9ced-11e4-a7ee-526210d665b4_story.html.

Chapter 4
Paying Attention

Recall your behavior in school, when the classroom was filled with laughter, mischief, and chatter. The teacher would dive in and say, "People, will you please pay attention?" While simplified to make a point, this sort of reminder to you—to pay attention—is central in sustaining your ethical behavior. As your values compete for priority, ask yourself: Do you have an inner voice that corrals your thoughts, reminding you to be aware of and think about the ethical elements of the given situation? Being ethical is not about being well versed in philosophy, decision-making models, or some profound reasoning strategy. Rather, it is about choosing to consciously be aware of your motives and intentions in your daily task actions and working to be your best. This effort is what ethicality is all about: striving to do the right thing as you navigate your everyday activities. However, this is easier said than done.

Our values often compete for attention, and short-term desires can easily intervene and trump the pursuit of being ethical. When this happens, personal wants tend to compete vigorously for supremacy. This can influence our willingness to be responsible, making our presumed ethicality much less effective than we realize. Striving to gain advantage in business, the desire to make money, save time, look good, and/or feel included can override a person's intent to be ethical. Values certainly fuel ethical action. But a multitude of other desires can steer you towards thoughts and actions that may block your ability to see the ethics of a situation. Do you consider how your values are reflected in the decisions you make? Are you really paying attention to whether or not you are actually behaving ethically? Do you assume you are ethical and then justify your behavior after you have already taken action?

Caught Up In Yourself

In business, paying attention to one's ethicality has never been more important. Leaders know that both visible actions and perceptions matter. In a world of instant messaging, combined with a shift in consumer demand for more corporate

© Springer International Publishing Switzerland 2016
L. E. Sekerka, *Ethics is a Daily Deal*, DOI 10.1007/978-3-319-18090-8_4

responsibility, being ethical has never been so vital to the health and welfare of the organization. When people get caught up in achieving their business goals, they can become distracted by other desires and even sidelined by a sense of entitlement. Being responsible can inadvertently take a back seat to fulfilling our immediate wants and desires.

Take Michael Hurd, former head of Hewlett-Packard (HP), as a case in point. Hurd resigned from HP in August of 2010, in the wake of a sexual harassment controversy. The HP board found falsified expense reports and other financial documents that apparently concealed Hurd's relationship with an HP contractor (Jodi Fisher) (Figs. 4.1 and 4.2). The company said its sexual harassment policy was not violated, but that its standards of business conduct had been breached. In unpacking the events of this story, the *San Francisco Chronicle* outlined what they thought happened (see Blodget 2010). Initially, Hurd and a female HP contractor started working together. For whatever reason, the personal and/or work relationship ended and Fisher stopped getting assignments. At some point she concluded that sexual harassment had occurred and she then sued Hurd based on allegations of impropriety.

HP's board members learned about this news and investigated Hurd, finding little to support the charge. But concerned about the potential for bad publicity, they examined the details of his activities and found inaccuracies in his expense reports. While his actions did not constitute proof of sexual harassment, fraud, or embezzlement, the Board stated he was in violation of HP's *Standards of Business*

Fig. 4.1 Michael Hurd. Image credited to drserg/Shutterstock.com

Fig. 4.2 Jodi Fisher. Image credited to s_bukley/ Shutterstock.com

Conduct and asked for his resignation (for more information see http://www.hp. com/hpinfo/globalcitizenship/csr/sbcbrochure.pdf). The company standards state that HP wants to be a company "known for its ethical leadership—a company where employees are proud to work." Hurd later stated, "I realized there were instances in which I did not live up to the standards and principles of trust, respect and integrity that I have espoused at HP" (Kim 2011).

Had this business leader thought more carefully about following company policies and understood that perceptions, along with actions truly mattered, he might still be at the helm of HP. Upon his departure, Hurd received anywhere from $12.2 to $40 million in his departure severance package (reports vary widely, depending upon the news source). Regardless of the exact amount, it is unlikely that any broad, sweeping lessons about ethical performance were learned by him or anyone else at HP. Ironically, what stands out most from this case is the fact that organizations can inadvertently reward bad behavior, which all but assures its continuation. Everyone in this situation would have likely benefited from thinking about the perceptions and unintended consequences associated with their actions.

Ambition and passion, qualities we often value in business management, can, at times, interfere with the value of being responsible. A desire for accomplishment and the gratification that accompanies it can inadvertently narrow the ability to see who we are, or who we are becoming. The values we say we hold, the principles that support our ethical identity, can become obfuscated as we aspire to advance our careers and work to achieve business success. Left unchallenged, personal desires can promote selfish thinking and misguided decision-making. Saying what is "right" or "wrong" is not for certain experts to declare (e.g., a professor of ethics). Rather, responsibility is the role of every organizational member. We must all take care to consider the circumstances, the implications of our choices on others, and choose behavior that befits our organizational and professional identities.

With every incoming message we observe, hear, or absorb, the intent to "do the right thing" can be cut short, distracted, or set aside for what may seem to be a more desirable option in the moment. Pleasing our immediate desires can inadvertently take center stage and blunt the best of our intentions to be ethical. Amplifying this tendency for speedy gratification, we are bombarded with information telling us we need to want more things and are deluged with an exhaustive list of choices.

Too Many Decisions

Whether it is status, material goods, food, sex, or power, the Western consumer-oriented society often makes being ethical subservient to consumption. The notion of "more is better" has perhaps gotten the better of us (see Fig. 4.3). For example, in the United States, we are presented with an absurd array of abundance. This manifests into so many choices, we cannot possibly consider them all. Starbucks offers over 87,000 drink combinations, Comcast presents over 1,000 entertainment channels (Worth 2009), and something as simple as jelly for our toast appears on grocery store shelves with anywhere from twenty-four to fifty different choice options. As far as snack foods, in many stores there are no longer sections for such products—there are aisles. The technology accompanying our lives adds a cacophony of alternatives, driving decisions influenced by a stream of ongoing calls, texts, emails, tweets, and other website and app offerings (not to mention pop-ups and ads appearing as we read and consume all of this information).

Human beings are thought to make over 35,000 decisions in any given 24 h period (Fig. 4.4). Scientists suggest that only about 70 of them are actually made with deliberate conscious attention (Iyengar 2010). The United States Department of Labor (2013) statistics show that adults in the United States sleep, on average, 7.7 h per day, leaving them with 16.3 available hours for activity. Given that about half of a typical day is spent at work, it stands to reason that half of our consciously made decisions (35) are made on the job (Tasler 2012). Whether it is a decision to meet someone or call them, share information or keep it to yourself, lend a hand or stay focused on achieving your own goals, every move you make is a reflection of what you value. It's like looking at your checkbook or credit card statement; where you spend your money actually says a lot about what is important to you.

Whether it is money spent on rent, food, phone, or television, paying for personal care, church, or school, these costs all reflect what you care about. Your daily actions also create a picture of what you value. Because most decisions are actually made without conscious deliberation, that, in itself, is part of the problem. Unconsciously

Fig. 4.3 Bling bling hip hop jewelry as an ostentatious statement of power and wealth. Image is in the public domain, courtesy of Jon Feinstein

Fig. 4.4 A barrage of options and choices. Images credited to Leslie E. Sekerka

made decisions create a kind of mindless cruise control or automatic pilot type of decision-making operation, one that is unlikely to be conducive for employing moral responsibility. Being ethical may happen by accident, but the reality is that many of us are asleep at the proverbial ethics "wheel" and don't even realize it.

Cognitive processes of decision-making are complex and can wear you down. Research in decision fatigue describes how making choices in today's everyday life can be exhausting. Scholars describe how we have a limited reserve of stamina for making choices, a capacity that depletes gradually as we navigate our day. Upon awakening until we retire, we make decisions ranging in impact and importance;

from the simple choice of what to eat to more complicated decisions that can have significant impact on our well-being, health, and financial security. Knowing which ones are important, requiring your deliberate attention and care, and applying prudential judgment, can be tiring. In a world where resources continue to shrink and responsibilities increase, the problem of decision fatigue is likely to become more troublesome rather than dissipate (Stewart et al. 2012). The mere act of resolving tradeoffs is taxing (Vohs et al. 2008). People not only have to work at being aware, we also have to manage our stamina in knowing when and where to apply our cognitive attention and emotionality. Effective ethical decision-making is not a trait. Rather, it is a reflection of regulating the power of self-control. Those who are effective at self-control often structure their lives to conserve their will-power. They don't over schedule themselves, avoid environments riddled with temptation, and establish habits that eliminate the mental effort of having to make multiple decisions all at once (Tierney 2011).

Tierney, another expert in this area of inquiry, explains that instead of deciding every morning whether or not we want to exercise, a prudent decision-maker sets up regular appointments for themselves. Instead of expecting or counting on personal willpower to be present, the person conserves and manages it as a limited and important resource. In so doing, the regulatory strength can be available in emergencies and for more important decision-making efforts. Effective decision-makers choose to avoid making choices when they are not well rested. Adding awareness of hunger to the watch list or caution zone is wise. For example, big decisions like making a major commitment to a project or firing someone are decisions that ought not be made late in the day, when you're likely to be mentally and perhaps physically tired and when your blood sugar is likely to be low. The best decision-makers, according to Baumeister, an expert on will power and self-control, are people who know when not to trust themselves (Baumeister and Tierney 2011). Prudent decision-makers conserve their willpower and are smart about when and where to apply it. Knowing when not to make decisions may be just as important as knowing when to make them. In becoming more mindful about decisions, we have a better chance at ensuring that our values match our choices.

In the United States, many of us are spoiled by living in a land of plenty. This opulence presents us with a lot of easy and available alternatives. Given all of this availability, our decision-making capacity is constantly susceptible to decay. We are in danger of being overloaded with too many choices, rendering our capacity for mindful decision-making susceptible to weakening—that is, unless we learn how to self-monitor and manage our decision-making processes. In sorting out how we make decisions, scientists have learned that cognitive control and value-based decision-making tasks appear to function in different brain regions within the prefrontal cortex (Gläscher and Adolphs 2003). When you are deluged with a host of options, with things you might want (rather than need), your valuation network strives to offer information about what is likely to be most rewarding. It can be exhausting trying to keep up with this, as the sea of choices seem like a deluge of overwhelming options that can flood our capacity to think, feel, and be mindful. Maintaining cognitive and emotional control is what keeps this process in check and balanced. Managing desires helps to keep you focused and, despite distractions and temptations, your internal valuation network can help guide and sort out appropriate and viable alternatives. Unfortunately, modern society surrounds us with constant reminders of things we want—or might want.

Of course, marketers have caught on to this weak spot and create clever campaigns that leverage our temptations with a myriad of products we are likely to buy (e.g., stationing cookies at the store entryway or displaying pop-up ads that correlate with our personal interests online). We are bombarded with distracting lures like junk food and other items that are likely to be desirable, often appealing to our short-term gratification. Cognitive and emotional control is what keeps this valuing network in balance. To be able to get to the grocery store checkout counter with what is on your list and nothing more, you have to be proficient at maintaining a focus on your intended goals. Thus, part of being an effective ethical decision-maker is teaching yourself to attend to longer-term goals when you are faced with short-term pleasures. For example, if you want to establish or maintain good health, you work to recall how you feel and look when you eat fruits and vegetables (rather than sugary treats). This practice of mindful awareness, paying attention to the motives and implications associated with your choices, can be a useful device when striving to overcome personal desires. Lures to deplete your decision-making energy can taunt you to give way to immediate gratification. With a persistent siren's song beckoning us to buy, buy, buy, it becomes all the more difficult to incentivize ethical mindfulness, becoming aware of the ethical elements of our daily choices.

What makes choosing to be ethical all the more difficult, is that it may not provide any tangible positive by-product. In fact, there may be perceived or actual negative consequences from doing "the right thing." This is a real problem. Without incentives, what could possibly motivate us? Philosophers and religious leaders have observed this concern, recognizing that the benefit of moral action is in the act itself. That is, being virtuous is its own reward. This presupposes that our internal valuing system functions in such a way that it self-affirms an ethical decision and action. When you do the ethical thing, do you feel good about it? When people are spoiled, getting used to short-term rewards for modest effort, the notion of doing something difficult and potentially threatening for an internally-driven reward over time is, well, a tough sell.

The Western culture has become, in largess, a society driven by wealth creation. Riches are typically considered money, power, fame, and/or status. Many of us have more than enough, yet want for more. While there are certainly many Americans who are in need, people living on the street and those who struggle from paycheck to paycheck to make ends meet, most of us do not have to think about our basic survival on a daily basis (like the original settlers). Now, rather than focusing on our needs to survive, many Americans compete to thrive. In this competition, being ethical may put you at a short-term disadvantage. By engaging in a moral action you might even place yourself in a vulnerable position, at risk of losing your job, reputation, riches, and/or relationships. In such a culture, it can become very difficult to encourage people to have a desire, to step up to the plate and choose to engage in the morally sound act.

It is hard to understand how being ethical has intrinsic benefits, unless you actually engage in the behavior. Working to do the right thing, over and over again, you can come to appreciate the intrinsic value of it for yourself (Fig. 4.5). This takes focused energy, commitment, and practice; especially because those extrinsic values can be appealing and receive attention in the workplace. Short-term organizational performance demands, like hitting sales quotas and revenue targets, often provide immediate external affirmations or reward. But in many cases, over time, right actions contribute to a deep sense of well-being, an inner confidence built from sustained ethical activity. Learning that a sense of personal achievement comes from repeated right action cannot be granted by external means. It is experiential wisdom that emerges from living ethically. But there is so much noise coming our way, it is easy to get distracted and forget to pay attention to the importance of being ethical in our everyday activities. Have we become so spoiled, busy, and distracted that we no longer want to work at being ethical?

Fig. 4.5 Extrinsic and intrinsic rewards. Figure credited to common cause 2014; see http:// valuesandframes.org/ handbook/2-how-values- work/

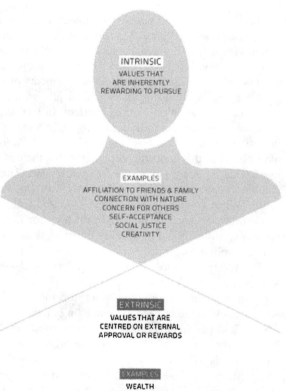

Corporations Mirror Our Ethicality

When we place our ethical decision-making efforts in the context of our work lives, we have the organization environment to consider. Organizations typically deal with their ethical responsibilities legally, with compliance serving as their moral baseline. So long as the firm is in compliance with the law, they often view themselves as being ethical. Responsible moral agency may be viewed as simply not breaking the law. In fact some managers may say, "Why should we do anything more?" Even more disconcerting, is that some business strategists consider punitive damages for being illegal a cost of doing business. They might ask, "How much will it cost us if we break the law?" rather than, "How can we achieve these business goals ethically?"

When corporate culture rewards those who cheat, cut corners, or leverage unethical practices (legal or illegal), the perpetuation of shoddy, less responsible behaviors are endorsed. This sort of environment can dull, mute, or even blind ethical decision-making, potentially making "doing the right thing" a less desirable course of action for organizational members. When individuals see corporations and those with power receive benefits by engaging in morally questionable activities, it makes wanting to be ethical difficult—and, therefore, that much more important. The cost of rewarding unethical performance is erosion of the value of personal responsibility. People begin to assume that morality is being addressed, that somewhere out there, a correcting mechanism is at work, which will eventually restore the ethical balance. What many people fail to realize is that *they are the system*. What you do is a reflection of the society you observe and want to see. The organization you work for is a reflection of your own morality. If you do not like what you see, it's up to you to change it. If you have hopes for the future, you are responsible for transferring these expectations into realities.

The ethical health of an organization can suffer when short-term performance is the primary objective. Researchers such as McKinsey (Dobbs et al. 2005) found that one firm achieved an impressive turnaround in its short-term financial performance, but simultaneously experienced falling customer service levels, a huge increase in staff turnover, and ultimately a decrease in its share price. Management complained that the financial market didn't understand what the company had achieved. But in reality the market reflected that short-term success had been purchased at the expense of the organization's underlying ethical health. Such short-sighted behavior is widespread. In a recent survey, a majority of managers said that they would forgo an investment offering a decent return on capital if it meant missing their quarterly earnings expectations. More than 80 % of the executives participating in the study said they would cut expenditures on research and development and marketing to ensure they met their quarterly earnings targets —even if they believed that the cuts were destroying long-term value. This illustrates that while leaders may talk the ethics talk, extolling the importance of moral strength, it is often superficial.

Fig. 4.6 Tempting, isn't it? Image credited to Maminau Mikalai/Shutterstock.com

Performance scorecards, a popular approach to balancing short- and long-term considerations, often consist of disconnected metrics that are confusing and/or lack impact. One public sector agency came up with nearly 100 key performance indicators, but the list was never actually implemented. Management chose to respond only to revenue targets and ignored the broader metrics that related to integrated integrity. Such breakdowns occur when long-term initiatives reside within departmental silos, rather than being incorporated across the organization as a whole. A systemic understanding of how to manage activities coherently, across the entire organization, is critical for integrated principled performance (Dobbs et al. 2005).

Outlandish pay schemes that stay in place when unethical activities occur endorse a future of similar actions (Fig. 4.6). Despite government efforts to address this problem, the vast majority of compensation policies across corporate America do not require the recovery of pay when executives take shortcuts or engage in other types of unethical behavior that imperils customers and the company itself. Changes in compensation laws are altering processes for retrieval of compensation, referred to as "clawbacks." As described by Morgenson (2014), under some new agreements retrieval can be sought not only for intentional misconduct and gross negligence, but also for violations of law or policies that cause significant financial or reputational harm to the institution. Clawback thresholds also state that executives can be forced to give back pay even if they did not commit the misconduct themselves; their pay can be revoked if they fail to monitor conduct or risk-taking by subordinates (e.g., as in the case of Citigroup, with the losses arising from its Banamex unit in Mexico). Unfortunately, such terms are not required. Exorbitant compensation packages can also be further insulated from criticism by ensuring that top management surrounding grossly paid leaders are also paid huge sums, which can quell employees' enthusiasm for raising ethical concerns.

Over the course of the past decade, we have seen an interest in the topic of morally generated revenue. The stakeholder approach to conscious capitalism has been adopted by a variety of firms in different industries around the world. The authenticity of this approach can be discerned by examining the organization's identity; more specifically, how they treat people and the planet in route to making a profit. While firms like Unilever and Whole Foods have been highlighted in case studies as modeling a more mindful form of business enterprise, it is important to question the genuine nature of such claims. Much of today's business is still largely driven by unmitigated self-serving motives. Selfishness and greed often pay, at least for a select few and those at the top. In the short term, they seem to come up the big winners. Meanwhile, the cost of such selfishness is typically shouldered by those with less power and money, as well as the natural environment. But eventually, over time, the truth comes out.

One truth that seems to be a constant is that money and power have palpable appeal. It is a source of temptation, not just for what it can buy, but for the power that is associated with it. Recall the infamous speech made by actor Michael Douglas in the original film *Wall Street*. The character of Gordon Gekko argues with every fiber of his being that greed is good (IMDb 1987). Explaining to the firm's shareholders he justifies his claim:

> The point is, ladies and gentleman, that greed—for lack of a better word—is good. Greed is right. Greed works. Greed clarifies, cuts through, and captures the essence of the evolutionary spirit. Greed, in all of its forms—greed for life, for money, for love, knowledge— has marked the upward surge of mankind. And greed—you mark my words—will not only save Teldar Paper, but that other malfunctioning corporation called the USA.

Plato (1992/365C) alluded to those who are like a greedy and crafty fox, people who wield actions effectively behind the illusory facade of justice . Similarly, Machiavelli describes the prince's ability to appear to have useful and virtuous qualities, rather than to really have them. Machiavelli (1940, translation) writes:

> It is not, therefore, necessary for a prince to have all the above–named qualities, but it is very necessary to seem to have them…he should seem to be all mercy, faith, integrity, humanity, and religion (p. 56).

More recently, in the film *The Wolf of Wall Street*, Leonardo DiCaprio (as Jordan Belfort), plays a New York stockbroker who runs a firm that engages in securities fraud and corruption (IMDb 2013). Here we see how the concept of wealth creation may initially be a righteous endeavor, but is fraught with a core moral issue of putting self above others. We can all be tempted by this fallacy, believing that voracity and self-interest is good for business. Primal competitiveness fuels a tendency to look out for ourselves and destroy the competition. The "selfish gene," as manifest within cells identified by their characteristic to destroy other cells, is a good metaphor to depict the dysfunctionality of greed (Dawkins 1976; Bull et al. 1992). We have probably all worked with someone who views business as "dog-eat-dog" or "survival of the fittest," earnestly believing that those "higher up the food chain" score big and that "winners take all." Those people who align with such beliefs are unlikely to be conducive toward engagement in socially responsible enterprise.

With too many choices and the desire for satiating short-term wants, complemented by selfish motives, we see how any one of us can come up ethically short, even when we start off with the best of intentions. While leaders like Hurd make the headlines, we all have a propensity to be susceptible to distractions, forgetting the ethical elements of our decision-making efforts and the potential implications that our behaviors convey to those around us. And yet, we know that people and the organizations they represent can make money and do so responsibly (Ozcelik et al. 2008). Academics, practitioners, and leaders around the world have rallied around this concept, extolling the power of conscious capitalism and moral markets, the ability to do well *and* to do good. Some companies that have successfully embraced this approach, and truly live up to it, sustaining a moral purpose driving their daily operations. The strategy within these organizations is to focus on achieving a profit, but to do so in an ethical manner. It can be done. But this takes a deep and systemic commitment to ethics, one that resides within the very core of the firm's operations and embedded into employees' daily task actions. This means incorporating both short- and long-term metrics in how performance is actually achieved, including socially responsible processes in route to individual and organizational goals.

Evidence shows that firms have been known to pursue aggressive unethical paths to profit. Some companies actively try to amend laws to their advantage, while they simultaneously promote new rules and seek special treatment for actions that would send anyone else off to jail. Through associations and industry special interest groups, lobbies and Political Action Committees strive to influence the government's expectations for sustainability and corporate responsibility. When powerful groups sway, influence and shape policy, they can encourage the development of laws that benefit the firm's objectives and do harm to people and the planet. These groups can also block legislation that may be beneficial, spending millions of dollars on ad campaigns that often shape public option. As described in the classic documentary "The Corporation," the firm, without leadership, is a legal entity designed to increase shareholder wealth.[1] Without ethical strength imposed from management, the firm will mechanistically press forward, driven by self-interest.

The issues raised by the Occupy protesters in 2011 were related to the systemic concerns of social and economic inequality, greed, corruption and the undue influence of corporations on government—particularly from the financial services sector (Fig. 4.7). The Occupy Wall Street slogan, "We are the 99 %," referred to income inequality and wealth distribution in the U.S. between the wealthiest 1 % and the rest of the population (although the movement's expression was voiced globally). The protest was, in some ways, a cry for more corporate social responsibility. Having a focus on mindful capitalism cannot just simply be declared by

---

[1]For more information on the film see: http://www.thecorporation.com/.

Fig. 4.7 Occupy movement protestors. Imaged credited to Miker/Shutterstock.com

firms. It must be demonstrated in what the corporation produces and sells, and how it works to establish profits and incentivize employee performance. A desire to "do good" and "do well" is manifest as a shared commitment at every level of the organization if it is genuinely striving to achieve socially responsible enterprise. This means achievement of success by a firm must reflect an ethical identity, manifest in its operations, throughout its supply chain.

Corporate ethics is influenced by law, but the personality of the firm is shaped by its leaders, managers, and employees. Every employee represents the organization that they work for. Similarly, the corporation is also a reflection of its members. Organizational members influence each other's identity, with refractive mirroring working to create a sort of isomorphic effect. If our leaders care about being socially responsible in business, it is likely that a majority of employees will as well. If the purported identity of the corporation is overshadowed by demands for quick profits, ethics will take a back seat to strategic decisions that enable short-term earnings.

A shared focus for creating socially responsible profits can be observed in companies like Patagonia and New Belgium Brewing. In these examples, business operations run based upon a corporate mission that focuses on addressing social and environmental concerns, and workers co-create a shared understanding that people and the planet are as—or more important—than short-term profit maximization. Work to establish the statistical validity of corporate social responsibility (CSR), Orlitsky et al. (2003) analyzed 30 years' worth of corporate data and affirmed a link between effective social performance and successful financial performance (the study included broader measures of CSR, not just ethics, per se). Drawing upon empirical data from a variety of studies, their research reflects that a firm's attention to social responsibility favorably influences corporate financial performance, up to 83 % of the time. While critics may raise concerns and issues with this type of research, another particularly thorny challenge is the glaring lack of congruency between a fiscal reporting system that demands quarterly earnings (doing well) and the types of long-term choices deemed necessary for responsible enterprise (doing good). Working to address and balance these broad-based competing values translates into a duty to be addressed by business leaders, managers, and employees, and it requires private and public professional moral courage. This implies that leaders have to make an explicit and sustained commitment to moral strength in their business enterprise, which likely requires focused attention, planning, and some level of investment (e.g., in strategies that incorporate ethics into performance).

Employees who work for socially responsible firms are encouraged to be ethically mindful, sensitive to issues, and to voluntarily seek out innovative solutions to social and ecological problems. In this sort of organizational culture it is possible to support morally justifiable and ecologically sustainable decision-making and to act in conjunction with performance goals. Employees are empowered and committed to doing what is right and responsible as they work to achieve their objectives and financial targets. This ability to make money and to do so with steadfast moral responsibility requires a durable and explicit commitment, along with buy-in from workers, management, shareholders, and extended stakeholders.

In describing the work being conducted at the Harvard School of Business, Blanding (2014) says that a wave of new insights are helping us unpack and expose how to determine if firms genuinely care about doing well and good in their quest to make a profit. For example, the language used in corporate reporting is a key cultural variable that turns out to be a strong predictor of CSR and sustainability. Examining thousands of global companies across 59 countries from 1999–2011, Liang (2014) and his colleagues found that the use of a future-time reference is associated with a reduced propensity to engage in CSR activities. A consideration of long-term consequences is essential for ethical performance; however, procrastinating or postponing CSR action and offering poetic rhetoric instead, is nothing more than a marketing proposal.

Rather than remaining an aspirational goal, being ethically responsible is a real-time effort achieved in the here and now. Members of genuinely responsible organizations strive to care about the ethicality of their business, on both a personal and organizational level in day to day operations. To create this type of approach means people come together and agree to pay attention to how their values are reflected in their regular decisions and actions, as they work to achieve the firm's overarching purpose. Simultaneously, employees have to stay mindful of where they are personally vulnerable, where their ethical and moral risks reside.

Takeaway Points

1. Moral strength typically requires deliberate forethought before taking action.
2. Pay attention to your everyday decisions—even the seemingly small stuff matters/counts.
3. Consider the long-term repercussions of your actions, being mindful of perception management. Actions speak louder than words.

Reflection Questions

How do you exercise social and environmental responsibility in your consumer choices? Does where you work reflect who you are? Do the choices you make on a daily basis reflect your best ethical self, decisions that make you feel good about who you are in the world?

References

Baumeister, R. F., & Tierney, J. (2011). *Willpower: Rediscovering the greatest human strength.* New York: Penguin Press.

Blanding, M. (2014, March 24). The surprising link between language and corporate responsibility. *Harvard Business School Working Knowledge.* Retrieved March 26, 2014 from http://hbswk.hbs.edu/item/7479.html.

Blodget, H. (2010, August 10). Here's the real reason HP CEO Mark Hurd was fired (As best we can tell). *San Francisco Chronicle.* Retrieved January 1, 2014 from http://www.sfchronicle.com/technology/businessinsider/article/Here-s-The-Real-Reason-HP-CEO-Mark-Hurd-Was-Fired-2535770.php.

Bull, J. J., Molineux, I. J., & Werren, J. H. (1992). Selfish genes. *Science, 256*(5053), 65.

Common Cause. (2014). *How values work.* Retrieved April 9, 2014 from http://valuesandframes.org/handbook/2-how-values-work/.

Dawkins, R. (1976). *The selfish gene.* New York, NY: Oxford University Press.

Dobbs, R., Leslie, K., & Mendonca, L. (2005). *Building the healthy organization.* San Francisco, CA: McKinsey & Company.

Glasher, J., & Adolphs, R. (2003). Processing of arousal of subliminal and supraliminal emotional stimuli by the human amygdale. *The Journal of Neuroscience, 23*(10), 274–282.

IMDb (1987). Wall street. *Twentieth century fox.* Retrieved January 3, 2014 from http://www.imdb.com/title/tt0094291/.

IMDb (2013). The wolf of wall street. *Paramount pictures.* Retrieved March 6, 2014 from http://www.imdb.com/title/tt0993846/.

Iyengar, S. S. (2010). *The art of choosing.* New York: Twelve Publishers.

Kim, S. (2011, December 30). Hewlett-packard former CEO mark hurd sex harassment scandal detailed in letter. *ABC News.* Retrieved April 6, 2014 from http://abcnews.go.com/blogs/business/2011/12/hewlett-packard-ceo-sex-harassment-scandal-detailed-in-letter/.

Liang, H., Marquis, C., Renneboog, L., & Li Sun, S. (March 2, 2014). Speaking of corporate social responsibility. *Harvard Business School Working Paper,* 14–082.

Machiavelli, N. (1940). *The prince* (L. Ricci, Trans. Revised by E. R. P. Vincent). New York: Random House, The Modern Library (ch. XV).

Morgenson, G. (2014, April 5). The wallet as ethics enforcer. *The New York Times*. Retrieved April 7, 2104 from http://www.nytimes.com/2014/04/06/business/the-wallet-as-ethics-enforcer.html#story-continues-2.

Orlitsky, M., Schmidt, F., & Rynes, S. (2003). Corporate social and financial performance: A meta-analysis. *Organization Studies, 24*(3), 403–441.

Ozcelik, H., Langton, N., & Aldrich, H. (2008). Doing well and doing good: The relationship between leadership practices that facilitate a positive emotional climate and organizational performance. *Journal of Managerial Psychology, 23*, 186–203.

Plato, *Republic* (1992/365C). (G. M. A. Grube, Trans. Revised by C. D. C. Reeve). Indianapolis: Hackett.

Stewart, A. F., Ferriero, D. M., Josephson, S. A., Lowenstein, D. H., Messing, R. O., Oksenberg, J. R., et al. (2012). Fighting decision fatigue. *Annals of Neurology, 71*(1), A5–A15.

Tasler, N. (2012, August 30). What is your momentum factor? You have 35 chances to change everything, every day. *Psychology Today: Strategic Thinking*. Retrieved December 31, 2013 from http://www.psychologytoday.com/blog/strategic-thinking/201208/what-is-your-momentum-factor.

Tierney, J. (2011, August 17). Do you suffer from decision fatigue? *The New York Times*. Retrieved January 1, 2014 from http://www.nytimes.com/2011/08/21/magazine/do-you-suffer-from-decision-fatigue.html?pagewanted=all&_r=0.

United Sates Department of Labor, Bureau of Labor Statistics (2013). *American Time Use Survey*. Retrieved January 1, 2014 from http://www.bls.gov/tus/charts/.

Vohs, K. D., Baumeister, R. F., Schmeichel, B. J., Twenge, J. M., Nelson, N. M., & Tice, D. M. (2008). Making choices impairs subsequent self-control: A limited-resource account of decision making, self-regulation, and active initiative. *Journal of Personality and Social Psychology, 94*(5), 883–898.

Worth, T. (2009, March 16). Too many choices can tax the brain, research shows. *Los Angeles Times*. Retrieved January 7, 2014 from http://articles.latimes.com/2009/mar/16/health/he-choices16.

Chapter 5
Recognizing Your Vulnerabilities

Regardless of the level of expertise or number of degrees you have received, no amount of education can *make* you genuinely care about being ethical. Being ethical means you have made a personal decision that this is who you want to be in the world and that you're willing to work at it. Recall a time when you became aware of others taking part in some activity that seemed inappropriate, perhaps doing something against the rules or even illegal. For example, someone padded an expense report, accepted a gift from a supplier without reporting it, or inappropriately used company resources. Such actions are not as benign as they can appear. While others around you may have pursued such activities, maybe you held your ground, staying above the moral line.

Exercising what it feels like to live your values, consciously being aware of their application, is one way to find out if your moral identity is as genuine or robust as you think. This is made particularly clear when those around you are engaged in ethically risky or questionable activities and you choose to maintain and exercise your character strengths. Everyone sees unethical behavior every day. Just drive on any highway or attend a public function or sporting event. Here, unethical activity around us becomes all too obvious. But what about your behavior? If you think about it, there are a variety of areas where you might have observed people cheat, lie, and steal. And, if we are really honest with ourselves, we might even recall a time when we have chosen to "bend the rules" or cut an ethical corner or two. If you think you are ethical, but you do not always behave ethically, you are not alone.

Confucius described real knowledge as knowing the extent of one's own ignorance. Understanding our limitations is central to being honest with ourselves and others. We are all fallible. But most of us can improve our ethical prowess, if we have a desire to do so. The good news is that if you do not have the resources for ethical fortitude, you can build them. This requires a decision, a conscious commitment to demonstrate personal responsibility, especially when those around you may not uphold the same commitment to being ethical. Being honest, kind, and mindful of the needs of others is a matter of personal choice. Workshops and seminars can inform and help people become aware of what is expected in their organization—what is right and wrong behavior according to company policy.

© Springer International Publishing Switzerland 2016
L. E. Sekerka, *Ethics is a Daily Deal*, DOI 10.1007/978-3-319-18090-8_5

Management can encourage the former and deter the latter. But because moral strength is about a person's character, you have to claim and exercise your ethical identity to actually possess it. Ethicality is a personal choice, one that requires your attention, care, and ongoing maintenance.

Do you have a desire to be your best ethical self? If you want to be ethical and encourage others to behave this way, you need to demonstrate and model behaviors that support moral courageous action. This entails becoming aware of how our thoughts and feelings can promote or diminish a willingness to "do the right thing." In tracking the success of a firm, accountants take stock and manage corporate assets. Similarly, if you expect to have the resources available to perform ethically, you need to maintain a sort of internal audit function. Do you have the necessary resources that enable you to be your best ethical self? We have considered how maintaining ethical awareness and committing to using the values you claim to hold is not a foregone conclusion. Rather, it is a sustained monitoring of thoughts and decisions, ensuring that what you value is in sync with what you actually do, each and every day. Thus, it is essential to understand the "self." But what you see and know about yourself is often different than what others observe. To this end, we can also benefit from input from others, in understanding how we are experienced and perceived.

What Others Perceive Matters

Working to understand the self, albeit imperfect, is critical if you want to pursue ongoing growth and development in adulthood. Most of us can look into the mirror and, in seeing our reflection, believe we have a reasonable idea of who we are. Yet the reality is that even when trying to be honest in this endeavor, to know the self, we cannot help but inadvertently distort the truth. The notion of self has been the topic of philosophy and science for centuries. Yet an ability to know who we really are remains elusive, skewed because of our own personal biases. An individual seeking self-understanding is the originator of the inquiry. Thus, an unbiased investigation of the self, by the self, is impossible. As the investigator, you can never be an impartial observer.

This tendency for producing inaccuracies in self-perception stem from our hard-wiring, evolutionary remnants of our will to survive, which can alter our perceptions. For some, biases cast a favorable light, elevating confidences that help them achieve success. For others, preconceptions cast a negative pallor, preventing them from engagement and potentially fueling their insecurities. Such distortions— good, bad, or indifferent—can foster imprecision in the knowledge of self. Adding complexity to this milieu of biases is the fact that we are social creatures, continuing to establish meaning in the context of our interaction with others. Therefore, our behavior and actions that represent our identity continue to unfold and remain continuously influenced by those around us. The ethical elements of our character may or may not be endorsed or supported by others. For many of us, ethical behavior is shaped by where we work and who we work with. While we may think we are ethical, our behaviors may not match our preconceived notions of self.

What does this have to do with business ethics? While most of us think we are ethical, we can be wrong—very wrong. The cost of this error can be detrimental to our personal life, to our families, friends, and employers, and to the community and society in which we live. Many ethical lapses go unnoticed, whereas other missteps result in embarrassment or financial cost. But unethical acts can also impose grave implications, such as the loss of our livelihood, and even put health and safety at risk. Being found guilty of an illegal action may cost you your reputation and even your freedom. Such a loss is not something we typically think about, until after we are already involved and what we care about is threatened.

When engaged in lucrative or self-fulfilling activities that reside on the edge of morality, we place the well-being of ourselves and others on the line. Perceptions matter. Regardless of whether or not it is fair or just to do so, leaders are held to an even higher standard. Expectations of ethicality are applied to the decisions and actions of leaders in both their business and personal life. Eliot Spitzer and David Petraeus were both embroiled in ethical scandals because of their personal indiscretions. Before deploying their decisions to engage in questionable activities, I wonder if either of them thought about how they would feel if their actions made front-page headlines? Did they think about what their constituents, colleagues, and family might say about what they were doing before they made the decision to engage inappropriate and even illegal behavior? This is not to judge them, to say they were wrong or bad; rather, it is to underscore that we are all vulnerable to temptation. Moreover, sometimes people simply do not think things through; they just act and then rationalize their behavior later. In the context of executive leadership, every decision reflects some level of judgment i.e., made automatically or via deliberate cognitive processing. In these cases, making the choice to engage in an extramarital affair or to share confidential information reflects profound carelessness. High level executives and leaders often possess exceptional talent and intellect in many areas, and are engaged in important and meaningful work. Yet, some experience shame, embarrassment, guilt and great loss, while also imposing harm on their loved ones as a result of a clumsy lack of ethical awareness and mindfulness (Figs. 5.1 and 5.2).

Was there a pause, stepping away from the situation, to think through the choices and potential ramifications of their behavior, before getting involved in these relationships? In the heat of the moment, when passions drive actions (sexual or otherwise), any one of us can act without taking time to consider how our behaviors may be perceived by those around us. Perhaps more importantly, considering how our choices and actions may impact the well-being of others, particularly those we care about and love. It is important to recognize behaviors are actualized decisions. These decisions are choices, regardless of whether or not you purposefully think about them or not. It would appear that some people, perhaps blinded by hubris, may not take the time to think things through. In the cases noted, only the people involved know their own truth (and in hindsight that is often skewed). What depth of reflection did they engage in before choosing to act in the way they did? It is

Fig. 5.1 Eliot Spitzer before his prostitute scandal. Image credited to Everett Collection/Shutterstock.com

unlikely that these people spent time forecasting how their actions could have massive ramifications, including bringing harm upon their reputations, families, and professional career paths. Rather, they ignored such potentialities or simply didn't care. In the workplace, management communicates the importance of moral responsibility by how they conduct themselves. And it is not just about conduct at work. Regardless of whether or not a choice is right, moral or ethical, what we do when we leave the workplace is not off limits in terms of its impact on the organization and its ethical health. In fact, given the reality that anything can and does show up online instantly, virtual appearances have never been more important. Ethical challenges in today's 24/7 workplace reflect that, as an extension of the corporate identity or brand, people need to be more mindful about their behavior during their down time.

The choices you make outside the boundaries of your work environment inadvertently reflect how you view the organization you work for. A decision to engage in an unethical or inappropriate activity can impact how others perceive you and your firm. Ovide (2013) describes a recent technology conference in the San Francisco Bay area where presenters made explicit and condescending remarks and jokes about women, sexual acts, and displayed rude and boorish behavior. In this article he describes how a dearth of women in high-level positions undermines the ability to weed out "loutish thinking and action" (2013). Of the private companies that received venture capital funding from 1997 to 2011, a mere 1.3 % of them had

Fig. 5.2 David Petraeus shakes hands with biographer Paula Broadwell. Image is in the public domain

a female founder and 6.5 % had a female chief executive, according to data from Dow Jones VentureSource. Prominent female technology executives like those presently at Facebook (Chief Operating Officer Sheryl Sandberg) and Yahoo (CEO Marissa Mayer) are not the norm. IT gatherings such as "TechCrunch Disrupt" seem to enjoy a boy's club atmosphere, which has a reputation of being ill-mannered. Organizational leaders who do not deter disrespect are accomplices to unethical behavior.

Help from Those Around Us

Leaders convey a message to organizational members, one that reflects how much (or how little) they value ethics, by what they do on a daily basis. But this duty, to support respect in the workplace, is not just a formal leadership function. We all have an ability to influence others, which can potentially sanction impolite, shady, or slippery behaviors or endorse ethically risky choices. Conversely, we can each work to cultivate the best in others by behaving with a commitment to respect, assuming personal responsibly with consistency. The message of living one's ethical code is often based on perceptions, which can be better understood with the help of those around us. Because perceptions are biased, rigorous self-awareness requires feedback from our colleagues, peers, and family members. The Johari window has been used in psychology and organizational behavior for decades to illustrate this point.

The Johari window illustrates the limitations of our own perceptions in how we see ourselves (Luft 1969). Using a square to depict what we know about the self, four quadrants reflect different aspects of how a person is perceived. Looking at Fig. 5.3, you see four quadrants of a box representing a complete view of the self. It is impossible to know the self without the help of others. This is because some elements are unknown to you. People who observe you, work with you, and have experienced being with you know who you are in a way that you cannot experience yourself. Given this challenge, a heuristic tool can help people see how the self can be better known, with the help of others.

Luft and Ingram (1955, 1961) refer to each block as a window. The visual is designed help you better understand how others may experience you, which may be different than your own perceptions. Reading Fig. 5.3 from top to bottom, people reveal information about themselves to others. From left to right, those around us can provide feedback on us that we may not be aware of (unknown to the self). This kind of two-way feedback reveals greater awareness and understanding of who you are by how you are being perceived. Application of this model can enhance personal self-awareness and foster adult development. For example, being quick to judge when presented with new ideas may be your typical reaction at staff meetings. Having a trusted colleague point this out, you can amend your quick response style to offer some pause for reflection and giving others opportunity to share. Imposing some change to your reactive tendency might benefit you and the group's collaborative decision-making. This is especially important in the context of addressing

1 OPEN *Known to self and to others*	**2 BLIND** *Not known to self but known to others*
3 HIDDEN *Known to self but not known to others*	**4 UNKNOWN** *Not known to self or others*

1. Open (Arena): Area visible to the self and others;
2. Blind (Blind Spot): Area known to others, but hidden from the self;
3. Hidden (Façade): Area known to the self, but kept hidden from others;
4. Unknown (Id): Area that exists, but is hidden to both the self and to others.

Fig. 5.3 The Johari window image credited to Luft and Ingram (1955)

ethical issues. Unintentional oversight or a simple lack of awareness can be problematic, potentially imposing costs and causing harm to others.

With information about the self from others, a person can use self-appraisal to access, study, and potentially improve their ethical behavior (Dumvill 1995). Processes and techniques, like 360 degree feedback, are often used in workplace settings to broaden self-awareness, learning to appreciate how your actions are perceived by others. Looking at the model, you can see how knowledge about the self is a combination of internal and external insight. Business ethics education and training needs to incorporate this sort of formalized process, as a means for employees to garner useful feedback about how they are perceived by their co-workers and customers. External feedback is typically incorporated within MBA programs and executive review processes, but rarely is this sort of feedback mechanism utilized as an ongoing ethical developmental tool in organizational settings.

Without help from those around us, a complete view of self is not possible. Intentionally or inadvertently, we may come to lean into our own perceptions of self that incorporate personal embellishments. We may even use denial as a cognitive tool to support the rationalization of our own unethical actions, decisions to proceed with choices that provide immediate gratification or leverage the means to get ahead. With or without conscious awareness, the perceptions of how we see ourselves can hide unwanted truths or veil what is threatening and/or embarrassing about the self, to the self. Admitting we are not as ethical as we think requires honest introspection and feedback from those around us. Looking at personal prejudices, hidden realities, or blind spots can be challenging and potentially disconcerting. But the cost of not paying attention to external feedback, ignoring what others see and perceive, can contribute to uninformed and potentially toxic decision-making. What you don't know or what you are not mindful of has the potential to detour your ethicality in business. Scholars describe how people have an uncanny tendency to attribute negative outcomes that stem from their own behavior to situational factors (Molinsky and Margolis 2005). We often assume that other people are wrong or bad when they act unethically. For ourselves, however, we assume that our own lack of ethics is the result of being trapped, forced, tricked, or some other "fill in the blank" rationalization i.e., we have reasons for taking such actions.

Coates (2010) describes how blind spots need to be examined for a person to learn to revise their image of self (mental schemas) in order to stave off decision-making errors. Character assets can become character defects, when out of proportion. While positive feelings like pride and favorable attributes such as self-efficacy often contribute to achievement and performance in the workplace, when out of balance or inflated they too can become deceptions that may contribute to ethical ineptitude. Garnering feedback from others allows us to ascertain a more robust form of self-awareness. When this awareness is combined with a desire to be ethical, people can develop a more rigorously honest starting point for their decision-making framework. From there, a person can better understand their character strengths and weaknesses. Such awareness is crucial when working to stave off potentially harmful blunders, establish balance, and to sustain a desire to detour temptation.

What you are not aware of regarding how others see and experience you may contribute to implicit social norms that can chip away at the moral strength of an organization. For example, managers may see themselves as transparent, proclaiming openness to ethical discourse. A manager may claim to hold a so-called "open door" policy, stating that he or she wants to hear from employees about ethical issues at any time. By the same token, this manager may impose excessive demands for goal achievement, making little or no time for employees to come forward with their issues. Leaders often say they care about ethics, but then engage in practices contrary to this claim. When there are pressures for employees to "make the numbers" or achieve a certain threshold of performance, and this is combined with cronyism, the message coming from management is, "Ethics comes first convenient. But only when it's required or convenient." When values compete for primacy, often those related to securing short-term performance objectives come out in front. This may result in the core values, central to the identity of the organization, being left behind in the dust (honesty, fairness, and quality).

We're All Ethical?

Managers typically say they care about creating an organizational culture that supports open dialogue, wanting employees to bring their ethical issues forward. And yet senior leaders may not provide viable opportunities for this to occur. Ethical congruence in organizational performance is the *sine qua non* of business ethics. But the workplace is often hypocritical. As employees, we hear that ethics is or should be an important element of performance. But, by the same token, organizations do not always support the viability of ethics in how we go about achieving our goals. No doubt, most managers see themselves as ethical and responsible for creating their firm's path for performance. But does management check in with organizational members, continually striving to identify and address the ethical challenges and risks employees face in pursing their objectives, targets, and/or quotas? If you are a manager, do you create a climate and culture of trust, open dialogue, and collaborative discourse around ethics being embedded in everyday and longer-term performance? Do you support employees by helping them to achieve their goals in an ethical manner? If you say you want to hear about employees' ethical issues, do you create the means for people to share their concerns, a path that engenders pride (versus guilt, shame, or fear)? Identifying and dealing with the ethical elements within a path to action is a constant in business enterprise. Therefore, ethical discourse must become part of the fabric of how people conduct and deal with their everyday tasks. Remaining blind to such concerns says a lot about ourselves and those around us. And, most of us recognize that being in denial often ends up badly.

Ask the former CFO of HealthSouth Corporation, Aaron Beam, about this very point (image on the left) of (Fig. 5.4). Beam describes how he came to expect a life that offered him all the splendors and accoutrements of luxury. After being

Fig. 5.4 Convicted Felons share "lessons learned". Images credited to Leslie E. Sekerka (Aaron Beam (*left*) and Mark Faris (*right*))

convicted of fraud and serving time in prison, he now works with business students to help them understand the nature of the "slippery slope" and how he lost hold of his own personal values. In sharing his story, Beam talks about how quickly he got used to having a table waiting for him at five-star restaurants, sipping fine wines, buying whatever he wanted, and being treated like a "rock star" (Beam and Warner 2009). For his role in approving fraudulent financial reports, Beam served three months in federal prison and was stripped of his CPA credentials. Now he uses his very trying experience to warn students and managers about the pitfalls of hubris and its association with unethical thinking and action. He describes how it started out small—an extra perk here and there—but eventually blossomed into a lifestyle that was beyond his means, and how his perceptions of self and others become grossly distorted.

Similarly, Mark Faris shares his experiential wisdom with business students. Pictured above (right) of (Fig. 5.4), he reads a letter out loud, what he wrote to the judge as he awaited his sentencing fate. He explains his moral failing and contrition for it. After serving time for several white collar crimes, he now supports educators interested in teaching the next generation of managers, helping them understand that they are susceptible to making the same mistakes. In opening his talk, he says:

> My name is Mark Faris. I am a loving husband of 23 years and a proud parent of two teenage boys, 18 and 15 years of age. I am an active member of my local Catholic church, a small business owner, and support a number of charities in the Minneapolis-St. Paul area. I also have the distinction of being a convicted felon. When you look at me, you might not think that. After all, I am well dressed, seem semi-polished, semi-poised, and am well

educated. My friends, the slippery slope is an easy path for all of us to find. I wouldn't wish my fate on any of you. I think the single biggest problem we have today is the lack of personal ethics and significant amount of moral and systemic rot.[1]

According to Johnson (2007), inflated egos are a particular problem among the higher levels of management. Executives are particularly vulnerable to excusing their own unethical behavior, while holding other employees accountable to organizational standards and rules. It's as though they see themselves as having a different "playbook," one that affords them a unique sense of entitlement. Johnson writes, "Unlike the rest of us, they (*executives*) don't have to wait in line for products or services or for a ride to work. Subordinates tell them what they want to hear and stroke their egos" (p. 67). This behavior is often buoyed by exorbitant compensation packages, which seem to be supported by upper levels of management (Sorkin 2014). Despite these inordinate salaries, executives are often tempted to use corporate funds for personal use. Such activities are typically justified as being well-deserved or somehow contributing to the overall success of the firm.

In studying people with great power, such as Bill Clinton (former President), Bernie Ebbers (former WorldCom CEO), and Tom Delay (former House majority leader), we observe that smart people can make really foolish decisions. As Sternberg's (2002) research describes this phenomenon, having "access" to people and information lulls those with power into a sense of belief that they have control and actually know more than others. Top officials and business leaders mistakenly begin to think that they can do whatever they want in or outside of their organizations—with a sense of omnipotence. With swarming subservient staff members and an entourage-like support system, smart and powerful people are seduced into believing that they are special, unique, insulated and protected from the consequences of their actions. As with descriptive elements used to explicate the concept of "groupthink" (Janis 1972), there is a sense of invulnerability. Johnson (2007) suggests that such "formidable forces of insecurity, greed, and ego" are further enhanced and fueled by a short-term performance orientation (p. 68).

Returning to Beam's story, he goes on to describe how his boss, the founder/leader of HealthSouth, Richard Scrushy, pressured him and others to pursue unrealistic performance goals, demanding favorable quarterly performance numbers. According to Beam, Scrushy was known for pushing his employees around with fear tactics, becoming angry and verbally abusive when his demands were not met. When people experience this type of pressure, ethically risky activities and potentially illegal actions start to seem "less bad" when the "heat is on." Unlike Enron, however, HealthSouth did not collapse. Beam writes, "The firm didn't declare bankruptcy and never missed a day of business, and is still in business on the NYSE today (personal communication December 17, 2014). Scrushy did not serve time in prison for the HealthSouth fraud (acquitted in 2005 on 36 counts of fraud) Davidson and Beasley (2009). Four months later, however, Scrushy was indicted on new charges of bribery and mail fraud in connection with

---

[1]Cited from: http://mpvethics.com/how-ethics-moral-compasses-can-improve-our-planet/.

former Alabama governor Don Siegelman. Scrushy was accused of donating $500,000 to Siegelman's campaign in exchange for a seat on a state hospital regulatory board. Both Scrushy and Siegleman were convicted on multiple charges, including bribery, mail fraud, and obstruction of justice. Both received sentences of or close to 7 years in prison. Later, in 2009, Scrushy was ordered to pay approximately $2.9 billion to HealthSouth shareholders to settle a civil suit.[2]

Leadership that drives performance via excessive pressure to succeed has been associated with organizational environments where unethical activities are seeded and thrive. In this case, one has to ask, did Beam ever pause to consider the repercussions of his actions? Why didn't he challenge his boss? Why were his perceptions of self and who he was becoming seemingly blocked from his own view? Once unethical activities start to unfold, a person can become blinded from seeing the truth about themselves. And, after you engage in one wrong act, unethical or immoral behavior can more readily increase with frequency and in magnitude over time. When unethical actions are accompanied with affirmations, praise and riches, it is also hard to turn back. In describing the snowball effect of his own unethical choices, Beam explains how maintaining an awareness of the everyday little things really matters. Those first steps of cheating, lying, embellishments and/or fabrications on exams, accounts, and forms start small. But they have the propensity to "get away from us," he explains. Doing one unethical action makes it easier to engage in another. What's more, the magnitude of unethicality tends to increase, once you start moving in this direction. By looking the other way, you are also, on some level, working to protect your own innocence, even if you know you are in the wrong. This point is consistent with research that describes how people can be lured and morally blinded by the spoils of money and the sense of immunity that comes with prestige and false pride (Bird 2002; Drumwright and Murphy 2004).

When we think of ethics, we tend to conjure up in our minds the most extreme cases. Most people recall stories about others who have engaged in really bad acts of deceit. Although seeming not as gripping to human interest, we hear accounts of those who engage in acts of character strength. Given the human propensity to be attracted to, focus on, or even crave negativity in its grandest form (shock and awe), our first thoughts about "ethics" might be regarding those who have constructed elaborate hoaxes, strategic deceptions designed to accrue profit, power, and/or fame, based upon lies and trickery. From Berni Madoff and his notorious Ponzi scheme, to the acclaimed composer cheat Mamoru Samuragochi, such egregious lack of ethics stirs both anger and outrage. Mr. Madoff's scheme was compelling on the face of it, simply because of its grandiosity ($50 billion). It claimed additional appeal because of his celebrity clientele. But the unmasking of this fraud came amid an overall market meltdown that had a direct, personal effect on people at every rung of the financial ladder. Many investors felt cheated, and Madoff became a sort of poster person for the lack of ethics on Wall Street (Fig. 5.5).

---

[2]For additional information see: http://www.biography.com/people/richard-scrushy-235385#profile.

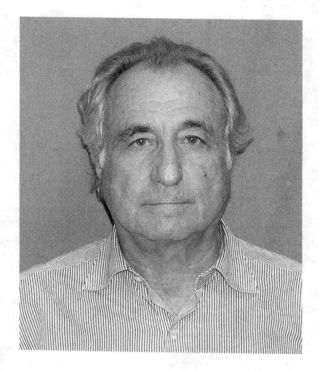

A very different story, but one similarly based on corruptible personal character, was the revelation of the hailed Japanese "Beethoven"—Mamoru Samuragochi— found to fake deafness and having a ghostwriter compose works ascribed to his own name. While this event was not at the same level of mainstream news as the Madoff ordeal, images of guilt are all too familiar. He bowed his head in shame and looked particularly distraught as he admitted his guilt at a world press conference (Tokyo, Japan, March 7, 2014). The images shown in the press that day reflect the tragedy of his disgrace and dishonor. Samuragochi publically apologized for misleading audiences, admitting he had employed a ghostwriter for years. He became famous as a deaf composer of classical music and for well known videogame themes. Dubbed as the modern Beethoven by the media, because of the deafness he shares with the famous German composer, Samuragochi said he was actually never diagnosed as having a full hearing disability (for more information see Kelts 2014). The scandal came amid revelations by Niigaki that he penned works for Samuragochi for 18 years, including the composer's most acclaimed piece, the Hiroshima Symphony.

Despite their differences, both Maddoff and Samuragochi serve as unethical exemplars. Once hailed as trusted agents and prodigies of their expertise and craft, they used talent, insight, and selected bits of truth to surreptitiously lure people with information that they wanted to know or hear. Masters of deceit spin yarns that get bigger and bigger, telling people elaborations of what they probably know that –on some level– is simply too good to be true. In the case of these two con-men, both were artists of dishonesty, building success from elaborate webs of trickery. Madoff was known as a magician of investment returns and Samuragochi was headlined as a musical genius of our time (Fig. 5.6).

In the end, there was no financial or melodic legacy of greatness, only memories of hoaxes, heartache, disappointment, and profound deep loss. While investors lost lifetime savings, the Madoff family was destroyed by the overwhelming guilt and shame. Madoff's son, Mark, the one who came forward to blow the whistle on his father, took his own life. Mark Madoff's widow said he could not separate himself from the ordeal. When the pain of lawsuits, accusations, and hostile investors became overwhelming, he committed suicide. Madoff bears the shame of his past actions and endures the horrific guilt over the loss of his son, while he sits in a federal prison (Stebner 2013). Meanwhile, Samuragochi is busy contesting a suit filed over his nationwide tour that was canceled, following the revelation of his composing scam (Kyodo 2014). Those listening to music associated that bear his name now hear chords that lack integrity, coming off way out of tune with sound ethical practices.

Fig. 5.6 Cheating and deceit comes in many forms. Image credited to the European PressPhoto Agency/KIMIMASA MAYAMA

Fooling Others and Yourself

These kinds of dramatic stories end up in the headlines. But there are many more schemes, perhaps not as grand or shocking, yet nevertheless unfolding in business every day. At this very moment, there are a whole lot of people at work who consider themselves to be ethical people. Simultaneously these very same people are actively engaged in committing unethical acts! It is doubtful they see themselves as being below average in ethicality or lacking in moral character. Seeing yourself as above average (Kruger and Dunning 1999) reflects the human tendency to embellish the truth about ourselves. We all have an inclination to self-bias in a favorable manner. This phenomenon can become clearer to the individual when a person takes an honest look at themselves and tracks their own behavior.

One of my students, a young man in my business ethics class, kept a weekly journal about the ethical issues he encountered. This was a part of a class assignment to reflect on the ethical aspects of one's everyday life. His journal contained a series of entries about riding the public transit system to and from school. He initially describes how he came to realize that he really should be paying for his travel, but admittedly, was not doing so at present. He justified the use of the transportation and his lack of ethicality by explaining that, as a student, he had little money to pay the fare. Lamenting the cost of books, food, and other expenses, he rationalized an inability to pay. As the weeks pass, he gradually admits to feeling a bit guilty for not paying the toll.

He writes about seeing that this behavior is actually revealing an important ethical issue: he believes himself to be an ethical person, and yet, his actions didn't seem to match his view of self. The journal continues with another entry, outlining, much to his chagrin, that the train conductor pulled him aside that day and told him that if he was found riding the train again without paying the fare, he'd be thrown off and given a probation period. He writes about how he now recognizes that this official warning was a huge signal—a proverbial "wake-up call." Realizing he had better change his ways, he goes on to extol the virtues of paying one's way in life. He doesn't want to get into trouble and he's worried that if he is thrown off the train he will have no way to get to school. His journal goes on to explain a rationale for why he really ought to pay, because he is sure he is an ethical person. Vowing to pay the next week, the very next entry in his journal is: "I got thrown off the train." Indeed, people rarely see themselves as being unethical even when they're in the act of doing something that they know is wrong!

Writer and host of National Public Radio's Program *Prairie Home Companion*, Garrison Keillor, describes the population of Lake Wobegon as a place where "all the women are strong, all the men are good looking, and all the children are above average." The perception that the youthful inhabitants of this fictional town are better than others is supported by research: people tend to see themselves as slightly better than those around them (Kleinke and Miller 1998). Now dubbed the "Lake Wobegon effect" (Harrison and Shaffer 1994), the phenomenon is based upon

Cannell's (1988) research that studied the national standardized achievement test (SAT) performance, finding that all 50 states reported being above the national average.

While an inflated view of self has coping and motivational advantages in some circumstances, it may not be particularly useful in motivating pursuit of an ethical action. This is especially the case when internal defense mechanisms rationalize inaction or block a person from sustaining their commitment to being ethical. Wanting to present information about ourselves that displays a favorable image can also endorse distortions and blind us from seeing the truth about our actual behavior. This sort of self-biasing can influence the way we think about and frame ethical issues in the workplace. Seeing yourself as an ethical person, you might be remiss in asking important questions, self-imposed diagnostics that help to ensure that your perceptions of self and actual behavior are congruent. Given this propensity for believing favorable assumptions about the self, it's important to look for how, when, and where we may be easing up on exercising our values as we pursue our goals (Fig. 5.7).

People have a tendency to express a rather large favorable bias when describing their adherence to ethical standards in organizational settings. For example, when asked, "Did you follow the rules on this project?" Your response might be, "Yes, everything is ready to go." By implication, this suggests you are aware of and employed the rules in your efforts. But several interesting self-imposed follow-up prompts might be, "What is the organization's policy as it relates to this project?

Fig. 5.7 Unregulated favorable self-biasing may inhibit genuine ethical strength. Image credited to lassedesignen/Shutterstock.com

What specific rules are applicable? What ethical risks might be present in this activity? Where have ethical issues surfaced in the past? What practices have been applied to overcome prior or potential ethical challenges?" In the heat of the moment, with pressures (real or self-imposed) to achieve goals in a timely manner, people may inadvertently skim over the ethical elements embedded within their everyday task actions. We may even get into a habit of inflating or exaggerating our ethical stance in an effort, as a means to achieve our objectives and/or endorse our capabilities. When puffery becomes a norm and is modeled by management, it's easy to see how lapses in ethical judgment occur.

Takeaway Points

1. How others perceive you may be different from how you see yourself.
2. Know what temps you, watch for areas of ethical risk and stay mindful of your vulnerabilities and/or character defects.
3. Guard against an inflated ego and self-bias that can shroud ethical awareness and truth.
4. If it sounds too good to be true, it probably is.

Reflection Questions

Become an observer of your own actions in the context of others. Do you continually strive to stay open, suspend judgment, and welcome alternative views and/or ways of knowing? Do you have a desire to be more thoughtful, caring, and mindful of other's vantage points? If so, how do you plan to improve upon your current abilities?

References

Beam, A., & Warner, C. (2009). *HealthSouth: A wagon to disaster.* Fairhope, AL: Wagon Publishing.

Bird, F. B. (2002). *The muted conscience: Moral silence and the practice of business ethics.* Westport, CT: Quorum Books.

Cannell, J. J. (1988). Nationally normed elementary achievement testing in America's public schools: How all 0 states are above the national average. *Educational Measurement: Issues and Practice, 7*(2), 5–9.

Coates, B. (2010). Cracking into the panes of corporate denial. *Business Renaissance Quarterly, 5* (3), 23–46.

Davidson, L. V., & Beasley, D. (2009, June 18). HealthSouth's Scrushy Liable in $2.88 Billion Fraud (Update3). *Bloomberg News*. Retrieved March 26, 2014 from http://www.bloomberg.com/apps/news?pid=newsarchive&sid=a89tFKR4OevM.

Dumville, J. D. (1995). Business ethics: A model to position a relative business ethics decision and a model to strengthen its application. *Employee Responsibilities and Rights Journal, 8*(3), 231–243.

Drumwright, M. E., & Murphy, P. E. (2004). How advertising practitioners view ethics: Moral muteness, moral myopia, and moral imagination. *Journal of Advertising, 33*(2), 7–25.

Harrison, D. A., & Shaffer, M. A. (1994). Comparative examinations of self-reports and perceived absenteeism norms: Wading through Lake Wobegon. *Journal of Applied Psychology, 79*(2), 240–251.

Janis, I. L. (1972). *Victims of groupthink: A psychological study of foreign policy decisions and fiascoes*. Boston: Houghton Mifflin Company.

Johnson, C. E. (2007). *Ethics in the workplace: Tools and tactics for organizational transformation*. Thousand Oaks, CA: Sage.

Kelts, R. (May 2, 2014). The Unmasking of "Japan's Beethoven". *The New Yorker*. Retrieved June 3, 2015 from http://www.newyorker.com/culture/culture-desk/the-unmasking-of-japans-beethoven.

Kleinke, C. L., & Miller, W. F. (1998). How comparing oneself favorably with others relates to well-being. *Journal of Social & Clinical Psychology, 17*(1), 107–123.

Kruger, J., & Dunning, D. (1999). Unskilled and unaware of it: How difficulties in recognizing one's own incompetence lead to inflated self-assessments. *Journal of Personality and Social Psychology, 77*, 1121–1134.

Kyodo News. (November 16, 2014). Quack composer Samuragochi contests ¥61 million damages over canceled tour. *The Japan Times*. Retrieved January 1, 2015 from http://www.japantimes.co.jp/news/2014/11/26/national/crime-legal/composer-accused-faking-deafness-contests-damages-suit-tour-canceled/#.VKhOQUZ0zX4.

Luft, J. (1969). *Of human interaction*. Palo Alto, CA: National Press.

Luft, J., & Ingram, H. (1955). The Johari Window: A graphic model of interpersonal awareness. *Proceeding of the western training laboratory in group development*. Los Angeles: University of California Extension Office

Luft, J., & Ingham, H. (1961). The Johari Window: A graphic model of awareness in interpersonal relations. *Human relations training news, 5*(9), 6–7.

Molinsky, A., & Margolis, J. D. (2005). Necessary evils and interpersonal sensitivity in organizations. *Academy of Management Review, 30*(2), 245–268.

Ovide, S. (2013, September 10). Boorish behavior by techies? There's no app for that. *Wall Street Journal*. Retrieved February 5, 2014 from http://online.wsj.com/news/articles/SB10001424127887323864604579065592682833608.

Sorkin, A. R. (2014, March 24). A question of what's a reasonable reward. *The New York Times*. Retrieved March 26, 2014 from http://dealbook.nytimes.com/2014/03/24/a-question-of-whats-a-reasonable-reward/.

Stebner, B. (2013, May 17). 'I'm responsible for my son's death': Convicted Ponzi schemer Bernie Madoff admits he is to blame for son's suicide. *New York Daily News*. Retrieved March 21, 2014 from http://www.nydailynews.com/new-york/bernie-madoff-claims-responsibility-son-suicide-article-1.1346512.

Sternberg, R. J. (2002). Smart people are not stupid, but they sure can be foolish. In R. J. Sternberg (Ed.), *Why smart people can be so stupid* (232–242). New Haven, CT: Yale University Press.

Chapter 6
Small Deceptions Matter

The reality of being human is that we all bend the truth. *We lie.* Whether intentionally for unethical reasons or in a backward manner to try and do good, mistruths are everywhere we go. We lie, and we lie a lot. One study found that telling lies to partners, bosses, and coworkers occurred, on average, six times a day for men and three times a day for women (Daily Mail Reporter 2009). In the workplace people share social fictions all the time, claiming that "nothing is wrong" (when something is wrong) or that we go along with something "that's fine" (when it is really troubling).

While personal biases can, in some cases, provide a motivation to act, they may also spur inaccuracies that can hinder or even block our willingness to act ethically. This is especially the case when internal defense mechanisms rationalize inaction or even fuel unethical action. Over time, if inaccuracies are endorsed by those around us, we may find ways to further justify unethical behavior. In organizations where there is a fixed hierarchy and an abundance of rules, managers often refer to their unethical actions as "rule-bending" rather than "rule-breaking" activities (Sekerka and Zolin 2007). Over the years I have noticed clichés being used to soften unethical activities. Adding to the above, terms like "sandbagging" and "parking it" were ways to talk about how and when to book a sale. The truth is, pun intended, these terms represent deceptions.

As Sam Harris writes in his treatise on lying (2013), infamous characters found among the classics in literature—*Anna Karenina, Madame Bovary,* and *Othello*—drove plot lines that were based entirely upon lives driven by more lies (Fig. 6.1). Both private and public vice are kindled and sustained by lies. When white lies go from grey to black, evil rears its ugly head. As Harris observes, acts of betrayal, deceit, adultery, fraud, cheating, evasion, corruption—even murder—are supported by a personal moral defect: the willingness to lie (2013).

When we're young, lies can manifest into social norms that show up in everyday online communications. People, especially Millenials, often exaggerate stories about themselves or information about their lives on Facebook, referring to such embellishments as "social oil," rather than lies or distortions of the truth (Underwood et al. 2011). One report suggests that people lie over 200 times a day (Jellison 1977), a number that's hard to believe until you think about how those little white lies can really add up. Of course, the number depends upon how you define "a lie" and if you

© Springer International Publishing Switzerland 2016

L. E. Sekerka, *Ethics is a Daily Deal*, DOI 10.1007/978-3-319-18090-8_6

Fig. 6.1 Madame Bovary.
Illustration by Charles
Léandre, engraved by Eugène
Decisy (fr). (1930, p. 322).
Image is in the public domain

are even aware of the fact that you are telling a lie. Another report, related to the lies we are consciously aware of telling and willing to admit, suggests that men are bigger liars than women (three times a day as compared to two times a day for women), and feel less guilty about it (BBC 2010); CBS News (2010).

I'm on My Way

Your motive behind telling a falsehood may be morally justifiable, such as when someone asks for your opinion about their weight or capability, and you don't want to hurt their feelings. But researchers have found that most of our everyday fibbing is designed for self-serving reasons (e.g., not revealing something). According to a survey commissioned by the Science Museum of London, some of the most popular lies we tell are:

- I'm on my way;
- It wasn't that expensive;
- I'm stuck in traffic;
- I didn't have that much to drink; and
- I missed your call.

Fig. 6.2 Lying in daily interactions is a regular happenstance. Image credited vvoe/Shutterstock. com

Consider, for example, you are behind schedule for a 1 pm meeting, one that requires you to drive across town. As you are leaving, you realize you are going to be late. Your meeting is with Jim, a supplier you need to see, based upon a direct request from your boss. There's no time to stop for lunch and you are a bit tired. You worked late the night before trying to catch up on paperwork. As a courtesy, you call Jim to let him know you'll be a few minutes late. In the process of doing this, you hear a message he's left for you. In it, he says it's important to bring along a particular file. You feel certain that bringing the file will alter the meeting agenda, bleeding into your time and ability to handle what your boss wants covered in the short time period allotted. You are walking from your office to the parking lot when Jim's voice mail kicks in. You act as though you didn't receive his call and leave a message saying you're stuck in traffic and will be there ASAP. When you get to the meeting and Jim asks for the file, you say you didn't hear the message. A seemingly harmless distortion of the actual truth, rounding corners, cutting off the edges, so to speak, are the little white lies we inadvertently let slip by, especially when we are task focused (Fig. 6.2).[1]

Specialists who study lying have learned that we tend to lie even more when we're talking to people we don't know well (Tyler and Feldman 2004). Talk show hosts and the news media make fun of this human vulnerability by asking people on

---

[1]A YouTube on the "Science of Lying" can be found at: https://www.youtube.com/watch?v= MX3Hu8loXTE.

the street what they think about something that's blatantly fictitious and ridiculous. For example, a feature of ABC's late-night Jimmy Kimmel Live is a segment called "Lie Witness News" (Opelka 2014). Instead of asking people for their opinions on something real, Kimmel's staff exposes the amazing propensity of people on the street to lie and to do so with apparent ease. Whether the impetus to lie to a stranger is a fear of looking ignorant, a burning desire to be on television, or some other reason, people seem to be readily armed to lie on the spot.

People on the streets of Los Angeles, California were recently asked, "What did you think of Obama's State of the Union address?" Interviewees describe their experience of watching something that had not yet even happened! Some people were also willing to dig into the lying more deeply, commenting on blatantly fictitious elements, prompted by the interviewer (e.g., "What did you make of Joe Biden falling asleep?"). In one especially funny segment, a reporter asks pedestrians what they thought about 12 *Years a Slave* having an all-white cast and whether or not Matt Damon really deserved the Oscar for his starring role in *I Made Love to My Sandwich*. With or without a microphone in front of us, many of us may automatically buy into trusting someone and vicariously also buy into the lies they project. The phenomenon of lying to strangers is more common than most of us may realize. When coupled with the influence of a professional role or position of authority, we can see how this tendency can be an ethical liability.

To understand the phenomenon, researchers created a study asking people to chat with someone they did not know for 10 min. Participants were asked to describe how honest they were in the dialogue. The vast majority of people reported that they had been completely honest and accurate in their statements. But researchers determined that 60 % of the subjects lied at least once and, on average, lied three times during the period (Feldman et al. 2002). Feldman and his colleagues explain that people's motives are not designed or intended to be deceptive; rather, we often lie to give others the impression that we are who we want to be, rather than who we really are. This seemingly innocent bit of insecurity may give way to developing a habit of lying. Some argue this is merely day-to-day perception management and/or "just a part of business." But such actions can contribute to patterns of behavior that fuel a slippery slope, making falsehoods seem less and less bothersome. A regular diet of lying can get out of hand and, before we know it, we can become involved in outright deception. While telling those little white lies, taking a shortcut here or there, or turning a blind eye to a wrongdoing may seem like a long trek from fraud and corruption, it's actually creating the path. When your expectations for what constitutes right action continue to be downgraded, before long the notion of workplace ethics is more about staying out of trouble than about being honest and forthright.

I hear students in my management classes say, "To succeed and accomplish your goals in business, you have to be shrewd, you have to do whatever it takes to get ahead." To help explain why these attitudes are present in business schools today, Laura Kray, a researcher at the Hass School of Business at the University of California, Berkeley, looked at how students respond to ethical challenges. Explaining her research (Kray and Haselhuhn 2012) on a National Public Radio program, she described how she gives her students a real estate negotiation problem that presents them with a moral dilemma (Vedantam 2014). Buyers want to turn a property into a commercial project and the sellers want their homes to be preserved. She puts it to the students: "Should the buyers reveal their intentions to the sellers?" To her surprise, Kray found that men have more lenient ethical standards than women, but that negotiators of either gender are more likely to tell a blatant lie to a female versus male counterpart. Both men and women are more likely to lie when they are dealing with a woman. So, in business, women appear to be the more common targets for blatant deception.

When it comes to ethical standards and ethical choices, men and women tend to be different. As buyers, men are more willing to lie and women are more likely to tell the truth. Interestingly, Kray and her colleagues also found that men tend to apply ethical principles according to egocentric convenience. For example, when an ethical decision affects a man negatively, he is likely to perceive the situation as being unethical. But when this same situation benefits the man, he is likely to perceive it as a "gray area," and "not that big of a big deal" or "it's fine, this is just business." Women, on the other hand, are more likely to view an ethical decision in a consistent manner and to resolve it accordingly. They don't tend to frame it in terms of personal benefit.

Kennedy and Kray (2013) took this research forward to see if students would be willing to include an inferior ingredient in a product (e.g., food, drugs, and vehicles). In this situation, it is not only an ethical matter; the decision has to do with the health and safety of human lives. In resolving such issues, the differences in ethical responsiveness seems to be linked to the fact that women experience moral emotions more often than men. What's more, men seem to be less plagued by ethical doubt. This "doubt" can be an important motivator in choosing to take more time, seek help, get more information, etc. These are the kinds of steps that people employ when they are responding to an ethical challenge with moral courage (see Chap. 9). Any professor in a university business school setting will tell you there are typically more men than women in their classes. Taking these ideas together, we can see why it is absolutely necessary to bring this information forward to our students and to challenge men, in particular, to rise above self-centered justifications that might substantiate choosing shrewd over ethical thinking in business. In turning to the experts in the science of honesty, living more honestly contributes to better health. It turns out that when people work to reduce the number of lies they tell, they encounter improved health.

Kelly and Wang (2012) found that people who purposefully worked to reduce telling lies for a 10-week period reported fewer mental and physical health complaints, such as feeling tense or having sore throats and headaches. As compared to the control group, participants who worked to be more truthful felt better as they became more honest throughout the period. In weeks when participants told fewer lies, they also reported that their close personal relationships had improved and social interactions had gone more smoothly overall. At this point, researchers believe that improvement in relationships significantly accounts for the improvements in health, associated with less lying. Current studies also show that people have an idea, albeit on a less conscious level, of when someone is lying to them or not (ten Brinke et al. 2014). The detection of lies is of great importance in personal, professional, and civic ethics, with the potential to guide business thoughts and actions at a subconscious level (Fig. 6.3).

Recent research also illustrates that even when the truth is difficult to share, honesty is usually the best policy in the long-run, in terms of building trust (John et al. 2015). To learn more about this concept, scientists had participants play a game, whereby person A is given an amount of money and must then decide how much of that money will be shared with person B (an assigned partner). The amount is then tripled, and person B has to decide how much to give back to person A. In making decisions about how much money to give, it turns out that the amount of money people decide to give back, is heavily influenced by how much they trust their partner. This trust factor is heavily influenced by whether or not the person A decides to share information, or not. When shown profile questionnaires filled out by their partners (who had been induced to either answer the questions or leave them blank), person B routinely gave less money back to person A if they the person chose not to answer the questions. This turned out to be a more powerful determinant for sharing, even if the person admitted to engaging in an unethical behavior (e.g., frequently tried to gain access to another person's email account or faked a sick day at work). John and her colleagues concluded that people tend to favor others who are honest, those who are forthright in sharing information—even negative information—with us. This work illustrates that signals of openness in sharing information can be a powerful determinant of trustworthiness, perhaps more so than even knowing about activities that signal less than ethical behavioral choice-actions. There appears to be a positive "halo" effect if you share information; such that people are willing to overlook an honest person's less than stellar behavior so long as they are open about it.

Taking these research findings together, it would appear that paying explicit attention to our own patterns of thinking and behavior around lying and truth-telling in the workplace is warranted. If lying is unhealthy, and others know (or eventually will know) that you are doing it, continuously ignoring such behavior is ultimately

Fig. 6.3 Lying to yourself is still lying. Image credited to Anchiy/Shutterstock.com

going to be both unproductive and unhealthy. If telling the truth casts a positive halo upon us and our associated actions, fostering trust and reciprocity, why wouldn't we want to aspire to be more honest in our business transactions?

Being Honest with Yourself

If people have a propensity to lie, but feel better when they are honest, it seems worthwhile to be a bit more truthful with ourselves about who we really are. Even though we probably intend to be ethical, we generally rely upon past actions as the basis for assuming we will behave ethically today. Unfortunately, biases of presumed goodness can inadvertently block us from seeing the need to focus on the elements of our current situation and to examine our role in it. It's easy to expect we will do the right thing if we see ourselves as ethical. When individuals rely on their expectations to address an issue, they may overlook the ethical implications of that issue because their workplace expectations may not include "moral" criteria (Moore and Loewenstein 2004). Are you in the habit of examining a situation and your motives thoroughly? If you hold an expectation that you are a moral person and see yourself as someone with sound moral character, it is still essential that you actually work to pursue right action—not just assume you have it.

What moves people to feel they need to embellish the truth in order to succeed? You might ask yourself, "What motivates me to lie or exaggerate in business? What do I have to gain by not being truthful?" Self-aggrandizement may be an underlying motive for lying, in the form of overstating realities (e.g., "We can have it there within a week"). Some people feel insecure or are worried about appearing as good as or better than others (e.g., "I make my goal every quarter, regardless of hurdles"). Competition can certainly fuel dishonesty. But interestingly, some people simply lie and cheat because it is easy to do. Unfortunately, if you don't pay attention to your truthfulness, lying can become habitual. In unpacking what drives people to be dishonest, it is often because a person is lazy and wants to take a short-cut (e.g., "I read the values statement and code of conduct before I signed it". Or, sometimes it is because a person is just plain greedy (e.g., "This was booked and shipped, so it should count for this month's commission", "I had my numbers in before the deadline"). In many ways, lying is a form of risk-taking, a trait associated with competitive individuals. Business naturally attracts people who tend to be competitive and highly motivated to achieve their goals. Rationalizing lies in business is far from unusual behavior. But lying goes hand in hand with a devaluing of ethics. Perhaps, when engaging in a less than ethical manner you have said to yourself, "What does it matter? Everyone does it."

If you think you are an ethical person, do you consider how you go about achieving this aspect of your character in your regular activities? For example, alerting someone that you will be late is, on the face of it, a thoughtful gesture—a courteous and "right" thing to do. But texting this information while you are driving is not an ethical way to address this matter. Even if your motive is good, it doesn't necessarily mean you will execute it in an ethical way. So, for starters, you need to ascertain your underlying motives for what you say and do. What is your intent, the genuine reasoning behind distortions of the truth. Understanding what drives your dishonesty is an essential step in learning how to get honest with yourself. Then, along with your motives, you must also consider how you go about deploying your activities.

When people communicate online, many are driven by the desire to promote their group cohesion. This may be achieved by telling "white lies." Some people regularly indulge in outright deceptive behavior in online platforms like Facebook, sharing information designed to self-promote or aggrandize themselves (Underwood et al. 2011). Discourse continues as to whether people are more truthful (ethical) in face to face or online communications. Take for example in emails, where people might be more truthful as they know whatever they say is being documented (Conger 2011). In communicating face to face, avoiding or giving eye contact does not suggest someone's lying to you, or telling the truth (respectively). But there are clues, like gaze aversion, that do signal deception (Sporer and Schwandt 2007). In online settings we do not have these sorts of non-verbal cues to consider. Certainly, a person's attributes and traits (being shy, risk aversion, etc.), along with the particular context or situation, influence the likelihood of someone being more or less truthful. It would seem, however, that taking the time to meet with people face to face, whenever possible, might help us better understand and deal with the socio-emotional challenges present in the workplace (Warkentin, Sayeed and Hightower 1999).

In business, we strive and sometimes struggle to achieve our performance goals. This includes hitting targets, making quotas, making deadlines, and addressing a variety of performance demands. Often missing from performance criteria is an explicit focus on how we achieved these goals. The means, or *how* we achieve ethical action in route to performance, is rarely valued as much as the achievement of the goal itself. If there is limited focus on how we achieve our goals, the motive for doing so may be based upon less than moral motives. When the context focuses more on "making the goal," over "how do we go about achieving the goal," it can be a crucible that breeds dishonesty. It is important to recognize that even when your motives are good, how we carry them out can be questionable ethically (Fig. 6.4).

Ethical people engage in unethical acts for many different reasons. Studies in social psychology reflect how we are susceptible to the influence of social norms. Interpersonal and environmental forces can certainly be deleterious to a person's character. We are all vulnerable to the influence of social, peer, and group behaviors around us (Shadnam and Lawrence 2011). Perhaps the most famous experiment in this regard was when Milgram (1963) demonstrated how reasonably thoughtful individuals could easily be swayed, choosing to engage in behavior that actually imposed harm on others (participants did not actually harm anyone, but they were led to believe they were doing so in the experimental setting). As stated by Milgram (1974), "[I]t is not so much the kind of person a man is—as the kind of situation in

Fig. 6.4 Achieving performance goals is essential, but *how* you go about achieving them matters. Image credited to Andor Bujdoso/Shutterstock.com

which he finds himself that determines how he will act." Social psychologists have continued to reflect on this disconcerting aspect of human nature, working to better understand our inherent ethical vulnerability, so that we may guard against it.

While ethical people engage in unethical behaviors for many different reasons, Milgram's work focused on the conflict between obedience to authority and personal conscience. He was interested in understanding justifications for acts of genocide by those accused at the Nuremberg War Criminal trials. Their defense was typically based on obedience, following the orders of their superiors. Milgram wanted to investigate whether Germans were particularly obedient to authority figures, as this was a common explanation for the Nazi killings. He found that any ordinary person may follow orders given by an authority figure, even to the extent of killing an innocent human being. Obedience to authority is ingrained in us, from the way we are brought up. Learning to obey parents, teachers, and authority figures cultivates what Milgram called an agentic state (we come to accept others directing, shaping, and/or being the agent of our ethical self).

As described by Nissani 1990, "the essence of obedience consists in the fact that a person comes to view themselves as the instrument for carrying out another person's wishes, and they therefore no longer see themselves as responsible for their actions. Once this critical shift of viewpoint has occurred in the person, all of the essential features of obedience follow" (pp. 1384–1385). Thus, we see how people tend to allow others to direct their actions, and then pass off the responsibility for the consequences to the person who has given the orders. In other words, superiors act as agents of your will. Social psychologists continue to reflect on this disconcerting aspect of human nature, working to better understand this inherent source of ethical malleability.

Recipe for Corruption

Carrying this concern for human moral vulnerability forward, other scholars have focused on the context and situations that seem to cultivate unseemly decisions and actions. Perhaps most well known in this regard, Phil Zimbardo became interested in the potential of environmental setting to shape behavior. The Stanford University professor of psychology is best known for his 1971 "Prison Experiment," in which average students descended into abuse when they were randomly assigned roles as "guards" over other student "prisoners."

This work, as well as other studies of environmental systems like Abu Ghraib prison, led Zimbardo to identify systemic factors that make good people do bad things. The Stanford Prison Experiment foreshadowed how such conditions can lead to horrific acts, like those enacted by military personnel at the Abu Ghraib prison (2007). In testifying as an expert witness, Zimbardo described how certain environments can serve to corrupt even those who have vowed to uphold ethical standards as a part of their social identity—i.e., military service personnel. In talking to Zimbardo, I learned he has been determined to learn how and why people can become so grossly separated from their ethical or moral selves (personal conversation, April 23, 2008). This scholarly pursuit led to his creation of a list of criteria that contribute to the corruption of people's identity in social settings (2004).

While amoral acts of atrocity toward other living and sentient beings (as depicted by the image at Abu Ghraib), may seem a far stretch from organizational life, those involved in such scandals did not expect to forget their values, morality, and humanity (Fig. 6.5).

To illustrate just how susceptible people are to ethical corrosion, Zimbardo drafted a list of circumstances that can move good people to do bad things. The components he offers are outlined below. They are modified for application to the workplace, showing how management and the organizational environment itself can become framed as the authority figures. Examples follow each item to help relate the elements to everyday organizational experiences.[2]

1. A workplace performance ideology justifies questionable actions, which are legitimated with rewards. People comply with and model this method.

   Let us say you are a member of work team where there is pressure and competition to perform. Stress to accomplish performance goals seems to take priority over fully vetting ethical risks. Management seems to turn a "blind eye" toward how goals are achieved. Cutting corners and taking shortcuts go unquestioned. Compensation is associated with meeting performance goals. Everyone seems to be going along with this approach and it is understood that this is the accepted practice. It is "just business," and people are making good money.

---

[2]Some of this material originally appeared in Sekerka, L. E. 2012.

Fig. 6.5 Abu Ghraib prisoner
abuse and torture. Images are
in the public domain

2. Those modeling this performance ideology reflect organizational compliance.

Many of us recognize that "rule-bending" occurs in organizational settings, in
route to achieving performance goals. Organizations may even tout their
compliance-driven ethics programs that supposedly drive their ethical performance,

pointing to values, standards, policies, and a reported commitment to adhering to industry regulations. However, management may still engage in rule-bending, as they profess to having complied with the required regulatory demands. Such efforts may follow the *letter* of the law, but lack the *spirit* of the law's intent.

3. Management appears to be just and, at times, even compassionate; yet, can also become dictatorial.

Your team leader, supervisor, or boss is inconsistent in mood or temperament. On Monday the boss seems to support your request for time off to care for a sick relative. Then later, that same week, she demands that quotas be met and current tasks be accomplished in an expedited time frame. You have to curtail your vacation time, hire outside help to care for your relative, and work overtime (without pay) to try to meet the goals. In the end, the boss is pleased with your efforts and suggests you need to ensure that future deadlines are met and exceeded. The morale of your team decreases measurably.

4. Rules are vague and changing.

Perhaps the performance policies or rules at your organization are amended without providing time to reflect and discuss the ramifications of the changes with coworkers and management. Before you can even figure out how these rules actually affect the existing processes or their implementation, another email arrives announcing another revision to the compliance standards.

5. Exiting the situation is difficult.

We count on employers because we make lifestyle decisions based on the expectation of earning money in exchange for our efforts. Many of us owe the government for student loans and have amassed credit card debt. While striving to pay off these bills, we often face additional unexpected financial burdens (e.g., medical, automotive, inflation). Jobs are scarce, or they are low-wage labor offerings, and it is seemingly impossible to relocate because our extended family helps provide childcare. Leaving the job is simply out of the question. When we rely upon our organization to keep our household going, we cannot just quit. People have to make the best of it and "make do," even if management is less than ethical. Quitting is not an option for most of us.

The points noted and examples accompanying them illustrate how easily people can be placed in situations that might work against their desire or intent to engage in principled performance. When any one or a combination of these elements is present, organizational members may be prompted to redirect ethical and moral responsibility externally. They may choose to go along with a situation and say nothing. People may even engage in decisions and actions that they might not otherwise engage in. As a result, moral agency may be postponed or thwarted, and the person might not even realize it.

These examples show how people are, in a sense, often at the mercy of an unjust, unfair, or tainted system. When people's basic survival relies on their employment, what solutions can be offered aside from leaving the organization? There is no short answer to this question. Nor are there convenient bullet points that can be offered with suggestions for here's how "next steps." If you are in management, it is your job to create a context for ethical performance. This means you are a role model for moral responsibility, provide emotional support and care for others, and demonstrate and reward moral competency in performance. To begin to address these aspirational ideas as goals, we can begin by modifying the typical business ethics philosophy. The notion of moving from "ethics as compliance" to "ethics as moral strength" creates a platform for this discussion (see also Chap. 9).

In review of the literature on the moral self, Jennings et al. (2014) describe moral strength as the capacity and conation (impetus to act) to achieve moral ends. In outlining the constructs associated with the action-taking features of the moral self, they discuss how moral character promotes the ability to uphold moral principles (Narvaez et al. 2006). Other constructs that support this actionable side of the moral self include moral attitudes (Jackson et al. 2008), moral confidence (Krettenauer and Eichler 2006), and moral conviction (Skitka et al. 2005). Moral chronicity (Narvaez et al. 2006), a lesser known support function, refers to those who tend to interpret social information in terms of chronically activated moral schemas. This is represented by an implicit moral personality which may influence the interpretation of social information and account for the automaticity of moral behavior (Warren 2008).

The state of moral potency (Hannah and Avolio 2010; Hannah et al. 2011) involves ownership of the moral aspects of one's environment (moral ownership), reinforced by beliefs in an ability to achieve moral purposes in that domain (moral efficacy), and the courage to perform ethically in the face of adversity and to persevere (moral courage). A duty orientation represents a loyalty to serve and faithfully support group members, striving to accomplish the mission of the group, and to honor its codes and principles (Hannah et al. 2013). The concept of moral strength itself reflects the intensity with which individuals rely on and seek to integrate moral notions into their actual behavior (Jennings et al. 2014).

Going Beyond Compliance

When working to achieve performance goals and objectives, people may not be aware of how their choices and actions may inadvertently deteriorate, leading them to become less ethical. This lack of forthrightness often stems from personal weaknesses fueled by self-interest, greed, hubris, and laziness, along with perceived social pressure. Fear of job loss and lack of information may also contribute to a person's ethical fallibility. Furthermore, small steps toward harmful actions tend to gradually increase in magnitude. Said differently, once people engage in an unethical act, there appears to be propensity to not only repeat that act, but to increase the size of its unethical proportion. For example, an employee pads their expense account by $100 in January. Nothing seems amiss by the accounting department, so the reimbursement check is cut and paid. In March or April, the employee repeats the action but increases the amount to $150. This might be rationalized by the individual, thinking, "the company owes me" or maybe it just feels like they are "due" or entitled to that money. Campbell et al. (2004) describe how such narcissistic entitlement reflects an attitude that one ought to have what one wants, presumably linked to the sense that one is a special, superior person. Narcissistic entitlement is defined as "a stable and pervasive sense that one deserves more and is entitled to more than others" (Campbell et al. 2004, p. 31). It would be no surprise then, to find that people who possess an over abundance in self-interest end up in business, where the focus can be largely directed toward achieving their personal success.

But let's say we're not the offender in this case; rather the innocent observer or co-worker. As fraudulent expenditures continue within a company, people may not report them. Perhaps it may be to avoid conflict. But another reason is that we tend to accept incoming information as the "new normal." Similar to the parable of the boiled frog, people are often unaware of the gradual change in their behavior or in the behaviors of those around them. To explain this phenomenon, the story describes how a frog being thrown into a pot of boiling water will react. Immediately becoming aware of the scalding temperature, the frog jumps out. However, putting that same frog into a pot of water at room temperature and then slowly turning up the heat, the frog stays in the pot and boils to death. Grim as the comparison may be, the workplace is like that pot of water, with the heat gradually rising (metaphorically speaking). With an incremental ethical degradation occurring around us, it can influence our judgment in surreptitious ways. A subtle ethical change in the environment may not allow employees to realize that the unethical heat (corruption) is being raised (increasing in frequency and magnitude) around them.

Given that people have personal weak spots in their character and that the organization's culture and climate can bring out the best or the worst in people, it becomes evident how a seemingly ethical organization can, as a whole, become unethical over time. As suggested by Moberg, an expert in organizational ethics, employees may not be aware that they are losing clarity of thought around ethical discernment and prudential judgment (2006). Organizational environments where moral myopia exists can cloud decision-making. Employees' ability to give voice to ethical concerns may become thwarted (i.e., moral muteness) (Bazerman and Tenbrunsel 2011; Bird and Waters 1989; Drumwright and Murphy 2004). Scholars have taken great care to ascertain how unethical acts form, spread, and can establish a negative influence on processes and even entire industries. If the hope is to create organizations that are ethically strong, it is necessary to aim higher than achieving a compliance-driven baseline. It is important to establish organizations that not only focus on helping employees adhere to rules and regulations, but in which leaders and management foster an organizational environment where ongoing moral development is a part of employees' expected performance.

Figure 6.6 depicts how firms relate ethics to performance (Sekerka and Godwin 2010). The center section represents an ethical baseline, achieved through compliance. Most organizations work to adhere to federal, state, and regional laws,

Unethical Action	Ethical Compliance	Ethical Action
Does harm	Does no harm	Reduces harm
Non-adherence to regulation	Adherence to regulation	Supersedes regulation
Punishment	Control	Empowerment
Disobedience and noncompliance	Obedience and compliance	Growth and development

|--|--|

Moral Weakness   Moral Minimum   Moral Strength

Fig. 6.6 The organizational ethics continuum. Figure adapted from Sekerka (2012)

along with industry regulatory standards. Adherence, however, does not necessarily include any efforts to build moral strength. The far left illustrates firms that fall below the baseline, those that are deficient and morally weak. The far right exemplifies what it looks like to go beyond compliance, doing more than what is required by law, cultivating ethical development at the individual and organizational levels in a way that instills the practice of principled performance. This perspective goes beyond ensuring compliance, as employees work to adhere to the letter along with the spirit of the law's intent. This approach considers how creating value for the firm impacts others, with focused concern to make money for investors while also being socially responsible.

If moral strength is to become routine, self-regulation is a necessary function at the organizational, group, and individual levels. To engage in ethical action in organizational settings, external support is needed. A proactive ethics culture—one that encourages empowerment—is essential if superseding regulation is to become an everyday workplace practice. To create organizational cultures of empowerment, where ethical growth and development is the norm, a focus on compliance must be expanded so that processes, norms, and routines support principled performance. While some organizations lack a sincere care for ethical considerations, firms in the United States are required to attend to the laws of the land, including rules from governmental regulatory agencies. On the face of it, an organization's ethical identity is visible via its mission, code of conduct, and operating stance. But sometimes these values are stated but not fully exercised.

Because most firms are compliance-driven, they move to do what is necessary to maintain their fiduciary duty to investors and do what's necessary to address legal requirements. But compliance programs are often behind the curve, guarding against yesterday's corporate problems, which can fail to identify and prevent tomorrow's ethical exposures. When confronted with misconduct, organizations must answer to the government, and senior management to their board. The best of risk assessment may not be forward thinking, and therefore leaves the organization exposed and vulnerable to ethical issues. Some firms consider the cost of an unethical action strategically, actually calculating how much the move will cost the firm in terms of legal fees, fines, and court costs. Of course, the cost to the organization's reputation is also real.

While such efforts are intended to avoid wrongdoing, organizations that work to achieve compliance are unlikely to exceed it. However, there are firms that possess norms and values that go beyond the legal baseline. These organizations create practices within their operations that meet and exceed the moral minimum. Such organizations aspire to achieve social responsibility as a part of their mission. Cameron illustrates this point by framing performance as driven by negative or positive deviance (referring to harmful functioning on one end of the spectrum and virtuous functioning on the other) (2007).

Cynics who insist that corporate ethics policies are rarely worth the paper they are written on might refer to Enron's 64-page Code of Ethics, published in July 2000.[3] Enron's ethics code was based on respect, integrity, communication, and excellence. The corporate values were described as follows:

Respect. We treat others as we would like to be treated ourselves. We do not tolerate abusive or disrespectful treatment. Ruthlessness, callousness and arrogance don't belong here.
Integrity. We work with customers and prospects openly, honestly and sincerely. When we say we will do something, we will do it; when we say we cannot or will not do something, then we won't do it.
Communication. We have an obligation to communicate. Here we take the time to talk with one another ... and to listen. We believe that information is meant to move and that information moves people.
Excellence. We are satisfied with nothing less than the very best in everything we do. We will continue to raise the bar for everyone. The great fun here will be for all of us to discover just how good we can really be.

Complementing their exemplary ethics handbook was a first rate training program crafted by their associates at Arthur Anderson, with input from the leading scholars of the time (e.g., Velasquez). For decades, Anderson was a firm known for its ardent commitment to rigorous accounting practices. Who better to craft your ethics training materials than a first rate accounting firm? Since this program was developed (1992), we have more empirically-driven insight about how ethical decision-making can be impacted by emotions, social norms, and a host of other psychological influences. However, looking at one of the original instruction manuals from the program (see Fig. 6.7), some of the pages look very similar to

---

[3]A commentary can be found at: http://blogs.cfainstitute.org/insideinvesting/2013/10/14/the-enron-code-of-ethics-handbook-from-July-2000-is-a-fascinating-read/.

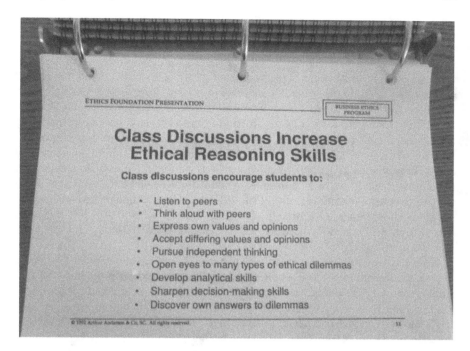

Fig. 6.7 A page from the Arthur Anderson ethics training notebook. Image courtesy of Leslie E. Sekerka, materials donated by Ken Euske

what we still teach today. Obviously, you have to actually apply this information to your daily efforts. For it to work, you have to own it and live it. It has become profoundly clear that the culture of an organization can bring out the best or worst in people. If the culture, as shaped, modeled and led does not encourage, promote and support ethics in performance, codebooks, training and policies are a charade.

Eighteen months after this carefully crafted Code was written, the ethical scandal broke, leading to the firm's ultimate self-destruction (Amble 2014). Having read and reviewed their ethics code and ethics training program documents, the problem was not in either. Rather, the crux of the issue was that neither were applied to the organizational life of the firm. In reality, the culture and climate of Enron had nothing to do with their corporate values. It has always amazed me that one of their core mottos was, "Ask why," inferring that if ethical risks emerged, employees were encouraged to raise the red flag (i.e., openness, transparency, and questions were welcomed).

Nothing could have been further from the truth. In fact, many, if not all, of Zimbardo's elements aptly describe this organization's operational environment. At the time, Enron was hailed as the darling of Wall Street. But over time, the charade of smoke and mirrors was revealed to be a fraudulent scam. Ask Ken Lay, Jeff Skilling, and Andy Fastow how this worked out for them.

The "Smartest Guys" Had a Hard Time with Ethics

In 2006, following four and a half years of government prosecutor preparation, the Lay and Skilling trials began. Lay was found guilty of securities fraud and related charges. Lay could have faced 20–30 years in prison; however, he died suddenly, just three and a half months before his scheduled sentencing. In reviewing the case history, analysts felt he did a good job building the company, but not in managing the legal and ethical risks, nor in shouldering the firm's downturn in performance. Lay was not active in looking for and finding misconduct within his management team. He continued to claim publicly that all was well with the company, even after he found out that Enron was in trouble. While Ken Lay said he did not know about any misconduct, internal reports told a different story. Although Lay claimed to never recall seeing the reports in question, internal whistle-blowing increased 300 % during the period that Lay was CEO and when Skilling took the helm (Brewer et al. 2006).

Both Lay as CEO and the Board of Directors should have examined this rise in reports to determine the causes. If Lay had investigated the problems and told employees and the public the truth, Enron might have survived. While Lay, Skilling, and Fastow were held accountable, analysts explained in retrospect that Lay's business model had actually never been tested under the existing legal system. He relied on accountants, lawyers, and his board of directors for guidance. While he made mistakes, without the regulatory constraints imposed by the Sarbanes-Oxley Act of 2002 (created in response to the post-Enron crisis) Enron imploded, and Lay, Skilling, and Fastow became the figure-heads (some say scapegoats) for the entire scandal.

Skilling, the former president of Enron, was convicted in 2006 of multiple federal felonies related to the firm's financial collapse, and is currently serving a 24-year prison sentence at the Federal Correctional Institution in Englewood, Colorado (Partington 2011). Under a new plea agreement, Skilling could receive early parole in 2017. Enron collapsed into bankruptcy, under the weight of years of illicit business deals and accounting tricks, putting more than 5,000 people out of work, wiping out more than $2 billion in employee pensions and rendering $60 billion in Enron stocks worthless. Its aftershocks were felt across Texas and the entire energy industry for years. It was a firm built on a foundation of deceit, which eventually self-destructed. I wonder, not if, but how often, Skilling manipulated the truth and used lies to gain strategic advantage (Fig. 6.8).

Former Enron CFO Andy Fastow spent more than five years in federal prison for his role in the Enron fraud. In 2010 he spoke to the Association of Certified Fraud Examiners, explaining how he became a "fraudster" and sounding provocative warnings about today's corporate practices. He said:

> I'm here because I'm guilty ... I caused immeasurable damage...I can never repair that. But I try, by doing these presentations, especially by meeting with students or directors, to help them understand why I did the things I did, how I went down that path, and how they might think about things so they also don't make the mistakes I made...I'm here because, in

Fig. 6.8 Jeff Skilling's mug shot. Image retrieved from the U.S. Marshals Service, in the public domain

my opinion, the problem today is 10 times worse than when Enron had its implosion…The things that Enron did, and that I did, are being done today, and in many cases they're being done in such a manner that makes me blush—and I was the CFO of Enron. (quote from Elkind 2013)

He posed this question to the audience, "How can it be that you get approvals… and it's still fraud?" Answering his own question, he says, "because my actions were misleading, and they knew it. I knew it was wrong…I knew that what I was doing was misleading. But I didn't think it was illegal. I thought, 'That's how the game is played. You have a complex set of rules, and the objective is to use the rules to your advantage. And that was the mistake I made." He insists that he got approval for every single deal he made—from corporate lawyers, accountants, management, and directors. Overreliance on accountants and lawyers, who were so well compensated that they lost professional objectivity, seems to have been part of the problem (Ferrell and Ferrell 2011). Moreover, Fastow 2015 says the accounting rules and regulations, along with the securities laws and regulations, were exceptionally vague and complex. What he and others at Enron did was to take and use this complexity, leveraging it as a business opportunity. He goes on to say, "The way we looked at it was 'do the rules allow it' or 'do the rules allow an interpretation that will allow it?'"

Enron is still considered the largest accounting fraud in history. Fastow and many other people believe that there continues to be widespread use of off-balance-sheet vehicles, as well as inflated financial assumptions that are embedded into corporate pension plans. The continuation of such practices makes it all but certain that more ethical scandals will unfold. He says that many people in business look at the rules and find ways to structure their way around them, noting that, "the more complex the rules, the more opportunity." In reflecting on his path he says, "The question I should have asked is not, 'What is the rule?' but 'What is the principle?'"

Adding another layer to the Enron story is the simultaneous fall of Arthur Anderson. As mentioned, this firm was closely aligned with the energy company, performing both accounting and consulting duties. The blend of accounting and consulting can be a dangerous mix, given they possess cultural norms. The highly respected accounting firm began to change, as the leaders at the time experienced the big dollar signs, and began to shift the focus from accounting to consulting. As they became more of a sales organization, the core of the firm's original mission suffered. The way in which business was conducted changed; cutting corners became the norm and rigor was passé. Similar to Enron, "It came down to doing the job as quickly as possible and making the most money. They pushed the edge of the envelope–pushed it too far," said Dean Christensen, who ran Andersen's Columbus, Ohio, office for more than 15 years. "I just think it got out of control. What it ended up being is greed. Total greed" (as cited in McRoberts 2002).

Breaking rules carries a negative connotation, especially when you are caught and charged. But in all fairness, it is also linked with a talent often sought out in managers: creative strategic thinking. The goal of my own academic institution, along with countless other schools and business organizations, is to "think outside the box." We encourage, motivate, and reward the use of divergent thinking to resolve problems (Torrance 1981; Runco 2010). This capability, by definition, necessitates breaking some of the rules (Bailin 1987). The resulting clever mental associations provide a basis for novel ideas and creativity (Sternberg 1998). So, in truth, managers and leaders can be inadvertently encouraged to break or bend the rules and to take advantage of existing opportunities or to create and find new ones (Brenkert 2009). Organizations that foster and embolden aggressive innovation or creativity may actually be giving people tacit or even explicit permission to break away from accepted practices (Winslow and Solomon 1993), or, for that matter, to actually break the rules (Baucus et al. 2008; Kelley and Littman 2001).

Research by Gino and Wiltermuth (2014) argues that creative and dishonest thinkers may be one and the same people. Highly creative people are more likely than less creative people to bend rules or break laws (Cropley et al. 2003; Sternberg and Lubart 1995; Sulloway 1996). Stories and news articles have used the term "evil genius" to describe everyone from Bernie Madoff (Ponzi artist) to Lex Luther (fictitious schemer in Superman). Researchers suggest a causal relationship between creativity and unethical behavior, which triggers dishonesty (Beaussart et al. 2013; Gino and Ariely 2012). Acting unethically is coupled with creativity, a coveted capability for innovation and establishing new sources for revenue and growth (Gino and Wiltermuth 2014).

Business ethicists largely concur that we will never be able to create enough laws to prevent schemes that are designed to cheat, beat, or usurp the spirit of honest enterprise (Ferrell and Ferrell 2011). The corporate ethical culture, governance, and reward systems have to change, if we expect to see different behavior. Many of the conditions that caused the collapse of Enron still pervade corporate America. The lessons from the tragedy underscore the fact that ethical tone starts at the top. Top management and the board of directors are responsible for risk assessment, ethics audits, and the development of an ethical culture. Ethics is more than the character of a few individuals, combined with an annual training program, code, and an anonymous reporting hotline. Living ethics in operational performance requires resources and proactive management associated with understanding and preventing misconduct, while also promoting right action through sustained development.

Tempering Talent

Building moral strength is a bit like becoming adept at a talent or sport. It calls for a set of skills that must be developed and honed, rather than relying solely on a particular inherent attribute or trait. Adult moral development requires a decision that being ethical is a capability that is important to you. Once identified as an important goal, the ability must be practiced as a skill. Aristotle believed ethics, as a practice, was neither an art nor a technique. He explained that a moral person addresses the situation and then considers what the appropriate response should be, then executes a right action.

Perhaps less often addressed is that we also need to ensure our character strengths are in balance. Even positive actions, like moral courage (where a person endures threat in route to achieving a moral goal), need to be prudently applied, lest they become foolhardy (e.g., taxing one's mental or physical health). Similarly, creativity, enthusiasm, zeal, curiosity, passion, and being competitive can all be tremendous assets in business. However, unbalanced, when moderation and self-regulation are not present, such excesses or extremes can blind us from seeing and/or being aware of ethical issues.

Managing this process can be prompted by looking at how you go about making everyday decisions, being more deliberate about your focus on the ethical elements embedded within your daily actions. Practicing ethical awareness and mindful decision-making can help you identify where you tend to be myopic, distracted, or influenced by external variables. To better understand the process, we now turn to conventional research on ethical decision-making and moral action.

Takeaway Points

1. Everyone has the capacity to be unethical. Similarly, we can choose to be our best, continually striving to be ethical and exercise moral strength.
2. Unethical behavior often starts with white lies, embellishments, and/or seemingly innocuous offenses.

3. There are no secrets. The truth eventually surfaces.
4. Ethical compliance is a moral minimum; it does not confer moral strength.

Reflection Questions

Count the number of lies you tell in one 24 hour period. Include white lies, omissions of truth, exaggerations and/or embellishments. Are you surprised, ashamed, or proud of your findings? Is honesty a part of integrity? Is integrity important in business? Why or why not?

References

Amble, B. (2014). *Corporate integrity undermined by the pursuit of shareholder value*, http://www.management-issues.com/news/6850/corporate-integrity-undermined-by-the-pursuit-of-shareholder-value/. Accessed on March 1, 2014.

Bailin, S. (1987). *Critical and creative thinking. Informal Logic, 9*, 23–30.

Baucus M. S., Norton W. I., Baucus D. A., & Human S. A. (2008). Fostering creativity and innovation without encouraging unethical behavior. *Journal of Business Ethics, 81*, 97–115.

Bazerman, M. H., & Tenbrunsel, A. E. (2011). *Blind spots: Why we fail to do what's right and what to do about it*. Princeton, NJ: Princeton University Press.

Beaussart, M. L., Andrews, C. J., & Kaufman, J. C. (2013). Creative liars: The relationship between creativity and integrity. *Thinking Skills and Creativity, 9*, 129–134.

Bird, F. B., & Waters, J. A. (1989). The moral muteness of managers. *California Management Review, 32*, 73–88.

Brenkert, G. G. (2009). Innovation, rule breaking and the ethics of entrepreneurship. *Journal of Business Venturing, 24*, 448–464.

Brewer, L., Chandler, R., & Ferrell, O. C. (2006). *Managing risks for corporate integrity: How to survive an ethical misconduct disaster*. Mason, OH: Thompson Higher Education.

British Broadcasting Corporation News. (2010, May 18). *Men are bigger liars than women, says poll*, http://news.bbc.co.uk/2/hi/8689010.stm. Accessed on March 22, 2014.

CBS News (2010). Science proves it: Men lie more than women,http://www.cbsnews.com/news/science-proves-it-men-lie-more-than-women/, Accessed on January 7, 2014.

Cameron, K. (2007). Positive organizational scholarship. In S. Clegg & J. Bailey (Eds.) *International Encyclopedia of Organization Studies, 1261*, 1261–67.

Campbell, W. K., Bonacci, A. M., Shelton, J., Exline, J. J., & Bushman, B. J. (2004). Psychological entitlement: Interpersonal consequences and validation of a self-report measure. *Journal of Personality Assessment, 83*, 29–45.

Conger, C. (2011, March 4). *Do people lie more online?*, http://news.discovery.com/tech/do-people-lie-more-online-110304.htm. Accessed on July 1, 2015.

Cropley D. H., Kaufman J. C., & Cropley A. J. (2003). Malevolent creativity: A functional model of creativity in terrorism and crime. *Creativity Research Journal, 20*, 105–115.

Drumwright, M. E., & Murphy, P. E. (2004). How advertising practitioners view ethics: Moral muteness, moral myopia, and moral imagination. *Journal of Advertising, 33*(2), 7–24.

Daily Mail Reporter. (2009, September 14). *Men lie six times a day and twice as often as women*, study finds. Retrieved March 21, 2014, from http://www.dailymail.co.uk/news/article-1213171/Men-lie-times-day-twice-women-study-finds.html#ixzz2we9LsMmH.

Elkind, P. (2013, July 1). The confessions of Andy Fastow. *CNN Money*. Retrieved April 12, 2014 from http://features.blogs.fortune.cnn.com/2013/07/01/the-confessions-of-andy-fastow/.

Fastow, A. (2015). *The Biography.com website*. Retrieved 10:13, January 02, 2015, from http://www.biography.com/people/andrew-fastow-234605.

Feldman, R. S., Forrest, J. A., & Happ, B. R. (2002). Self-presentation and verbal deception: Do self-presenters lie more? *Basic and Applied Social Psychology, 24*, 163–170.

Ferrell, O. C., & Ferrell, L. 2011. The responsibility and accountability of CEOs: The last interview with Ken Lay. *Journal of Business Ethics, 100*, 209–219.

Gino, F., & Ariely, D. (2012). The dark side of creativity: Original thinkers can be more dishonest. *Journal of Personality and Social Psychology, 102*, 445–459.

Gino, F., & Wiltermuth, S. S. (2014). Evil genius? How dishonesty can lead to greater creativity *Psychological Science*, 1–9. Retrieved 11 March, 2014 from http://pss.sagepub.com/content/early//02/18/0956797614520714.full.pdf+html.

Hannah, S. T., & Avolio, B. (2010). Moral potency: Building the capacity for character-based leadership. *Consulting Psychology Journal: Practice and Research, 62*, 291–310.

Hannah, S. T., Avolio, B., & May, D. (2011). Moral maturation and moral conation: A capacity approach to explaining moral thought and action. *Academy of Management Review, 36*, 663–685.

Hannah, S. T., Jennings, P. L., Bluhm, D., Peng, A. C., & Schaubroeck, J. M. (2013). Duty orientation: Theoretical development and preliminary construct testing. *Organizational Behavior and Human Decision Processes, 123*(2), 220–238.

Harris, S. (2013). *Lying*. http://www.elephantsbookshelfpress.com/: Four Elephants Press.

Jackson, L., Zhao, Y., Qiu, W., Kolenic, A., Fitzgerald, H., Harold, R., & Von Eye, A. (2008). Cultural differences in morality in the real and virtual worlds: A comparison of Chinese and U. S. youth. *Cyberpsychology and Behavior, 11*, 279–286.

Jellison, J. M. (1977). *I'm sorry, I didn't mean to, and other lies we love to tell*. Morris Plains, NJ: Chatham Square Press.

Jennings, P. L., Mitchell, M. S., & Hannah, S. T. (2014) The moral self: A review and integration of the literature. *Journal of Organizational Behavior*, DOI: 0.1002/job.1919.

John, L. K., Barasz, K., & Norton, M. I. (2015). What hiding reveals. *Harvard Business School*. Retrieved June 3, 2015 from http://hbswk.hbs.edu/pdf/HidingRevealsWKfinal.pdf.

Kelley, T., & Littman, J. (2001). *The art of innovation: Lessons in creativity from IDEO, America's leading design firm*. New York: Currency.

Kelly, A. E., & Wang, L. (2012, August 4). A life without Lies: How living honestly can affect health. *American Psychological Association Annual Conference*, Orange County Convention Center, Orlando, FL. Retrieved February 2, 2014 from http://www.apa.org/news/press/releases/2012/08/lying-less.aspx.

Kennedy, J., & Kray, L. J. (2013). Who is willing to sacrifice sacred values for money and social status? Gender differences in reactions to ethical compromises. Social *Psychological and Personality Science*.

Kray, L. J., & Haselhuhn, M. P. (2012). Male pragmatism in negotiators' ethical reasoning. *Journal of Experimental Social Psychology, 48*, 1124–1131.

Krettenauer, T., & Eichler, D. (2006). Adolescents' self-attributed moral emotions following a moral transgression: Relations with delinquency, confidence in moral judgment and age. *British Journal of Developmental Psychology, 24*, 489–506.

McRoberts, F. (September 1, 2002). The fall of Anderson. *Chicago Tribune*. Retrieved July 17, 2015 from http://www.chicagotribune.com/news/chi-0209010315sep01-story.html#page=1.

Milgram, S. (1963). Behavioral study of obedience. *Journal of Abnormal and Social Psychology, 67*, 371–378.

Milgram, S. (1974). *Obedience to authority: An experimental view*. New York: HarperCollins.

Moberg, D. J. (2006). Ethics blind spots in organizations: How systematic errors in person perception undermine moral agency, *Organizational Studies, 27*(3),413–428.

Moore, D. A., & Loewenstein, G. (2004). Self-interest, automaticity, and the psychology of conflict of interest. *Social Justice Research, 17*, 189–202.

Narvaez, D., Lapsley, D., Hagele, S., & Lasky, B. (2006). Moral chronicity and social information processing: Tests of a social cognitive approach to the moral personality. *Journal of Research in Personality, 40*, 966–985.

Nissani, M. (1990). A cognitive reinterpretation of Stanley Milgram's observations on obedience to authority. *American Psychologist, 45*, 1384–1385.

Opelka, M. (2014, January 29). See people react to Obama's speech…BEFORE it happened, *The Blaze*. Retrieved April 8, 2014 from http://www.theblaze.com/stories/2014/01/29/people-react-to-obamas-speechbefore-it-happened-jimmy-kimmel-does-it-again/.

Partington, R. (2011). The Enron cast: Where are they now? *Financial News*, December 1. Retrieved January 25, 2014 from http://www.efinancialnews.com/story/2011-12-01/enron-ten-years-on-where-they-are-now.

Runco, M. A. (2010). Creativity has no dark side. In D. H. Cropley, A. J. Cropley, J. C. Kaufman, & M. A. Runco (Eds.), *The dark side of creativity* (pp. 15–32). New York: Cambridge University Press.

Sekerka, L.E. (2012). Compliance as a subtle precursor to ethical corrosion: A strength-based approach as a way forward. *Wyoming Law Review,12*(2), 277–302.

Sekerka, L. E., & Godwin, L. (2010). Strengthening professional moral courage: A balanced approach to ethics training. *Training & Management Development Methods, 24*(5), 63–74.

Sekerka, L. E., & Zolin, R. (2007). Rule bending: Can prudential judgment affect rule compliance and values in the workplace? *Public Integrity, 9*(3), 225–244.

Sporer, S. L., & Schwandt, B. (2007). Moderators of nonverbal indicators of deception: A meta-analytic synthesis. *Psychology, Public Policy, and Law, 13*(1), 1–34.

Sternberg, R. J. (1998). Cognitive mechanisms in human creativity: Is variation blind or sighted? *The Journal of Creative Behavior, 32*(3), 159–176.

Sternberg, R. J., & Lubart, T. I. (1995). *Defying the crowd: Cultivating creativity in a culture of conformity*. New York: Free Press.

Sulloway, F. (1996). *Born to rebel*. New York: Pantheon.

Shadnam, M., & Lawrence, T. B. (2011). Understanding widespread misconduct in organizations. An institutional theory of moral collapse. *Business Ethics Quarterly, 21*(3), 379.

Skitka, L. J., Bauman, C., & Sargis, E. (2005). Moral conviction: Another contributor to attitude strength or something more? *Journal of Personality and Social Psychology, 88*, 895–917.

ten Brinke, L., Stimson, D., & Carney, D. R. (2014, March 21). Some evidence for unconscious lie detection. *Psychological Science*, 1–8. Retrieved April 6, 2014 from http://pss.sagepub.com/content/early/2014/03/19/0956797614524421.full.pdf+html.

Torrance, E. P. (1981). Empirical validation of criterion-referenced indicators of creative ability through a longitudinal study. *Creative Child and Adult Quarterly, 6*, 134–140.

Tyler, J. M, & Feldman, R. S. (2004). Truth, lies, and self-presentation: How gender and anticipated future interaction relate to deceptive behavior. *Journal of Applied Social Psychology, 34*(12), 2602–2615.

Underwood, J. D., Kerlin, M., & Farrington-Flint, L. (2011). The lies we tell and what they say about us: Using behavioural characteristics to explain Facebook activity. *Computers in Human Behavior, 27*(5), 1621–1626.

Vedantam, S. (2014, April 9). Why men outnumber women attending business schools, *NPR, Morning Edition*. Retrieved April 10, 2014 http://www.npr.org/2014/04/09/300836825/why-men-outnumber-women-attending-business-schools?utm_medium=Email&utm_source=npr_email_a_friend&utm_campaign=storyshare.

Warkentin, M., Sayeed, L., & Hightower, R. (1999). Virtual teams versus face to face teams: An exploratory study of a web-based conference system. In Kenneth E. Kendall (Ed.), *Emerging information technologies: Improving decisions, cooperation, and infrastructure* (pp. 241–262). New York: Sage Publications.

Warren, E. A. (2008). Modeling moral personality: Moral chronicity, moral identity, and moral cognition, *Dissertation: Columbia University*, 120 pp. DAI/A, 69–01, 3299303.

Winslow E. K., & Solomon G. T. (1993). Entrepreneurs: Architects of innovation, paradigm pioneers and change. *Journal of Creative Behavior, 27*, 75–88.

Zimbardo, P. G. (2007). *The Lucifer effect: Understanding how good people turn evil*. New York: Random House.

Zimbardo, P. G. (2004). A situationist perspective on the psychology of evil: Understanding how good people are transformed into perpetrators. In A. Miller (Ed.), *The social psychology of good and evil* (pp. 21–25). New York: Guilford Press.

Chapter 7
Choosing to Be Ethical

People often "go with the flow," emulating other people's behaviors in how they go about completing their work or assigned tasks. In many instances, we put very little thought or conscious effort into determining how we respond to our daily decisions. It's like when you see someone jaywalk—you are easily tempted to do the same thing. Being ethical at work requires an overarching personal decision to be mindful of the ethical elements embedded within your everyday activities. This requires self-awareness, and being honest with yourself about identifying your moral strengths and weaknesses. Underutilizing the capacity for moral mindfulness, you are, in some ways, denying or even shirking a civic responsibility. In choosing to walk across the street against the light, aware or unaware of this decision, you are still accountable for your actions and must accept the punitive response if rendered.

Offering excuses when caught breaking the rules may get you out of an ethical jam. But when swift action and corrective punishment are not rendered, unethical behavior is subtly reinforced. As considered previously, getting away with an unethical action increases the likelihood of the person, and others, doing it again. Owning your ethical missteps and accepting the consequences that accompany your choices is a part of being ethically responsible. Occasionally, people "get away" with their unethical actions—they may have chosen to avoid, blot out, or curtail a rule to achieve other gains. Inadvertently or intentionally, this deflection of responsibility may even be rewarded with compensation, prestige, or additional power. Such affirmations, of course, all but ensure the continuation of similar actions.

Ethics is about choosing to be morally aware and applying this moral awareness to your daily life. In ascertaining the ethical elements within a situation, both challenges and opportunities, a person has committed to being a moral agent, looking for the ethical features of decisions and choosing to address them with prudential judgment. The reality, however, is that many of us go through our day without a careful consideration of the ethical elements embedded in many of our choices. If you have a desire to be ethical, it is essential that you are rigorously honest with yourself about your motives and intentions as you make decisions.

Elements of this research original appeared in (Sekerka and Bagozzi 2007).

© Springer International Publishing Switzerland 2016
L. E. Sekerka, *Ethics is a Daily Deal*, DOI 10.1007/978-3-319-18090-8_7

Being Aware of Mindfulness

Humans have an innate ability to be reflective. We have an amazing capacity to consider our options and to form and revise our perceptions. Being aware of this ability, it is therefore a choice to react without thought or to choose to be mindful (Fig. 7.1). An overarching aspect for every decision you make is, "How aware do I want to be of the ethical elements of this circumstance?" How considerate do you want to be in terms of the ethical aspects of your thoughts and actions? It takes effort to reflect on the ethics of any situation. Do you take the time to look for where and how you can exercise your character? Do you look for the moral concerns or ethical risks within an activity before you act? Do you look for how to broach a situation with character strength? Many people toss their power of ethicality away, allowing decisions to be made without reflective consideration. Relying upon assumptions about the self, other people, and the business context, we often proceed without ethical forethought. People frequently respond to a situation, then justify what they have done after they have already acted! Backdating explanations for behavior can potentially shroud a person from seeing their real (versus perceived) ethical identity. Sustained justification of your actions, rather than mindful reflective consideration, may block you from seeing how your behavior is incongruent with your personal values.

Have you ever done something without thinking it through? When you arrive at an outcome, you explain your thinking in retrospect. Post hoc explication can become a habit, one that can inadvertently inhibit an ability to see who we are, or who we are becoming. After engaging in an unethical practice you might rationalize your decision, explaining that, "Everyone was doing it that way." The problem here is that your reasoning is crafted after the fact. A simple example where you might see this happen is when you go to the grocery store. You might walk by the bakery section, placing something into your cart that's not on your list. At the checkout,

Fig. 7.1 Millenials pause to consider the value of ethical awareness

when your grocery bill is \$20 higher than you expected, you then justify the purchase decision. You might tell yourself you rarely buy this sort of thing, you deserve a treat or, that on this occasion it looked particularly fresh.

If it's only a few dollars and you are not on a tight budget, you may not even notice you made the decision without deliberate thought. Or, you may have continued to justify your decision as you continued to shop. Perhaps you returned the item to the shelf after you neared the end of your visit, realizing the money would be more wisely spent elsewhere. While this may not seem like a question of ethics, when people make a habit of buying things they do not need and cannot afford, debt can build up over time. The assumption of financial obligations beyond one's means can become an ethical issue, when people are unable to pay. Of course, small items at the grocery store are not homes, cars, or large ticket luxury items. However, a mindset of frugal use of purchasing power is a discipline that requires mindfulness —especially in a culture that overwhelmingly encourages a lack of prudential judgment in ethical consumption.

Another kind of automatic decision-making happens when we go about our daily tasks. When we drive, we all know to put on a seatbelt, attend to the speed limit, and slow down in the rain or on ice. Embedded tacit knowledge helps us to navigate automatically and to do things simultaneously. We don't think about how to ride a bike once we know how to do it. We just hop on and go! Such tacit or implicit knowledge provides unconscious processing capabilities for many of our everyday decisions. But such cognitive ease may contribute to a potential habit of being less attentive to the ethical elements within our everyday work lives. This may be especially so when ethics are framed as compliance-driven rules, as opposed to a broader duty to moral responsible performance.

The myth of effective multitasking is another area of concern, especially in today's technologically saturated lifestyle. Many of us seem to think we are great at doing multiple things simultaneously (e.g., talking on the phone, sending emails, looking up something online, and perhaps even reading a document—at the same time). Some even take pride in this so-called capacity for productivity and efficiency, being able to accomplish many things all at once. But simultaneous task accomplishment is actually only possible if two conditions are met: (1) at least one of the tasks is so well learned that it is automatic (no focus or thought is necessary to engage in the task) and (2) the tasks involve different types of brain processing (Taylor 2011). For example, you can read while listening to a symphony because reading comprehension and processing instrumental music engage different parts of the brain.

However, your ability to retain information while reading as you listen to music with lyrics declines significantly (as compared to music without lyrics), because both tasks activate the language center of the brain. Despite expectations and appearances, a person cannot effectively talk on the phone, read email, send an instant message, and watch YouTube videos all at once. The modern myth of multitasking may inadvertently underwrite a belief that as we accomplish our work we are also considering the ethical elements. Ironically, those who consider themselves to be great multitaskers have been found to be the least effective at doing it (Ophir et al. 2009).

The Decision-Making Path

Theories of planned behavior, reasoned action, and ethical decision-making are used to help us understand the processes involved in ethical behavior. The idea has always been to look at what stages or steps contribute to a decision-making effort that lead to a moral action (Ferrell and Gresham 1985). Rest's (1986) traditional cognitive theory outlines a sequential process, leading off with moral awareness, followed by the development of moral intention, forming a moral judgment, and then engaging in the appropriate moral action. The complexity of a decision-making effort increases tremendously when it takes place in a social context—that is, when other people are involved. In such conditions, as in organizational settings, decision-makers not only try to maximize their own utility, but also need to take into account the interdependent nature of the situation. Information about others' preferences, characteristics, and actions plays an important role in decision-making and impacts evaluative efforts before a decision is made and enacted. Anen's (2013) research on neural functioning in moral decisions helps us understand how the brain evaluates social situations and how we use social measures like trust, agency, strategic interaction, and fairness to make decisions in the context of working with others.

Prior research shows how movement toward moral action can be influenced by factors such as attitude, perceived importance, subjective norms, and the nuances of a particular situation (Hegarty and Sims 1979; Treviño and Youngblood 1990; Mayo et al. 1991; Dubinsky and Loken 1989). Progress along the ethical decision-making path can be influenced by moral approbation (i.e., approval from self and others) (Jones and Ryan 1997, 1998) and moral intensity (i.e., issue-related moral imperatives in a situation) (Jones 1991). Research over the last two decades has shown how affect and cognitions work together with individual and social forces to influence the path to ethical action (Sekerka and Bagozzi 2007). Rather than discrete steps, an overarching decision to be ethically mindful (looking for the ethical challenges and opportunities) and then staying committed to proceeding with moral action, are critical factors in being able to endure the rigors of moral decision-making. These elementary choices can then be further supported by moral competency, abilities that help support movement from ethical awareness into action.

Sonenshein (2007) takes the classic cognitive ethical decision-making theory to task, refuting the notion that individuals use deliberate and extensive moral reasoning. He raises an important concern that ethical issues frequently involve equivocality and uncertainty. In addressing the limitations of purely rationalist approaches, he presents an alternative explanation drawing upon social psychological and sense-making perspectives. His theoretical model frames the process as issue construction, intuitive judgment, and post hoc explanation and justification. While his model explains how many decision-makers make sense of their ethical issues at work, most ethics education and training still tends to focus on reactions to issues that are clearly presented. Sonenshein's work has brought attention to the value and potential influence of intuitive judgment, as it pertains to ethical issue framing, decision-making, and action.

Being ethical means actually having a desire to seek out the ethical features of a situation, before you find yourself in a "must-act" moment. If you have a desire to live congruently with your values, this choice requires a deliberate and ongoing effort. Being ethical means you learn to look for the ethical elements within each situation and then consider where your character strengths and personal and organizational values can be applied. In some regards, this is similar to the idea of ethical issue identification (construction), but on a much broader scale.

A responsible person in the workplace strives to identify ethical issues before they become full-blown problems. Maintaining a desire to seek out where ethical risks might raise issues, where opportunities for moral strength lie dormant, and maintaining the willingness to address the ethical challenges with moral courage, calls for a durable commitment to being responsible (see Chap. 9). This foundational decision, to look for the ethical potentials and be prepared to take action, is not something that gets "turned on and off." Because ethical issues, once spotted, are often difficult to address, endurance is needed as you look for and move to determine what the best response may be, given the current circumstances.

A related example is the ethical controversy that Reddit now finds itself embroiled in, over material shared on its Internet website. The popular social news portal's troubles escalated because of a lack of swift action to prohibit "subreddits" that shared inappropriate information online (e.g., homophobic or racist views). It could be argued that the recently removed CEO Ellen Pao demonstrated moral strength, standing firmly behind the rights of Reddit's users, protecting free speech. In this light, a decision was apparently made to not ban distasteful subreddits, even when they were deemed odious or the organization personally condemned the material (Issac 2015). The concern about the ethics of maintaining anonymity with these shares, added another layer of complexity to the issue. To date (July 2015), Steve Huffman, the co-founded Reddit (in 2005), has returned to lead the organization and address these ethical challenges. After being away for 6 years, Huffman is now charged with turning around the company and winning back the confidence of its users (Fig. 7.2).

Under Huffman's leadership, Reddit immediately *proposed a new content policy* for the site that would effectively ban spam, illegal activity and harassment, as well as the posting of "private or confidential information" and sexual content involving minors. As the site grew, Huffman explained, the company's views on what sort of content should/should not be allowed needed to evolve, and they did not. As cited in *The New York Times*, referring to the type of shares posted, Huffman added, "We cannot turn a blind eye to it like we have in the past" (Issac 2015, np.).

It would be presumptuous to argue what the proper course of action should have been by the former leader, or, if what she did was right or wrong. Given I don't have all the facts, there are multiple vantage points, and it's easy to criticize in retrospect. That was not the objective of sharing this story. Rather, it is interesting to consider that Reddit's prior policy was unsustainable in today's world. I wonder if the management team thought about this, and consciously decided to stay true to

Fig. 7.2 Pao steps down after an ethics controversy at Reddit. Image courtesy of Christopher Michel, Flickr https://www.flickr.com/photos/cmichel67/18330347136. Creative Commons Attribution 2.0 Generic

the original mission? Perhaps Pao "fell on her sword" so to speak, to protect the right to share anything, even it is deemed immoral.

When we look at ethic issues in our own lives, it is helpful to visualize the path of the decision. Conventional ethical decision-making models show the process as steps. This sort of simplicity does not reflect real-time sense-making and the sort of back-dating processes that often occur in real time i.e., explaining decisions after one has already engaged in an action. That said, they do offer educational insight. Models can illustrate what might fuel or weaken a person's desire or resolve to act, helping a person learn what they might do and why, and what influences a path to moral action. In examining your own ethical decision-making efforts, there are a number of affective and cognitive elements that can mitigate or bolster your resolve and efforts to "do the right thing" (Sekerka and Bagozzi 2007).

Starting with a general moral awareness, which is referred to more discretely as the identification of an ethical challenge or opportunity, we then consider our willingness to proceed. A host of personal and group influences impact the extent of a person's desire to act ethically, which can then thwart or fuel the motivation to proceed with a decision to act. Bear in mind that "a desire to act", at this point in the model, refers to thoughts and actions congruent with that desire (as opposed to a general wanting to act, per se). Having the "will to proceed" must be established, maintained, and reinforced throughout the entire ethical decision-making process. Indeed, the "will" to be ethical is at the center of moral agency itself.

Willingness to Be Willing

William James wrote extensively about the importance of human will in our lives (James 1890a, b) (Fig. 7.3). He argued that moral opinions are based on personal proof of what a person wants (wills) to believe. In describing our psychological propensity to have different personas with varying desires, James called the self a "fluctuating material" (p. 291, 1890b). While one aspect of the self may have a desire to "do the right thing" another aspect may be compelled to move to achieve other goals, fulfilling other wants and desires. Scholars have sustained their interest in constructs related to self-will. Research has been conducted to better understand the influence of desire on the *will* to do right, to choose to behave ethically or to do otherwise (Bagozzi et al. 2009, 2013). But this remains a particularly challenging area of inquiry because willingness is an effort made up of a combination of unconscious (automatic) and conscious (deliberate) choices (Fig. 7.4), (see also Fig. 8.4).

Ethics is not a matter of convenience. We should not cherry-pick when we want to be ethical, applying ethical considerations to some areas of our life and not in others. However, within your varying self-schemas there are likely to be varying levels of the willingness to pursue the ethicality of your actions. The desire to be ethical must therefore be integrated among our various personas, selves, identities, roles, etc. This is a particular element of concern, as it is noteworthy that many leaders who have been caught up in ethical scandals seem to have forgotten this crucial fact. By definition, your character implies some element of consistency, congruency, and integration across your identity. A willingness to be willing (to be ethical) must be nurtured in every element, feature, and facet of your selfhood.

Fig. 7.3 Philosopher William James. Image credited to the Houghton Library, Harvard University (1902)

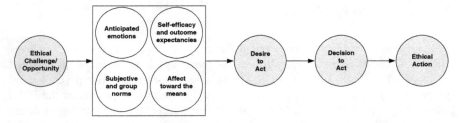

Fig. 7.4 Ethical decision-making process. Figure adapted from Sekerka and Bagozzi (2007)

This suggests that being ethical is a never-ending process and one that can never be perfected. But, by the same token, it also means that you only need a modicum of desire to move forward, improve, and or to become more ethical.

Being ethical consistently means learning how to become more aware of your decision-making efforts, ensuring that what you choose to do is in alignment with the overall character you believe you possess. People who choose to be ethical recognize that this often requires a concentrated deliberate act of attention. Past experiences build up a repertoire of how you think and feel about a given circumstance. Thus, our past actions may unconsciously direct our will in the current moment. Similarly, how you think about or perceive the future can also influence how you experience the present. Taken together, we see how perceptions compete for attention and commitment, both real and perceived, putting pressure on us to formulate a reason to act (or not to act) ethically in any given circumstance.

Your ethicality manifests as a felt desire to respond in a particular way. But because we have multiple self-schemas (identities), our scripts for these various roles (manager, son/daughter, or father/mother) may conflict as our desires within these identities compete for supremacy. The development of a desire to proceed with an ethical action is influenced by many personal factors. These factors are, in turn, dependent upon social forces around you, such as your culture, the company you work for, your profession, and the surrounding community. Additionally, directives, social norms, perceived rewards or punishments, social pressures, and other situational variables that shape your willingness to be ethical can also impact your resolve. Distractions often deter our focus; hence a desire to move ahead with an ethical act can be thrown off course. Rorty (1986, 1988) describes how a person must garner a willingness to act as they move toward potential engagement and then work to sustain this willingness throughout their ethical decision-making effort. In other words, you have to continue to muster your desire to do the right thing, up to the point of when the action is taken, and then even after the action is deployed.

In the workplace, getting people to behave in responsible ways can be encouraged via positive reinforcement. This can be done by establishing an organizational climate and culture that encourages ethical action and discourages unethical behavior. There is a saying in business that "what you measure is what gets done." If organizations track and reward *how* performance objectives are achieved, making the process of ethical goal achievement valued, goals are more likely to be accomplished ethically. Organizational members need tracking mechanisms and support activities to ensure they understand that ongoing moral development is essential, embedding ethics within the organization's goal-setting and -striving processes. If someone does not want to be ethical, you cannot make them want it for themselves. But you can create an environment that supports ethicality, a system where performance goals are designed to be achieved ethically and are rewarded.

Once a desire to act ethically is established (referred to as first- or lower-order decision-making), a person fuels their motivation to achieve ethical action by framing it as an achievable goal. This latter process involves second- or higher-order decision-making efforts, as the person determines whether or not to bolster their desire and then to act on it. This self-regulatory process is governed by appraisal, determining if acting is consistent with the type of person the individual is, wants to be, or hopes to become. Similar to features set forth by Jones and Ryan (1997) in their theory of moral approbation, first-order desires to behave ethically precede a commitment to act (Rest 1986). This commitment to sustain the willingness and movement to engage in moral action is governed by second-order desires, fueled by personal moral standards.

If you are the kind of person who demonstrates moral strength at work, you have likely developed a habit of considering whether or not your actions contribute to your personal and the organization's standards of excellence. In recognizing the ethical concerns within a situation or surfacing an ethical issue, both a desire and decision to act need your endorsement. This process (as seen in Fig. 7.3) is influenced by a myriad of variables, including different forms of anticipated and felt emotions. For example, affect toward the means, is what you think you might feel if you proceed with a particular course of action. So too can what you actually feel in that moment influence your willingness to move from issue identification to having a desire to act (in the particular situation). In this stage, personal values, traits, and virtues often come into play, along with social identity processes. These variables can influence a person's ability to perceive the ethical elements of the situation and help them form an appraisal.

Theoretical research and its empirical substantiation outline how these higher-order decision-making processes are choices that we can control (Bagozzi et al. 2009, 2013). But a person's efforts are also shaped by other social factors from their past and present encounters, which they may not even be aware of, factors that can influence motivation toward or away from pursuit of ethical action. For example, let's say your company is about to launch a very exciting new product line. Sharing information about the line is forbidden until the campaign is launched in the coming weeks. You are well versed in the corporate rules about secrecy and recognize that protecting information is essential for the good of the firm. You are excited about the product and your role in its forthcoming success. Over the weekend, you unexpectedly run into an old college friend at a social gathering. Back in the day, this guy (Alex) always seemed to trump your best efforts. Regardless of whether it was on exams or the playing field, he was always upstaging you. You exchange pleasantries and he asks, "So what's new at that company of yours anyway? Things have been quiet there for a bit too long, don't you think?" At first you appease him with a generalized response. But he keeps egging you on. It feels like he's daring you to prove you have "made it." You really want to share the news about the new product launch.

At this point, some might fail to pause and recognize they might be feeling angry, irritated, or maybe even a bit insecure (Fig. 7.5). Being aware of your feelings in the moment is important. But so too is playing out how you might feel, given how you might respond to the situation (thinking ahead before reacting). In this case, you might consider how you would likely feel a momentary sense of pride in sharing the product information with Alex. You might rationalize this action, because he's not in the industry and you're only sharing a modest overview of the new product line. But how would you feel if something happened as a result of your revealing the information? Say word gets back to the firm that you were a leak or somehow instrumental in thwarting the success of the product launch. You really have no idea what sort of person Alex is today, who he is connected with, or for that matter, why you even care about what he thinks.

In considering how you feel as well as how you might feel if you were to engage in a particular action, your emotions provide useful information. Awareness of your affective cues provides you with insights that can help keep you in check as you work to maintain an ethical path. In this case, choosing not to share information about the product and ending the tête-à-tête may be the cleanest response. By exposing the new product information you may experience a short-term spark in pride, but at what potential cost? The possible expense of a short-term gain to your ego may be associated with long-term guilt, shame, and embarrassment. Worth noting as it relates to this kind of scenario, executive coaches also warn leaders, managers, and employees about sharing information at parties, in online forums, while traveling, etc. Recall the old saying, "loose lips sink ships." It is also important to be aware that alcohol consumption often sets the stage for ethical risk, especially when it comes to information sharing. Maintaining privacy, keeping trade secrets, and protecting yourself from vulnerable set-ups, known to leverage corporate espionage, requires all of your keen sensibilities (Bencie 2013).

Fig. 7.5 Pausing and recognizing how you feel is essential. Image courtesy of Sebastian Gauert/ Shutterstock.com

Emotions at Work

Aristotle left us with some uncertainty about the function of emotion in exercising ethical action. His clues suggest that virtuousness occurs because the "spirit operates" within us (1999, NE 7.8.1116). He considers moral strength (moral courage) as perfect harmony between body and soul (Ward 2001). This adds depth to the emotional side of ethical decision-making, how affect is experienced (consciously or unconsciously) and if emotions experienced in similar encounters in the past serve as influences in the present. The somatic marker hypothesis (SMH, Damasio 1994) describes how affective somatic states associated with prior decisions unconsciously guide future decisions by serving as valuations of the personal significance of criteria entering into the decision process (see also Hinson et al. 2002).

The SMH suggests that learned affective reactions help shape choices and simplify decision-making. Damasio and his colleagues demonstrated how making choices (decisions) is influenced by signals that arise in bio-regulatory processes, including emotional expressions. These signals (somatic markers) occur at multiple levels of cognitive and emotional operations, helping to establish motivation to act. Related to the SMH is the work by Carver and Scheier (1990, 1998) and Johnson-Laird and Oately (1989), reflecting how emotion is linked with a sense of progress in pursuing desired goals in a cybernetic system of control. As one makes progress in goal pursuit or fails to do so, emotional reactions to these outcomes emerge in the form of (a) positive affect to sustain goal thriving and (b) negative affect to spur one on or discourage one, depending on specific negative emotional reactions and their intensity and how one copes.

How people convey their affective states outwardly varies. How you express your emotions in public depends on social norms of display, along with other variables like gender and cultural influences, as well as conscious emotional self-management. Emotional display is also influenced by situational circumstances and individual traits and attributes. But recognizing emotions in others is not simple. Examining the four photographs in Fig. 7.6, it is hard to tell what emotions are being conveyed. Starting with the upper left image, is the man expressing determination? Or, perhaps it is anger. Looking at the upper right image, do you see cheerfulness? Maybe the man is simply being attentive. The image in the lower left might convey shame, but it could also be guilt. Finally, in the last image (lower right), would you say his expression is one of daringness or irritability? Taking another look, maybe he's just concentrating. Perhaps you see something altogether different than any of the observations mentioned thus far.

While social and emotional intelligence (Salovey & Mayer 1990; Schachter & Singer 1962) is a central competency in leadership (Goleman 2004), accurately reading the affective states of others may be difficult if not altogether impossible. This makes understanding your own emotions all the more important. A cornerstone of ethical action is learning to recognize your own feelings and emotions, and then dealing with them appropriately in social settings. If you do not learn how to do this, the values you say you hold, being ethical in route to achieving

Fig. 7.6 Emotions influence ethical behavior, but display does not always send a clear message. Images courtesy of freeimages.com

a goal, can be easily thwarted. Emotions serve as useful guideposts, directive clues that can encourage us to move forward or discontinue pursuit of an ethical goal.

Carver and Scheier (1998) describe how when negative emotions are aroused, based on an unfavorable outcome being compared to a reference value, it signals that continued engagement is not expected to turn out well. For example, if you were caught cheating and got into trouble, you may recall feelings of embarrassment, shame, guilt, fear, or anger. Thus, when you have a thought to cheat, skim, pad, or lie (or to engage in some similar activity) in the present, those negative emotions are recalled and linked to a reference value. Similarly, the arousal of positive emotions, when a favorable outcome is compared to a reference value, signals that further activity will likely lead to successful outcomes.

If you were tempted but decide not to cheat, you might be signaled by a sense of pride for doing the right thing. In choosing not to cheat, you are cued to recall that things will probably turn out better if you select the 'right' path. You are likely to act in accordance with your reference value of honesty. However, a person's decision-making typically reflects their motivational power, which is often endorsed by avoiding negative outcomes (rather than prompting positive outcomes). This is likely related to the human negativity bias previously described (bad is stronger than good), but may also occur because ethical issues are rarely framed as opportunities for virtuousness. Instead, ethical issues are seen as problems that require a solution and/or are regarded as issues that present some level of threat.

In the work by Carver and his colleagues, depicting the influence of emotions on performance, positive feelings tend to relate to high performance (e.g., doing better than expected) and negative feelings tend to relate to low performance (e.g., doing worse than expected) (Carver et al. 2000). A person's positive and negative emotional reactions to prior outcomes from past choices often guide their current responses. To some extent, then, how we construe the present depends upon emotions previously experienced and currently interpreted. Past outcomes and their association with our emotions and affective processes often color and shape our feelings and the subjective experience we presently encounter. In the context of facing an ethical challenge, such reactions will influence cognitive associations to past events where similar choices have been made, as well as to the current situation. Associations, cues, and subsequent affective arousals will impact a decision to act, and sustain our willingness to engage.

Referring back to the scenario with "Alex" at the party, being mindful of your emotions is central to sustaining your ethicality. Being more aware of your anticipated emotions, what you expect to feel as you render a forecast of the situation, and then considering what potential actions might be employed, can provide useful information in ethical decision-making (Bagozzi et al. 1998; Perugini and Bagozzi 2001). Analogous to counterfactual thinking processes, people have the ability to imagine and reflect upon future goal achievement and goal failure. Gleicher et al. (1995) refer to such processes as prefactual elements in decision-making. Imagined goal success leads to positive anticipated emotions (e.g., pride, hope, joy); imagined goal failure leads to negative anticipated emotions (e.g., frustration, disappointment, worry). People are motivated to approach pleasant outcomes and avoid negative ones. Hence, anticipatory emotions serve to prompt desires to act that are functional for emotional well-being. Scholars believe there is a relationship between recognition of an ethical issue and the desire to act with moral strength, influenced by anticipated emotions (Sekerka and Bagozzi 2007).

Belief in Your Ability

Along with emotions, self-efficacy and outcome expectancies are important mental processes in forming a decision to respond ethically. In the workplace, what sense do you have about your ability to control or influence the situation you are in? Your perceptions of confidence and empowerment rely upon your belief that you have some level of control over the circumstances (Christensen and Kohl 2003). Picture being faced with an ethical challenge at work, then ask yourself, "Do I think I can influence the situation and make a difference?" Self-efficacy is a psychological state and refers to the confidence one has; a belief one can effectively perform a specific behavior in a particular situation. It differs from the concept of locus of control (e.g., Lefcourt 1992), which is a psychological trait referring to a general disposition to act consistently across multiple situations or domains.

Bandura's work reveals that perceptions of self-efficacy can enhance or impair one's motivation and performance in a variety of ways. This includes the kinds of activities people will ultimately choose to engage in (1982) and the effort and persistence exerted to achieve one's goals (Bandura and Cervone 1986). Self-efficacy, having a belief that you can accomplish what you set out to do (Bandura 1982), is linked with outstanding leadership (Bennis and Nanus 1985) and effective management performance under stress (Murphy 1992). Additionally, possessing self-efficacy is related to work motivation in general (Gist and Mitchell 1992). It is an important contributor to cultivating and sustaining a desire to act when facing an ethical challenge (Sekerka and Bagozzi 2007). Self-efficacy is relevant to acting ethically because it can influence not only what skills you think you have, but also what you think you can do with the skills you believe to possess (Chemers et al. 2000). A personal belief in the efficacy of self can affect cognitive processes, eliciting confidence or self-doubt (Bandura and Wood 1989).

If you set your alarm and get up, drive to work, and begin to tackle the tasks at hand, you have already demonstrated some degree of self-efficacy. You obviously have some level of confidence that you will effectively pursue your goals for the day and be able to accomplish something. Chemers and his colleagues (2000) examined dispositional affect and leadership effectiveness and found that self-efficacy is associated with both leadership potential and performance. Self-efficacy can impact levels of perseverance in the face of difficulty, which can be beneficial toward stimulating and maintaining a desire to engage in ethical action. Taking these elements together, scholars have outlined a relationship between recognition of an ethical challenge and the desire to act as being influenced by self-efficacy (Sekerka and Bagozzi 2007). In terms of the ethical decision-maker's experience, self-efficacy refers to a sense of personal control or causation.

In addition to self-efficacy, forces beyond one's control can also be influential in the path to moral action. Outcome expectancies are judgments that an action will lead to a desired goal, taking into account that there are external variables you do not have control over. As Carver and Scheier (1998) describe, outcome expectancies can be more determinative of action than self-efficacy. People often make judgments to act on the basis of the likelihood of a desired outcome happening. As a result, expectations of success and/or failure are important determinants of an urge to achieve a sought after goal. Locke and Latham (1990) recognized the roles of self-efficacy and outcome expectancies in their high performance cycle model of goal-directed behavior. It makes sense that as you recognize an ethical challenge, and begin to formulate a potential desire to act, you would consider your ability to be effective. Moreover, you are likely to think about your likelihood of being successful in achieving a particular desired outcome.

An important point to remember is that if a person never tries to exercise their competence, they may never know the moral strength they possess i.e., what they are capable of achieving. Take this scenario as an example: you learn information

Fig. 7.7 A leader expresses his views on ethical culture and self-efficacy. Image courtesy of the Naval Postgraduate School

that strongly suggests your boss is engaged in an unethical activity. The tip relates to her potentially falsifying some details on a company report. You mention this concern to a friend within your workgroup, someone you have known for years. He asks you not to say anything because he believes this will lead to an investigation into everyone's practices, adding, "An investigation would bring down morale, threaten long-overdue bonuses, and create conflict in our workgroup." "Besides," he adds, "it won't do any good." The report is going out at the end of the week. If you come forward, your friend, your boss, and possibly other people in your group, including you, may be questioned and possibly implicated.

As you envision this situation, you are prompted to think about what you might potentially do and the potential impact your actions could impose on you, others, and the organization itself (Fig. 7.7). You will likely consider the security of your job. You might think about whether or not saying something, which may put you at risk, will actually make a difference. You will probably consider what losses might be incurred if you take action. Influencing this path of decision-making (to act, not to act, or wait), Is raising a red flag worth losing a friend, maybe even losing your job? Is acting ethically worthwhile in this case? If you see merit in taking action, do you have confidence that your actions will be effective, that the outcomes will be favorable?

If you believe your actions will be ineffective and that nothing will change as a result of your efforts, it is unlikely you will have the necessary motivation and resolve to proceed. On the other hand, if you believe in your abilities, self-affirm your capability to be effective, and maintain that ethical congruence is important to you, it's likely you can muster the willingness to step up to the plate. In so doing, your actions may include information gathering, talking with trusted mentors, meeting with management, and/or reporting the problem to someone else within the organization or a whistle-blowing entity, like an anonymous hotline (a requirement of the Sarbanes-Oxley [SOX] legislation). Such actions are supported by self-awareness, preparation, and being able to relate and work with others.

Being a moral agent often requires moral courage, the ability to do the right thing, even when it is not valued by others. Unfortunately, many organizations profess to be ethical, and then thwart the efforts of those trying to proceed with right action. Therefore, it is also important to regulate one's self-efficacy and outcome expectations and to recognize the potential for such acts to be rejected. Seeking help and support before taking action and building a coalition versus going it alone, may be a prudent path for endurance and ultimate success, toward evoking change. Like people, organizations may not be as ethical as they purport to be; thus, acts of moral courage may be unrequited, leaving an employee discouraged or even harmed (financially, emotionally, and even physically) (Sekerka and Comer 2015). Preparation for ethical action is key to maintaining health and well being.

Self-efficacy, a kind of sister to self-confidence, certainly supports moral strength and endurance in achieving a moral goal. This skill enables you to take on a major challenge and to see it through to completion (Bandura and Wood 1989). So important is self-efficacy in moral action, that Hannah and Avolio (2010) identify this ability as a core element of what they call *moral potency*. They further distinguish self-efficacy in moral behavior as *moral efficacy*, depicting this as having self-confidence toward organizing and mobilizing motivation, having the cognitive resources, means, and course(s) of action needed to attain moral performance, and persisting in the face of adversity. When a person senses they can achieve their moral goals and persevere in the face of difficulty, moral efficacy supports a durable protracted effort, rather than succumbing to prevailing challenges.

A regulated form of moral efficacy takes into consideration a conscious or deliberate awareness of its balanced application. In short, too much self-efficacy and confidence prior to action, coupled with an effort that has not been fully vetted, planned, or thoughtfully prepared, may actually be foolhardiness; i.e., in an Aristotelian sense, character strengths must be balanced. Similarly, if the outcomes you expect (results) do not take into consideration aspects that are beyond your control, you may be setting yourself up for disappointment (failed efforts in your attempts to engage in an ethical act). Sekerka and Bagozzi (2007) underscore how both self-efficacy and outcome expectancies can help fuel the desire to proceed toward a morally courageous act. It's essential that these assets are "right sized", meaning in balance (not grandiose), to be fully effective and healthy (Sekerka and Comer 2015).

If you have decided to be an ethical person, it means you have agreed to be ethically vigilant, with a commitment to be ready to respond ethically at all times. Being primed for ethicality is like keeping a device, tool, or mechanism readied for peak performance. It also means not being overly grandiose with the perceptions of your capability. Take, for example, your car. Aside from the legal and procedural aspects (getting a license and automobile insurance and having proof of this information), you make sure the vehicle is properly maintained, fuel it up before a trip, put air in the spare tire, mind the rules of the road, and have rehearsed what you should do if you run into any problems. You are likely to call upon others if you need help. In keeping with the metaphor of vehicle maintenance and functionality, you might depend upon the expertise of others to clean, service, and repair the car.

It's also prudent in knowing the strengths and limitations of your car. If the muffler is dragging, you need to get it fixed. And, taking a trip to the grocery store is very different from driving across country i.e., a car may be fine for the former, but not well suited for the latter.

We have considered some of the internal elements that help support the ethical decision-making path, focusing on how perceptions and personal skills can influence ability and likely effectiveness. While personal aspects are tremendous factors in supporting moral action, the reality is that we engage in decision-making in the context of others. When we think about it, just about everything we do at work involves other people. Thus, being ethical at work depends upon the care and attention we put toward addressing moral issues and being able to sort them internally (within ourselves) and externally (with others).

Working with Others

Humans are social creatures, with a need to be with and support members of our family, friends, and extended communities. We learn with and from one another. Hopefully, this learning continues throughout our lives. Influential in this process are the collective behaviors of people that emerge as a result of working together in groups. As we engage in activities, our behavior serves as a role model to others as we are similarly influenced by the behavior of those around us. As a society, certain acts are deemed inappropriate or unacceptable, while others are deemed fruitful and desirable. Kelman (1974) identified several aspects of social behavior tied to norms. And, salient to any discussion regarding workplace ethics is the term compliance. Compliance refers to the guidelines for expected ethical behavioral norms in most organizations (Fig. 7.8).

The meaning of the word compliance (to comply) suggests a yielding to interpersonal pressure, based on the human need for approval and a desire to belong. We all have some desire to be accepted, included, liked, appreciated, and valued.

Fig. 7.8 Behavioral norms form and evolve in the workplace. Images credited to michaeljung (*left*); lightwavemedia/Shutterstock.com (*right*)

From the school lunchroom to the workplace cafeteria, most of us want to get along and be a part of some group. Compliance processes and standards of behavior pose effects similar to those of subjective norms i.e., a belief that other people you respect, like, or value believe you should behave in a particular way. Scholars have examined this phenomenon under the theories of reasoned action (Fishbein and Ajzen 1975) and planned behavior (Ajzen 1991, 2002). The basis for our personal subjectivity resides among normative beliefs, stemming from the culture we are born into and influenced by (i.e., what we come to know as being socially appropriate). Each person responds to how they believe their significant referents feel they should act, laden by their internal motivations to comply with the expectations of these referents. But some people place more value on compliance-based inclusion than others. The efficacy or usefulness of subjective norms has been demonstrated in organization research (e.g., Armitage and Conner 2001; Sheppard et al. 1988) and in ethical decision-making (Jones and Verstegen Ryan 1997). Sekerka and Bagozzi (2007) further describe the relationship between recognition of an ethical challenge and the desire to act with moral strength, mediated by subjective norms (e.g., degree of openness).

Group norms are the shared values or goals among members of a group. Do you put a napkin in your lap at meals? Do you arrive early or late to work? Do you smile frequently or remain guarded with your emotional display? These sorts of behaviors are elements of social behavior tied to subjective norms (Eagly and Chaiken 1993). Kelman (1974) described the processes underlying group norms as internalization. When group norms become adopted, desires or decisions to act are governed by the congruence of significant personal values with those within the group. The self-regulatory aspects of internalization originate through socialization processes, whereby standards of conduct conveyed by significant others help form self-guides for meeting commonly accepted idealized goals (Higgins 1991).

Norms of the group often find expression in the theory of reciprocity (Gouldner 1960), where members react in kind to benefits provided by fellow group members. Internalization processes can lead to feelings of obligation with respect to the welfare of group members and go beyond returning favors to include the initiation of beneficial actions on behalf of the group and its members (Cialdini et al. 1991; Tyler 1997). Group norms can support moral strength, even if they are not perfectly congruent with your own personal desires. For example, at one Silicon Valley Bay area firm, employees discuss "holding each other accountable" as a strength-based element of their organizational culture. Here, the norm is to actually tell peers, fellow organizational members, if what they are doing is ethically risky or potentially inappropriate. Group pressure to act ethically can influence actions via positive or negative incentives to be ethical.

Morally courageous acts are unlikely to become a habit, unless, over time, the person makes a decision that this is the type of person they want to be. Anticipated emotions (if I do this I will likely feel this way) and outcome expectancies (if I do this, this will likely happen) help a person review the consequences and likelihood, respectively, of goal achievement. Such emotional forecasting serves as a personal determinant that can motivate or thwart one's ethical decision-making effort.

Self-efficacy constitutes a personal felt power to act. Subjective norms and group norms address different kinds of social pressures to act in order to achieve a goal. In pursuing moral strength, the goal in question might be to right an injustice, choose between conflicting moral principles, or to ensure human dignity. The consequences of achievement or pressures to act to achieve a goal may also be influenced by an emotional reaction towards the means of how you broach the action. In other words, how you feel about the way you are moving to achieve an ethical goal impacts your willingness to continue. The expectation of being ostracized versus affirmed are likely to support or curtail your desire to proceed. Even the perception of potentially being shunned from inclusion with others can stunt or block a decision to act ethically.

In facing an ethical challenge, like reporting an unethical or illegal action, doing the "right" thing is not a simple task. Are you nervous, intimidated, worried, doubtful, fearful, or perhaps even angry, as you think about what you need to do to pursue right action? If you possess moral strength it is likely you have some or all of these feelings. Those with moral strength typically feel a negative reaction when they become aware of the situation. It can be difficult to do the right thing, as there are real and perceived dangers involved in speaking up. This is especially the case when the issue involves a supervisor, boss, or a senior official suspected of an inappropriate behavior. If you have a desire to do the right thing and you feel that reporting is the ethical thing to do, working through feelings that alert you of potential harm must be addressed.

But not everyone has the capacity to be forthright. Many people rationalize their silence when observing an unethical activity, stating, "Don't be a rat," "Who wants to be around a snitch," "It's not my job to tattle,", or "What if I'm wrong, then where will I be?" Dealing with the reality of pending threat from being a moral agent is learning how to deal with the negative affect that comes with being an ethical person. This suggests that to effectively navigate an ethical decision-making path, managers need to have the courage to be moral.

Forming a Plan

In thinking about what we might do in response to an ethical issue, we formulate potential action steps. Affect towards the means, the feelings toward your potential actions, is independent of a judgment value of a goal, normative pressure, or self-efficacy, per se. To elevate the ethical aspects of a situation and address a particular concern, the person has to decide not only whether or not to act—but also what to do. Some instrumental acts of goodness can be intrinsically enjoyable, leading to pleasant consequences. For example, telling the boss that you identified an ethical risk, which, left unattended, could cost the firm millions of dollars in legal exposure. This situation might elevate you to become a trusted colleague, bringing attention to the organization's ethical vulnerability. And yet, other circumstances (or the same issue perceived differently) may be so noxious or unpleasant that it leads to avoidance because you do not wish to be the bearer of bad news, be perceived as part of the problem, or take the fall for someone else's mistakes. It is especially difficult to want to proceed with right action when it is your boss or another person with authority who is instigating the behavior or is, on some level, aware of what is going on.

Feelings experienced as you consider the possible means toward right action can supply additional information to a decision-maker on the personal consequences of engaging in goal pursuit. Depending on the polarity and magnitude of emotional reactions towards the means of goal attainment, a decision to employ one method or another will be seen as favorable or unfavorable in and of itself. Affect towards the means has been studied by Bagozzi and his colleagues (Bagozzi et al. 1992; Bagozzi and Edwards 2000). Here we see that in making healthy ethical choices, affect toward the means interacts with self-efficacy and outcome expectancies to influence action.

This is especially challenging when impediments to act are strong. In terms of an ethical decision, your desire to not be the problem and feeling anxious about bringing an issue forward is likely to conflict with your desire to take action. Ethically challenging situations are demanding and pose risk, as they can induce strong impediments to act, both internally and externally. Therefore, the effect of an ethical challenge on the desire to act is influenced by the means under consideration and the person's self-efficacy, coupled with their outcome expectancies. The effect of an ethical challenge will vary by the degree of felt affect (towards the means needed to act), one's self-confidence (your belief that you can perform the means), and a belief that the effort will lead to a successful (effective, useful) outcome.

Awareness of inner affective and cognitive processes helps a person move forward, with a potential to demonstrate their best ethical self. As Rorty (1980) describes the complex structure of this effort, exposure to failure can occur at any point in the decision-making effort if we cave in—showing a weakness of will. Indeed, individuals are vulnerable as they move from one stage to the next (e.g., from awareness to desire, from desire to decision, and from decision to action). Although a behavioral action is perhaps the most visible outcome, the more granular features of your internal mental decision points make an impressionable mark on your willingness and desire to proceed down the ethical decision-making path.

Researchers studying moral action in the twenty-first century have shown that moral agency, the propensity to engage in ethical action, is associated with a discrete set of skills (Weaver 2006; Sekerka et al. 2011). The capacity for moral strength can, therefore, be developed in most people. But this requires having a *desire* to act, forming a personal goal to want to be ethical and to engage in moral action. Toward this end, it is important to not only be aware of the ethical elements of a decision and have a desire to "do the right thing," but you must also know how to act on this desire. Managing one's desires and striving to be ethical and moral at work takes practice. Selfish immediate desires often deter our longer-term moral goals. Learning how to manage your desires is therefore and important aspect of ethics as a daily deal.

Takeaway Points

1. Ethical decision-making is influenced by your emotions (realized or perceived).
2. Self-efficacy, the belief that you can be successful at accomplishing your targeted goals, is central for moral behavior.
3. Group and organizational norms can influence what we consider important in any given context, thereby influencing our behavior.

Reflection Questions

Under what circumstances would you choose not to report an unethical activity? What social norms support this decision? What needs to be present for you to take ownership of an ethical issue, assuming responsibility to address the matter?

References

Ajzen, I. (1991). The theory of planned behavior. *Organizational Behavior and Human Decision Processes, 50*, 179–211.

Ajzen, I. (2002). Perceived behavioral control, self-efficacy, locus of control, and the theory of planned behavior. *Journal of Applied Social Psychology, 32*, 1–20.

Anen, C. R. (2013). Neural correlates of economic and moral decision-making. California Institute of Technology, US. Source: Dissertation Abstracts International: Section B: *The Sciences and Engineering* 74(1-B)(E).

Aristotle [350BC]. (1999). *Nicomachean ethics*. T. Irwin (Trans.). Indianapolis, IN: Hackett Publishing.

Armitage, C. J., & Conner, M. (2001). Efficacy of the theory of planned behavior: A meta-analytic review. *British Journal of Social Psychology, 40*, 471–499.

Bagozzi, R. P., & Edwards, E. A. (2000). Goal-striving and the implementation of goal intentions in the regulation of body weight. *Psychology and Health, 15*, 255–270.

Bagozzi, R. P., Baumgartner, H., & Yi, Y. (1992). Appraisal processes in the enactment of intentions to use coupons. *Psychology and Marketing, 9*, 469–486.

Bagozzi, R. P., Baumgartner, H., & Pieters, R. (1998). Goal-directed emotions. *Cognition and Emotion, 12*, 1–26.

Bagozzi, R. P., Sekerka, L. E., & Hill, V. (2009). Hierarchical motive structures and their role in moral choices of managers. *Journal of Business Ethics, 90*(4), 461–486.

Bagozzi, R. P., Sekerka, L. E., Hill, V., & Seguera, F. (2013). The role of moral values in instigating morally responsible behavior. *Journal of Applied Behavior Sciences, 49*(1), 69–94.

Bandura, A. (1982). Self-efficacy mechanism in human agency. *American Psychologist, 37*(2), 122–147.

Bandura, A., & Cervone, D. (1986). Differential engagement of self-reactive influence in cognitive motivation. *Organization Behavior & Human Decision Processes, 38*(1), 92–113.

Bandura, A., & Wood, R. (1989). Effect of perceived controllability and performance standards on self-regulation of complex decision making. *Journal of Personality and Social Psychology, 56*(5), 805–814.

Bencie, L. (2013). *Among enemies: Counter-espionage for the business traveler*. Mountain Lake Park: D Street Books.

Bennis, W., & Nanus, B. (1985). *Leaders: The strategies for taking charge*. New York: Harper and Row.

Carver, C. S., & Scheier, M. F. (1990). Origins and functions of positive and negative affect: A control-process view. *Psychological Review, 97*, 19–35.

Carver, C. S., & Scheier, M. F. (1998). *On the self-regulation of behavior*. Cambridge: Cambridge University Press.

Carver, C. S., Sutton, S. K., & Scheier, M. F. (2000). Action, emotion, and personality: Emerging conceptual integration. *Personality and Social Psychology Bulletin, 26*(6), 741–751.

Chermers, M. M., Watson, C. B., & May, S. T. (2000). Dispositional affect and leadership effectiveness: A comparison of self-esteem, optimism, and efficacy. *Personality and Social Psychology Bulletin, 26*(3), 267–277.

Christensen, M. M., & Kohl, C. B. (2003). Ethical decision making in times of organizational crisis: A framework for analysis. *Business & Society, 42*(3), 328–358.

Cialdini, R. B., Kallgren, C. A., & Reno, R. (1991). A focus theory of normative conduct: A theoretical refinement and reevaluation of the role of norms in human behavior. In L. Berkowitz (Ed.), *Advances in experimental social psychology* (pp. 201–214). New York: Academic Press.

Damasio, A. R. (1994). *Descartes' error: Emotion, reason, and the human brain*. New York: Grosset/Putnam.

Dubinsky, A. J., & Loken, B. (1989). Analyzing ethical decision making in marketing. *Journal of Business Research, 19*(2), 83–108.

Eagly, A. H., & Chaiken, S. (1993). *The psychology of attitudes*. Fort Worth: Harcourt Brace Javanovich.

Ferrell, O. C., & Gresham, L. G. (1985). A contingency framework for understanding ethical decision making in marketing. *Journal of Marketing, 49*(3), 87–96.

Fishbein, M., & Ajzen, I. (1975). *Belief, attitude, intention, and behavior: An introduction to theory and research*. Reading: Addison-Wesley.

Gist, M. E., & Mitchell, T. R. (1992). Self-efficacy: A theoretical analysis of its determinants and malleability. *Academy Management Review, 17*(2), 183–212.

Gleicher, F., Boninger, D. S., Strathman, A., Armor, D., Hetts, J. & Ahn, M. (1995). With an eye toward the future: The impact of counterfactual thinking on affect, altitudes, and behavior. In N. J. Roese & J. M. Olson, et al. (Eds.), *What might have been: The social psychology of counterfactual thinking* (pp. 283–304). Mahwahy: Lawrence Erlbaum Associates.

Goleman, D. (2004). What makes a leader? Harvard Business Review (January). Retrieved September 20, 2015.

Gouldner, A. W. (1960). The norm of reciprocity. *American Sociological Review, 25*, 165–178.

Hannah, S. T., & Avolio, B. J. (2010). Moral potency: Building the capacity for character-based leadership. *Consulting Psychology Journal: Practice and Research, 62*(4), 291.

Hegarty, W., & Simms, H. P. Jr. (1979). Organizational philosophy, policies, and objectives related to unethical decision behavior: A laboratory experiment. *Journal of Applied Psychology, 64*, 331–338.

Higgins, E. T. (1991). Development of self-regulatory and self-evaluative processes: Costs, benefits, and tradeoffs. In M. R. Gunnar & L. A. Sroufe (Eds.), *Self processes and development: The Minnesota symposium on child development* (pp. 125–166). Hillsdale: Erlbaum.

Hinson, J. M., Jameson, T. L., & Whitney, P. (2002). Somatic markers, working memory, and decision making. *Cognitive, Affective, and Behavioral Neuroscience, 24*(3), 241–353.

Issac. M. (July 16, 2015). Reddit changes content rules as Steve Huffman takes charge. *The New York Times*. Retrieved July 17, 2015 from http://www.nytimes.com/2015/07/17/technology/reddit-steve-huffman.html?_r=0 .

James, W. (1842–1910). *Notman studios*. MS Am 1092 (1185), Series II, 23, Houghton Library, Harvard University.

James, W. (1890a). *Habit*. New York: H. Holt & Co.

James, W. (1890b). *The principles of psychology*. New York: H. Holt & Co.

Johnson-Laird, P. N., & Oately, K. (1989). The language of emotions: An analysis of a semantic field. *Emotion and Cognition, 3*, 81–123.

Jones, T. (1991). Ethical decision-making by individuals in organization: An issue-contingent model. *Academy of Management Review, 16*(2), 366–395.

Jones, T. M., & Verstegen Ryan, L. (1997a). The link between ethical judgment and action in organizations: A moral approbation approach. *Organization Science, 8*(6), 663–680.

Jones, T. M., & Verstegen Ryan, L. (1997b). The effect of organizational forces on individual morality: Judgment, moral approbation, and behavior. *Business Ethics Quarterly, 8*(3), 431–446.

Kelman, H. C. (1974). Further thoughts on the processes of compliance, identification, and internalization. In J. T. Tedeschi (Ed.), *Perspectives on social power* (pp. 126–171). Chicago: Aldine.

Lefcourt, H. M. (1997). Durability and impact of the locus of control construct. *Psychological Bulletin, 112*(3), 411–414.

Locke, E. A., & Latham, G. P. (1990). *A theory of goal setting and task performance*. Englewood Cliffs: Prentice-Hall.

Mayo, M. A., Marks, L. J., & Ryans, J. K. (1991). Perceptions of ethical problems in international marketing. *International Marketing Review, 8*(3), 61–75.

Murphy, J. (1992). Entrepreneurial organizations and self-evaluation: Learning. *Leadership & Organization Development Journal, 13*(5), 28–40.

Ophir, E. N., Wagner, C., & Anthony, D. (1991). Cognitive control in media multitaskers. *Proceedings of the National Academy of Sciences of the United States of America, 106*(37), 15583–15587.

Perugini, M., & Bagozzi, R. P. (2001). The role of desires and anticipated emotions in goal-directed behaviors: Broadening and deepening the theory of planned behavior. *British Journal of Social Psychology, 40*, 79–98.

Rest, J. R. (1986). The major component of morality. In W. M. Kurtines & J. L. Gerwitz (Eds.), *Morality, moral behavior, and moral development* (pp. 24–38). New York: Wiley.

Rorty, A. O. (1980). *Explaining emotions*. Berkeley: University of California Press.

Rorty, A. O. (1986). The two faces of courage. *Philosophy, 61*, 151–171.

Rorty, A. O. (1988). *Mind in action*. Boston: Beacon Press.

Salovey, P., & Mayer, J. D. (1990). Emotional intelligence. *Imagination, Cognition and Personality, 9*(3), 185–211.

Schachter, S., & Singer, J. E. (1962). Cognitive, social, and physiological determinants of emotional state. *Psychological Review, 69*, 379–399.

Sekerka, L. E., & Bagozzi, R. P. (2007). Moral courage in the workplace: Moving to and from the desire and decision to act. *Business Ethics: A European Review, 16*(2), 132–142.

Sekerka, L. E. & Comer, D. (2015). *Sustaining moral courage: Understanding and preventing demoralization in workplace settings*. Paper presented at the European Academy of Management Annual Meeting, Warsaw, Poland, 6/15.

Sekerka, L. E., McCarthy, J. D., & Bagozzi, R. (2011). Developing the capacity for professional moral courage: Facing daily ethical challenges in today's military workplace. In D. Comer and G. Vega (Eds.), *Moral courage in organizations: Doing the right thing at work* (pp. 130-141). Armonk, NY: M.E. Sharpe.

Sheppard, B. H., Hartwick, J., & Warshaw, P. R. (1988). The theory of reasoned action: A meta-analysis of past research with recommendations for modifications and future research. *Journal of Consumer Research, 15*, 325–343.

Sonenshein, S. (2007). The role of construction, intuition, and justification in responding to ethical issues at work: The sensemaking-intuition model. *Academy of Management Review, 32*(4), 1022–1040.

Taylor, J. (2011, March 30). The power of prime: The cluttered mind uncluttered. Technology: Myth of multitasking—Is multitasking really more efficient? *Psychology Today*. Retrieved

March   8,   2014   from   http://www.psychologytoday.com/blog/the-power-prime/201103/
technology-myth-multitasking.

Treviño, L. K., & Youngblood, S. A. (1990). Bad apples in bad barrels: A causal analysis of
ethical decision-making behavior. *Journal of Applied Psychology, 75*(4), 378–386.

Tyler, T. R. (1997). Why people cooperate with organizations. *Research in Organization
Behavior, 21*, 201–246.

Ward, L. (2001). Nobility and necessity: The problem of courage in Aristotle's Nicomachean
ethics. *The American Political Science Review, 95*(1), 71–84.

Weaver, G. R. (2006). Virtue in organizations: Moral identity as a foundation for moral agency.
Organization Studies, 27(3), 341–368.

Chapter 8
Managing Your Desires

Being ethical is about consciously making choices that reflect what you care about most, believe in, and *truly* value. The organizations we work for are platforms for executing our ethical values. Ask yourself, do you value being morally responsible at work? This means taking charge of your own behavior to ensure that your values are demonstrated in what you do.

Many of us end up spending time and energy in service of our immediate demands and/or fulfilling short-term wants and desires. Rather than valuing being responsible, which, in and of itself is at the crux of being ethical, we often behave in ways that demonstrate how much we value fulfilling short-term gratification or other priorities. This can happen at work, when we are bombarded with tasks that may be perceived as requiring immediate action. Given the ubiquitous demands for our attention and time, distractions can detour us from being aware of the ethical elements of what we are actually doing. Being consciously mindful of the ethical elements of the choices we make is central toward acting responsibly as employees, managers, consumers, parents, and citizens.

Valuing Self-regulation

To understand how values and even virtues can become habits of choice, let us consider Aristotle's explanation of how we acquire character strength through repeated right action:

> We do not act rightly because we have virtue or excellence, but rather we have those because we have acted rightly. We are what we repeatedly do. Excellence, then, is not an act but a habit (1985: NE 1103a20).

Valuing a desire to be ethical usually requires some deliberate effort. Personal values function as both automatic and deliberate self-regulatory mechanisms, similar to the role of traits. They are internalized pre-established guidelines to help direct our responses when we face an ethical situation (issue, concern, or challenge).

© Springer International Publishing Switzerland 2016
L. E. Sekerka, *Ethics is a Daily Deal*, DOI 10.1007/978-3-319-18090-8_8

These values, implicit and explicit, are inherent in our choices and behaviors, but vary depending upon the person and situation (Konrad 1982). Family and peer influences, religious values, organizational values, and personal needs shape our value sets and contribute to how we will act when we face an ethical challenge at work (Barry 1985). If you have a desire to do the right thing, learning to bring your values into your conscious thought process when you are engaged in ethical decision-making will help you to bolster the path to realized action.

Research shows that personal values influence moral behavior (DiBattista 1989; Gautschi 1977). For example, individual difference variables such as having an economic value orientation and a high degree of Machiavellianism are positively related to unethical behavior (Hegarty and Sim 1979). Think about it, if you crave money and take huge risks, trouncing on others' well-being to achieve this objective, your focus on ethical values is likely nullified. Only you can truly know how important your values are to you, and how much you value their application in your life. When you make a decision, how much weight do you attach to the welfare of others as compared to fulfilling your own desires? Do you have a tendency to be unemotional and detached, finding it easy to use deception and manipulation to gain personal advantage? Or maybe you are deeply empathetic and often think about how others will feel if you proceed with a particular course of action. While a predisposition to behave ethically or unethically is a strong predictor of workplace behavior, it does not assure ethical (or unethical) action. Moreover, adults can edify and improve their character strengths that support their second-order desires to act ethically. The standards that reside within our moral fiber, what Rokeach calls personal values (1977), prove useful in understanding and explaining sensitivity to the ethical dimensions of organizational life (Payne and Giacalone 1990). You might consider values as a starting point for your ethicality. But simply possessing a particular value is no assurance for right action. This is especially the case if you have difficulty in applying a desire to be ethical, should that desire compete with other, perhaps more salient values. To enact a value, you need practice at sustaining the desire to act with character strength. Values serve as a platform in guiding our daily decisions, but acting on them requires commitment and endurance (Fig. 8.1).

Personal and organizational values are principles that guide employee actions at work. You often hear employers say that their firms, "Only hire ethical people." Research confirms this is a ubiquitous assumption (Sekerka 2009, p. 93). This assumes you can accurately determine who is ethical and who is not, which isn't really possible in an interview process. But even if somehow you could, the idea is based upon the premise that ethical identity is fixed and/or finalized. Many people seem to believe that by the time you are an adult, you either are ethical or you are not. There a modicum of truth to this, as beliefs learned as a child help form some of our values as we grow up. But such simplistic explanations or declarations deny the reality that we continue to evolve as we age. Moreover, given the circumstances and the people involved in the particular situation, we may or may not have the necessary commitment required to sustain our desire to be ethical in that moment. A key point is that we have to continue to find worth (value) in the application of

Fig. 8.1 Aristotle (1999)
observed "we are what we
repeatedly do". Sculpted
portrait of Aristotle mid-2nd
century AD, artist unknown;
image credited to Szilas/in the
public domain

our values. As a character strength and moral competency, self-regulation is fore-most in demonstrating the capacity for values application. Morality is like a muscle, it can be strengthened in most adults with ongoing exercise.

While self-regulation is often framed as a technique or skill, it can also be a personal value and trait. In an ideal scenario, a person values self-regulation in the course of their ethical decision-making. Over time, self-regulation (as a personal value) can become second nature to us, evolving into or becoming ingrained as a character trait (Rokeach 1973). We can thereby augment our values and the desire to act ethically, learning to consciously self-regulate—directing positive emotions to fuel right action and managing negative emotions that might quell or diminish our desire to proceed. The frequent reference to self-regulation as a moral muscle (Baumeister and Exline 1999) implies that it can be strengthened with use.

Bandura (2002) points out that the ability to act as a moral agent has dual aspects: the power to refrain from behaving inappropriately (inhumanely) and the proactive power to behave appropriately (humanely). Embedding agency to act morally in social-cognitive self theory, he was one of the frontrunners in science to explain how affective self-regulatory mechanisms rooted in personal standards are linked to self-sanctioning. He describes how moral functioning is therefore governed by reactive self, rather than simple dispassionate abstract reasoning. The point is that self-regulatory mechanisms governing moral conduct do not come into play unless they are activated; working to learn how to activate these mechanisms for "good" is a central feature of maintaining the will to proceed (toward a moral act).

Self-regulation is a purposive effort to employ self-corrective adjustments to thoughts and feelings (Carver 2004; Carver and Scheier 1998). Therefore, it is a powerful mechanism for managing and bolstering the will to proceed throughout an ethical decision-making effort. It has also been identified as a moral competency that supports moral courage (see Chap. 9). Current states that can be regulated are desires, thoughts, feelings, and actions. The ability to alter our immediate reactions requires the capacity to initiate or change one's initial response to a more preferable one (Baumeister and Vohs 2004). The goal is to prevent negative outcomes and/or achieve positive ones. As a form of self-control, self-regulation refers to an ability to alter cognitive and affective states and their associated responses. Hence, this function is both key to adaptive success and central to ethical action, especially if the latter requires setting aside the pursuit of selfish goals (Baumeister and Exline 2000).

Living and working effectively requires that you restrain certain impulses and desires, while channeling others in the pursuit of valued goals. For example, perhaps you have attempted to change behavior with regards to exercise, deciding to incorporate regularly scheduled workout activities into your everyday routine. Assuming your goal is to feel better, have more energy to do your work, and live longer, on some level this could be considered a moral choice. In order for ethical awareness and action to become a habit of choice, you need to impose personal self-regulation to overcome inertia, resist temptations, and block impediments to imposing your plan. In short, you are working to create and support a new choice, while managing other desires that compete for your time and attention, which likely have (at least initially) more appeal.

Self-regulation is considered so important to human functioning that Baumeister and Exline (1999, 2000) refer to it as the "master virtue," inasmuch as the process can move individuals to overcome selfish impulses for the sake of others. With an association between self-regulation and high ethical commitment (Avshalom and Rachman-Moore 2004), it acts as a conduit for moral strength. Whether it is a trait or learned action, automatic or conscious, self-regulation can alter one's current state and pending response. Such efforts are central to the deliberate engagement of moral action (Sekerka and Bagozzi 2007). From a motivated cognition perspective, effective application of self-regulation can be of particular importance when personal, professional, and organization values conflict (Higgins and Spiegel 2004). To habitually pursue right action, however, people must work at postponing their automatic tendencies to react and consistently manage their emotions (Salovey et al. 2002; Goleman 2004). This requires control and restraint, coupled with an ability to know when to act. To master this capability takes practice. Self-regulation, as a practice, supports consistency and striving to achieve a goal when working to achieve moral good, especially when obstacles present a threat to self. Factors like self-regulation and other values and traits that support ethical action in decision-making are more established for some than others. This suggests there is potential for further development in most people (Fig. 8.2).

Personal values often arise through developmental and socialization processes and are often exercised as a response to explicit social influence (Schwartz 1996).

Fig. 8.2 Considering morality as a muscle. Images credited to Kzenon/ Shutterstock.com

Values motivate behavior and justify past actions; but they can also influence movement toward moral action. The operation of personal values, in the form of automatic self-regulation, can influence the effect of a desire (to engage in a moral action) on the decision to do so (to the extent that a person has acquired personal values, traits, and virtues to act morally). Individual differences augment or atten- uate the influence of this desire to demonstrate moral or ethical strength. When self-regulation is a value, trait or virtue, its effects are largely unconscious and automatic. But self-regulation may also be a controlled way that decision-makers can transform their desires into deliberate decisions to act.

Central to ethical action is a person's ability to respond to and/or alter their emotional and motivational states. We need certain skills or competencies to keep our emotions and motives in perspective, relative to others (Feldman Barrett and Gross 2001; Salovey et al. 1993). Those who research business ethics have argued that people who are aware of their emotions and motives, and use them effectively, impose self-regulation to their advantage (Sekerka and Bagozzi 2007). To facilitate moral strength, our emotions and motives need to inform but not overwhelm us. Building on self-regulation theory, emotional and motivational awareness coupled with self-control can be used to guide choices via incorporation of long-range considerations in decision-making. To consider a more systemic view over time, people must learn to manage their emotional and motivational behavior in the light of their present circumstances.

Ideas formulated by the philosopher Frankfurt (1971, 1988) help us to explain how self-regulation and desires may work together to moderate (i.e., attenuate or augment) the relationship between the desire to act and the decision to act with moral strength. Frankfurt suggested that people have the capacity for reflective self-evaluation in that they can become aware of their motives, feelings, thoughts, and desires. He proposed that everyone, albeit in varying degrees, has the capacity to evaluate their desires and decide whether they want (or do not want) to have these personal desires as they scrutinize them. Frankfurt termed these mental events second-order desires (Bagozzi 2006). For example, you are faced with an ethical challenge. Having a desire to act ethically is a first-order desire. But when you reflect upon this desire to act, in such a way as to cancel, override, or postpone further implementation of this desire to act, you deploy a second-order desire.

More specifically, when thinking about the desire to act, you ask yourself questions like:

- Am I the kind of person who should have a desire to act ethically?
- Am I the kind of person who acts on this desire?
- Is the desire I feel consistent with the kind of person I ought or wish to be?
- Will acting on this desire lead to my well-being?
- What effect will acting on this desire have on other people important to me?
- What effect will acting on this desire have on others, perhaps people I may not even know?
- Is my not feeling a desire to act consistent with the type of person I want to be?

In a parallel manner, a decision-maker can, in an ethically challenging situation, reflect on his/her lack of felt (first-order) desire to act (Fig. 8.3). Here, the person considers whether to embrace, accept, or construct a desire to act, and questions analogous to those noted above may be posed self-reflectively. Given the power of self-reflectivity, second-order desires can attenuate or augment the effect of one's first-order desire to act on the decision to act. Such acts of deliberate or conscious self-regulation, viewed as second-order desires, develop and are influenced by several social elements; namely, self-conscious emotions and social identity.

Fig. 8.3 Navigating choices and desires in decision-making. Image credited to wavebreakmedia/ Shutterstock.com

Making these questions a part of your internal cross-check or inventory process is vitally important to help you ensure and maintain ethical consistency. Running through these types of questions as you think through a given situation, can you at least get honest with yourself about your motives and reasons for acting (or not acting)? If nothing else, this type of cross-check effort helps to reveal your willingness to embolden or cheat your own values.

Acting on the Desire to Be Ethical

There is an overarching assumption that in facing an ethical challenge you will want to do the right thing. But even having a desire to be ethical or moral doesn't mean that you will necessarily act on it. Given the nuanced elements of desire, it is worth focusing directly on this aspect of the ethical decision-making process. Just because a person has a desire to be ethical doesn't mean they will have the requisite character strength needed to form a judgment and make a decision to act on this intention.

Like most constructs that describe human behavior, desire comes in different forms and is felt in varying ways. In working to understand the moral sciences, philosophers differentiate between appetitive and volitive desires. The former is an automatic response not based on reasoning; the latter, a more deliberative cognitive process (Davis 1984a, b). An appetitive desire occurs unconsciously, whereas a volitive desire is one where you consciously direct your energies to achieve it (becoming a deliberate goal). Being a part of the team or group is an example that might present itself in either form. In choosing to be ethical, your volitive desire to be an ethical person may have to outweigh your desire to be a part of the group (if acting ethically is perceived to be in contrast to the group's social norms).

Aside from the differences in the role of reasoning, forms of desire may also differ subtly in the way they are expressed. Synonyms for appetitive desires include craving, hungering, longing, and yearning, whereas volitive desires encompass wants, wishes, or coveting. The formation of an appetitive desire to do something ethically tends to generate and motivate a volitive desire to act (Marks 1986). Moral philosophers have a special role in mapping out the logical and ontological geography of desire—for deontologists (moral judgments create desires), utilitarians (moral actions serve desires), and virtue theorists (moral traits embody desires).

Regardless of the perspective, the intensity of your volitive desire to be ethical is generally a function of multiple elements, including anticipated emotions, self-efficacy, outcome expectancies, subjective norms, group norms, and affect towards the means (perceived feelings related to what you might do [as a course of action]). The intensity of our appetitive desire is based on internalized factors, which are often biological. Sometimes a desire to act, however arrived upon, will lead directly to a decision. This constitutes a deterministic outcome of your desire. Such a path influences an ethical decision when more basic or primitive habits, urges, compulsions, or impulses operate unhindered. This can occur when self-regulation is absent or thwarted, or when first-order desires go unchecked. It's possible that you may do the right thing automatically. But because many ethical issues are difficult challenges, they often require forethought and a plan of action, calling upon both forms of desire along with automatic and deliberate self-regulation (Fig. 8.4).

In contrast to a direct, deterministic path from desire to decision to act, a person can learn to self-regulate the influence of their desires on decision-making in several ways. Automatic or unconscious self-regulation of a desire to act occurs as a consequence of a behavioral orientation learned developmentally—often early in life (e.g., Kochanska 1994; Posner and Rothbart 2000). Such an orientation is manifest in particular values, traits, and/or virtues. Deliberate or conscious self-regulation occurs through the willful application of personal standards to one's desire. For example, in riding public transportation you might have been taught to give up your seat to someone in need (e.g., an elderly person or pregnant woman). You automatically hop up and offer your seat on a crowded bus. But let's say another passenger takes the seat you have offered, rendering the person in need still without a place to sit. You don't know if this was an accidental error or an intentional disregard. Believing it to be the latter, rather than getting mad or raising a fuss, you maintain composure and make eye contact with another seated passenger. You signal the need and/or ask them to offer their seat, so the person in need can still be helped. The former action, to get up, may be instinctive, as you learned from your parents it was right to do so. The latter, negotiating the circumstance effectively, requires more deliberate thought.

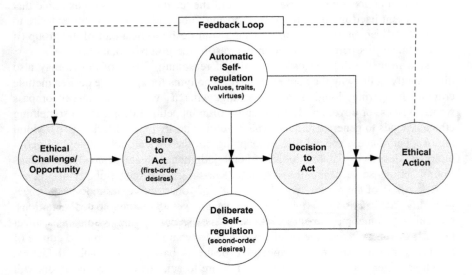

Fig. 8.4 The importance of automatic and deliberate self-regulation. Figure adapted from Sekerka and Bagozzi (2007)

As you work to resolve situations, determining how to act, you need to self-regulate your desires, which are typically coupled with emotions. Getting angry or resentful may create additional difficulties, so these emotions necessitate regulation, shaping and directing them as needed, to endorse your desire and decision to act ethically. For a specific workplace example, think about the meetings you have attended, when people are rude, impolite or sharing false information and you need to effectively navigate the situation. In some areas of social psychology a decision to act is termed an intention to act (e.g., Fishbein and Ajzen 1975) or an implementation intention (e.g., Gollwitzer 1993). The need to differentiate between the desire to act and the decision to act arises from the dissociation of a desire from an intention or commitment to act (Perugini and Bagozzi 2004). A direct link between desire and decision can be thought of as a habitual or compulsive pathway. This path can be activated immediately or straightaway, depending on the degree of a person's prior learning in classical conditioning, operant learning, or cognitive learning senses. In all of these cases, the effect is deterministic. To bolster and fuel your resolve in having a desire to act ethically often requires a more deliberate or conscious pursuit and/or endorsement.

"I Don't Do Emotions"

In a recent presentation, I asked listeners to consider an ethical challenge and what they were feeling at the time it occurred. Asking a male professorial colleague in the room to share his reflective insight, he replied, "I don't do emotions" (Sekerka 2014). I was not surprised. Having posed this question to well over a thousand people in my practice and research, whether in one-on-one meetings or group work, men often have difficulty responding. The typical answer is something like, "I feel fine." But with some encouragement, most people can come up with at least one feeling word to describe their emotional experience. Scholars studying emotional expression have found that emotion language is generally age-dependent and sensitive to gender-related "display rules" for talking about emotions (O'Kearney and Dadds 2004) (Fig. 8.5).

Scholars believe that language development processes are associated with emotional expression, the conditions for which can vary greatly among individuals (e.g., think about if and how often you were read to as a child). While some may recognize their emotions, it is difficult for some individuals to talk about them. We are often socialized to not recognize our feelings and/or not to share our personal sentiments in public. Regardless of verbal expression, it is important that people begin to understand the power of their emotions as helpful cues, central in shaping second-order desires and in signaling moral insight.

Emotions and cognition are deeply intertwined, working together to help us make sense of situations and give us clues about what we might or ought to do. To learn from our past actions, it is very important to reflect on what affective elements may have inadvertently guided our actions. Emotions direct cerebral processes

Fig. 8.5 Being aware of your emotions is key to moral action. Image credited to Viktor Gladkov/Shutterstock. com

within the ethical decision-making path. Haidt (2001) distilled four families of moral emotions, referring to them as: other-condemning (contempt, anger, and disgust), self-conscious (shame, embarrassment, and guilt), other-suffering (compassion), and other-praising (gratitude and elevation). From a young age, people are socialized to different degrees to feel these emotions, along with additional social self-conscious emotions like empathy, pride, envy, and jealousy (Lewis 2000; Tangney 2003; Tangney and Fischer 1995).

Empirical findings for research investigating the influence of the moral self on intentions and behaviors reflect the influence of self-conscious moral emotions (i.e., guilt and pride) and moral strength (i.e., moral chronicity and moral character) (Jennings et al. 2014). Moral emotions positively influence ethical behavior and intentions (Cohen 2010; de Hooge et al. 2007; Kim and Johnson 2013; Narvaez et al. 2006) and negatively influence unethical and counterproductive behavior and intentions (e.g., scapegoating, Rothschild et al. 2012). Consciously dealt with or not, our emotions often play a critical role in motivating or hindering our choice to engage in right action—or to step away from or ignore the matter. Second-order desires quite often depend upon self-conscious emotions. In terms of ethical action, our desires respond to the personal and social standards for conduct entailed by self-conscious affect. For example, in the case of pride, this emotion helps to maintain self-esteem, signaling important standards that can facilitate the acquisition of information about the self as an ethical agent. Pride also shows those around us that we have achieved valued outcomes and/or shared motives. Of course, pride must be self-managed in social settings, lest it lead to hubris, with negative social and unethical consequences (Lewis 2000, p. 630).

With a desire to be ethical and confronted with an opportunity to pursue right action, a decision-maker will typically experience that one or more of these emotions become activated, depending upon the nature of their developmental experiences and history of coping with these emotions. In particular, self-conscious emotions have personal and social connotations and foster the experience of considering the self as object and agent (Barret 1995). Other affective sentiments in moving to resolve an ethical challenge include worry, loneliness, fear, shock, surprise, and feelings of hurt—often stemming from a sense of betrayal (e.g., when colleagues or a supervisor are engaged in an unethical activity or are aware of unethical behavior occurring, and choose to let it go unreported/unaddressed) (Sekerka et al. 2011). A common theme among those who move to address an ethical challenge with moral courage is an initial sense of confusion, agitation, or helplessness. In such a state, there is a concern for the potential of personal harm (e.g., being fired), which is often accompanied by emotional discomfort and distress (Sekerka et al. 2011).

Another factor that shapes and constrains deliberate self-regulation and desire to do the right thing is social identity (Ashford and Mael 1989; Bergami and Bagozzi 2000; Dutton et al. 1994; Ellemers et al. 1999). Membership in a group or organization can promote certain values or standards which might be used as criteria in the application of second-order desires. Social identity entails self-awareness of group membership, feelings of attachment to the group, and evaluative connotations that you are an important and valued member. As social identity grows, the individual self can become depersonalized and group or organization standards become paramount. To the extent an organization instills its values and standards to support the resolution of ethical challenges, it can shape second-order desires of group members in ways that support the regulation of desires and a decision to act ethically.

Given that your desire and intent to engage in ethical action have remained steadfast, you can then determine what to do and move to deploy your selected mode of response. In Fig. 8.3, the dotted line from the final ethical action back to the initial step indicates that the process is never finalized. The completion of one ethical act informs your ability to be aware of other ethical challenges and opportunities. Having learned from the prior action, you can pursue the ethical decision-making path again, hopefully with experiential insights that will help your next action be that much more effective.

Principled Performance

On a broader scale, in terms of a desire in business to engage in ethical action via principled performance, some firms are starting to deliberately impose self-regulation in their decision-making efforts. We are beginning to see some signs of authentic ethical business with initiatives like the Benefit Corporation (B-Corp) (see http://www.bcorporation.net/). Instead of incorporating for shareholder wealth, a B-Corp platform is designed to use the power of business to solve social and environmental problems. Firms like Etsy, Patagonia, Seventh Generation, and Better World Books are examples of companies that have rallied to this way of thinking by defining, operating, and leading novel ways of conducting business that reflect a sustained moral awareness and intent. Those taking part in the B-Corp way of business are required to have three core elements:

Purpose: a resolve to create a material positive impact on society
and the environment;
Accountability: expand fiduciary duty to require consideration
of the interests of workers, community, and the environment; and
Transparency: annual public reporting on the firm's overall social and
environmental performance against a comprehensive, credible, independent,
and transparent third-party standard.

Another program, different although similar in name, is referred to as the B Team (see http://bteam.org/). The B Team initiative is designed to catalyze a better way of doing business that supports the well-being of people and the planet. Members of the B Team align with this not-for-profit initiative formed by a global group of leaders to create a future where the purpose of business is to be a driving force for social, environmental, and economic benefit. According to the plan, firms who join the team work under a new definition of business, joining with other B Team members to form sustainable alliances. The purpose of the firm is to serve the stakeholders, not solely to produce profits for shareholders.

As practitioners and business leaders become interested in new models for what it means to do business ethically, combining profit with well-being, scholars strive to build business models that outline how to create profit without causing harm and to explicate how to earn revenue and create value for stakeholders simultaneously (juxtaposed to shareholders alone). This can work, but it calls for a shift toward valuing longer-term values. Companies perceived by their employees to care about ethics (genuinely possessing an ethical organizational culture, not merely advertising claims), have been shown to produce higher profits and reflect strong performance on a variety of indicators (as compared to traditional shareholder-driven operations) (Guiso et al. 2015).

An example of this work has emerged from the *Value of Corporate Culture* (VCC) project. Researchers studied how companies described integrity and their approach to ethics on their organizational websites. They then compared this information to the survey responses collected by the Great Place to Work Institute (the resource for the annual list of "100 Best Companies to Work For" (see http://www.greatplacetowork.com/). The data from the VCC included responses from employees at 1000 public and private firms between 2007 and 2011. Findings show that high levels of perceived integrity are correlated with higher productivity, profitability, better industrial relations, and a higher level of attractiveness to prospective job applicants—over time (Guiso et al. 2015). Research has also shown that when comparing privately and publicly traded firms, the latter organizations are less able to sustain a focus on integrity. This result is linked with an excessive focus on shareholder value maximization, which can undermine integrity (Amble 2014). Recognizing that commitment, quality, and care take time, and that doing so can be profitable, are important signals to the next generation of leaders that ethics is a choice. We can choose to care, or choose to do otherwise. This choice reflects that profits can indeed be made, but the results of such success may not emerge as quickly as in more traditional forms of business, where the pressure for producing quarterly results imposes an unrelenting demand for short-term gains.

The multiple points of self-reflection, self-evaluation, and self-regulation that people face along the way to ethical action are like little mental acts of moral courage throughout the ethical decision-making path. Understanding the mechanisms that support the desire to engage in ethical action can instigate further learning and moral development. But it is especially important to recognize how varying emotions, dispositions, and values can come into conflict. While moral agency is often extolled as being valued by the organizations we work for, little is done to help people understand how to enact it. This is particularly difficult when organizational norms and processes are not congruent with supporting moral agency, or when pressures to perform do not support self-regulation in the path to securing organizational goals. If management hopes to ensure that values are applied toward decisions in the workplace, it is important to recognize that employees need to go beyond compliance, striving to achieve moral action in their daily decisions. But what exactly supports the ability to engage in moral strength? How might we study, examine, and measure the ability to engage in moral strength at work? What is professional moral courage? In the next chapter, we begin to address these questions.

Takeaway Points

1. Self-regulation is the primary moral muscle, considered a master virtue because it supports a desire and ability to use other character strengths in pursuit of ethical action.
2. The use of self-regulation may be deliberate or automatic. It is important to work at being more aware of its application i.e., not just assume it will be there when you need it.
3. Building moral strength is an ongoing effort that takes patience, care, and commitment.
4. Ethical behavior at work needs to be supported by ongoing open communication, explicit performance metrics, and addressing stakeholder concerns.

Reflection Questions

Do you have a desire to be ethical at work? If so, how do you act on this desire daily? Do you pay attention to your moral emotions and use this energy to advance right thinking and right action?

References

Amble, B. (2014). *Corporate integrity undermined by the pursuit of shareholder value*. Retrieved March 23, 2014, from http://www.management-issues.com/news/6850/corporate-integrity-undermined-by-the-pursuit-of-shareholder-value/.

Aristotle. [350BC] (1999). *Nicomachean Ethics*. T. Irwin (Trans.). Indianapolis: Hackett Publishing Co.

Ashford, B. E., & Mael, F. (1989). Social identity theory and the organization. *Academy of Management Review, 14*(1), 20–40.

Avshalom, M. A., & Rachman-Moore, D. (2004). The methods used to implement an ethical code of conduct and employee attitudes. *Journal of Business Ethics, 54*(3), 223–242.

Bagozzi, R. P. (2006). Consumer action: Automaticity, purposiveness, and self-regulation. In N. K. Malkotra (Ed.), *Review of Marketing Research, 2(3-42)*. Sharpe: Armonk, NY.

Bandura, A. (2002). Selective moral disengagement in the exercise of moral agency. *Journal of Moral Education, 31*(2), 2002.

Barret, K. C. (1995). A functionalist approach to shame and guilt. In J. P. Tangney & K. W. Fischer (Eds.), *Self-conscious emotions: The psychology of shame, guilt, embarrassment, and pride* (pp. 25–63). New York: Guilford Press.

Barry, V. (1985). *Moral issues in business*. Belmont, CA: Wadsworth.

Baumeister, R. F., & Exline, J. J. (1999). Virtue, personality and social relations: Self-control as the moral muscle. *Journal of Personality, 67*, 1165–1194.

Baumeister, R. F., & Exline, J. J. 2000. Self-control, morality, and human strength. *Journal of Social & Clinical Psychology. Special Issue: Classical Sources of Human Strength: A Psychological Analysis, 19*(1): 29–42.

Baumeister, R. F., & Vohs, K. D. (2004). *Handbook of self-regulation: Research, theory, and applications*. New York: Guildford Press.

Bergami, M., & Bagozzi, R. P. (2000). Self-categorization and commitment as distinct aspects of social identity in the organization: Conceptualization, measurement, and relation to antecedents and consequences. *British Journal of Social Psychology, 39*, 555–577.

Carver, C. S. (2004). Self-regulation of action and affect. In R. F. Baumeister & K. D. Vohs (Eds.), *Handbook of self-regulation: Research, theory, and applications* (pp. 13–39). New York: Guildford Press.

Carver, C. S., & Scheier, M. F. (1998). *On the self-regulation of behavior*. Cambridge, UK: Cambridge University Press.

Cohen, T. (2010). Moral emotions and unethical bargaining: The differential effects of empathy and perspective taking in deterring deceitful negotiation. *Journal of Business Ethics, 94*, 569–579.

Davis, W. A. (1984a). The two senses of desire. *Philosophical Studies, 45*, 181–195.

Davis, W. A. (1984b). A causal theory of intending. *American Philosophical Quarterly, 21*, 43–54.

de Hooge, I. E., Zeelenberg, M., & Breugelmans, S. (2007). Moral sentiments and cooperation: Differential influences of shame and guilt. *Cognition and Emotion, 21*, 1025–1042.

DiBattista, R. A. (1989). Providing a rationale for ethical conduct from alternatives taken in ethical dilemmas. *The Journal of General Psychology, 116*(2), 207–214.

Dutton, J. E., Dukerich, J. M., & Harquail, C. V. (1994). Organizational images and member identification. *Administrative Science Quarterly, 39*(2), 239–263.

Ellemers, N., Kortekaas, P., & Ouwerkerk, J. W. (1999). Self-categorisation, commitment to the group and group self-esteem as related but distinct aspects of social identity. *European Journal of Social Psychology, 29*(2–3), 371–389.

Feldman Barrett, L., & Gross, J. (2001). Emotional intelligence: A process model of emotion representation and regulation. In T. J. Mayne & G. A. Bonnano (Eds.), *Emotions: Current issues and future directions* (pp. 286–310). New York: Guilford.

Fishbein, M., & Ajzen, I. (1975). *Belief, attitude, intention, and behavior: An introduction to theory and research.* Reading, MA: Addison-Wesley.

Frankfurt, H. (1971). Freedom of the will and the concept of a person. *Journal of Philosophy, 68,* 5–20.

Frankfurt, H. (1988). *The importance of what we care about.* New York: Cambridge University Press.

Gautschi, T. F. (1977). *Ethics in change. Design News, 11,* 217–219.

Goleman, D. (2004). What makes a leader? *Harvard Business Review, 82*(1), 82.

Gollwitzer, P. M. (1993). Goal achievement: The role of intentions. *European Review of Social Psychology, 4,* 141–185.

Guiso, L., Sapienza, P., & Zingales, L. (2015). The value of corporate culture. *Journal of Financial Economics, 117*(1), 60–76.

Haidt, J. (2001). The emotional dog and its rational tail: A social intuitionist approach to moral judgment. *Psychological Review, 108*(4), 814–834.

Hegarty, W. & Sim, H. P. Jr. (1979). Organizational philosophy, policies, and objectives related to unethical decision behavior: A laboratory experiment. *Journal of Applied Psychology, 64,* 331–338.

Higgins, E. T., & Spiegel, S. (2004). Promotion and prevention strategies for self-regulation: A motivated cognition perspective. In R. F. Baumeister & K. D. Vohs (Eds.), *Handbook of self-regulation: Research, theory, and applications* (pp. 171–187). New York: Guildford Press.

Jennings, P. L., Mitchell, M. S., & Hannah, S. T. (2014) The moral self: A review and integration of the literature. *Journal of Organizational Behavior.* doi: 10.1002/job.1919.

Kim, J., & Johnson, K. P. (2013). The impact of moral emotions on cause-related marketing campaigns: A cross-cultural examination. *Journal of Business Ethics, 112,* 79–90.

Kochanska, G. (1994). Beyond cognition: Expanding the search for the early roots of internalization and conscience. *Developmental Psychology, 30,* 20–22.

Konrad, R. A. (1982). Business managers and moral sanctions. *Journal of Business Ethics, 1,* 195–200.

Lewis, M. (2000). Self-conscious emotions: Embarrassment, pride, shame, and guilt. In M. Lewis & J. M. Haviland-Jones (Eds.), *Handbook of emotion* (2nd ed., pp. 623–636). New York: Guilford.

Marks, J. (1986). *The ways of desire: New essays in philosophical psychology on the concept of wanting.* Piscataway, NJ: Transaction Publishers.

Narvaez, D., Lapsley, D., Hagele, S., & Lasky, B. (2006). Moral chronicity and social information processing: Tests of a social cognitive approach to the moral personality. *Journal of Research in Personality, 40,* 966–985.

O'Kearney, R., & Dadds, M. (2004). Developmental and gender differences in the language for emotions across the adolescent years. *Cognition and Emotion, 18*(7), 913–938.

Payne, S. L., & Giacalone, R. A. (1990). Social psychological approaches to the perception of ethical dilemmas. *Human Relations, 43*(7), 649–665.

Perugini, M., & Bagozzi, R. P. (2004). The distinction between desires and intentions. *European Journal of Social Psychology, 34,* 69–84.

Posner, M., & Rothbart, M. (2000). Developing mechanisms of self-regulation. *Development and Psychopathology, 12,* 427–441.

Rokeach, M. (1973). *The nature of human values*. New York: Free Press.

Rokeach, M. (1977). *The nature of human values*. New York: McGraw-Hill.

Rothschild, Z., Landau, M., Sullivan, D., & Keefer, L. (2012). A dual-motive model of scapegoating: Displacing blame to reduce guilt or increase control. *Journal of Personality and Social Psychology, 102,* 1148–1163.

Salovey, P., Hess, C. K., & Mayer, J. D. (1993). Emotional intelligence and the self-regulation of affect. In D. M. Wegner & J. W. Pennebaker (Eds.), *Handbook of mental control: think about business: How personal integrity leads to corporate success* (pp. 258–277). New York: Oxford University Press.

Salovey, P., Mayer, J. D., & Caruso, D. (2002). The positive psychology of emotional intelligence. In C. R. Snyder & S. J. Lopez (Eds.), *Handbook of positive psychology* (pp. 159–171). New York: Oxford University Press.

Schwartz, S. (1996). Value priorities and behavior: Applying a theory of integrated value systems. In C. Seligman, J. M. Olson, & M. P. Zanna (Eds.), *The psychology of values: The Ontario symposium, 8* (pp. 1–24). Mahwah, NJ: Lawrence Erlbaum.

Sekerka, L. E. (2009). Organizational ethics education and training: A review of best practices and their application. *International Journal of Training and Development, 13*(2), 77–95.

Sekerka, L. E. (2014, February 20). *Driving business with ethical strength*. Presentation at John Carroll University, Boler School of Business, University Heights, Ohio.

Sekerka, L. E., & Bagozzi, R. P. (2007). Moral courage in the workplace: Moving to and from the desire and decision to act. *Business Ethics: A European Review, 16*(2), 132–142.

Sekerka, L. E., McCarthy, J. D., & Bagozzi, R. (2011). Developing the capacity for professional moral courage: Facing daily ethical challenges in today's military workplace. In D. Comer & G. Vega (Eds.), *Moral courage in organizations: Doing the right thing at work: 130-141*. M.E. Sharpe: Armonk, NY.

Tangney, J. P. (2003). Self-relevant emotions. In M. R. Leary & J. P. Tangney (Eds.), *Handbook of self and identity* (pp. 384–400). New York: Guilford.

Tangney, J. P., & Fischer, K. W. (Eds.). (1995). *Self-conscious emotions: The psychology of shame, guilt, embarrassment, and pride*. New York: Guilford.

Chapter 9
Professional Moral Courage

The desire and decision to be an ethical and moral person needs to be durable—continuously maintained and strengthened. Managers, leaders, and employees at every level of the organization have come to some level of agreement that there is both necessity and value in being ethical in business. Despite the jokes that the combination of business and ethics is an apparent oxymoron, many of us believe that the two can go hand-in-hand. Although temptations of selfishness and greed seem to accompany profit-driven motives, people are capable of conducting commercial enterprise in a fair and honest manner if they make up their mind to do so. To help managers develop the skills necessary to support ethical choices and actions at work, it is important to begin by defining and articulating the overall behavior. We must come to a shared understanding of what moral strength looks like. Presumably, this is an ability to recognize the ethical elements of decisions and actions and to address and resolve challenges and opportunities in a morally sound manner.

To better understand how to support moral strength in organizational settings, scholars have pursued the topic of moral agency (Wilcox 2012; Watson et al. 2008). My colleagues and I augmented this work, in an effort to identify, define, and explain the discrete elements of moral strength. When managers, as moral agents, respond to a specific ethical challenge with moral fortitude, they demonstrate *professional moral courage* (Sekerka et al. 2009). To help people better understand and learn how to respond to ethical challenges when they are performing their work, we felt greater clarity was needed in order to measure the capacity. From that point, we could move to identify specific skills that are needed to help make professional moral courage possible, to actually enable and fortify the behavior.

Some of this research originally appeared in Sekerka, Bagozzi et al. (2011), Sekerka, McCarthy et al. (2011), Sekerka et al. (2009), Sekerka, Marar Yacobian et al. (2014), Sekerka, Godwin et al. (2014).

L. E. Sekerka, *Ethics is a Daily Deal*, DOI 10.1007/978-3-319-18090-8_9

Moral Courage

The practice of courage is an important trait for organizational members (Verschoor 2003). It is a quality and attribute necessary for ethical behavior in organizational settings (Hesselbein 2005; Pears 2004). Employers assume that the managers they hire will exercise moral principles in accomplishing their performance goals. But each manager must determine how to establish the will to act and maintain that willingness as they traverse their management decisions with moral strength. If organizations expect managers to possess moral courage as a part of their professional role, we must explain, describe, and measure the ability.

The construct of courage has been explored in broad terms (Woodard and Pury 2007). Described as perseverance, authenticity and zest, courage has been depicted in multiple forms of bravery, both mental and physical (Peterson and Seligman 2004). However, our work looked directly at its management application. We wanted to understand the kind of moral courage needed for moral action, specifically what is necessary for managers to tackle their daily ethical challenges with fortitude. Some suggest that this may not be moral courage, but moral conduct. As described in Chaps. 7 and 8, there are countless influences in the ethical decision-making path that can derail a person's intent to act, including competing values, social norms, emotions, and higher-order decision-making processes (Sekerka and Bagozzi 2007; Steenhaut and Van Kenhove 2006). Managers do indeed act with professional moral courage if they can traverse this path with moral strength.

In consulting with the existing literature, we see a variety of detailed accounts of what it means to have moral courage. Aristotle (c350BC) set the stage for understanding the idea, considering it as both an ends and means toward creating comprehensive good (1999, NE 2.6.1103). In general, moral courage reflects a personal fortitude to face ethical issues, challenges, or dilemmas and to pursue virtuous action. This type of courage is not bravery in the sense of risking physical harm to rescue another living being. Cavanaugh and Moberg (1999) suggest that moral courage is the consideration of right and wrong, with a conscious choice to engage in doing moral good.

Other scholars describe moral courage as an ability to consistently make decisions in the light of what is good for others, despite the potential for personal risk. Kidder's (2005) treatise depicts moral courage as the "intersection between three conceptual fields: principles, danger, and endurance" (p. 73). Courage has also been highlighted as a management virtue (Harris 1999; Srivastva and Cooperrider 1998), with professional courage described as an attribute that motivates and enables individuals to take the right course of action, given the ethics of their profession (Sekerka and Zolin 2005). Viewed in the context of daily work performance, professional moral courage implies that it entails an active attempt to set and

Fig. 9.1 Putting a stop to unethical practices. Image credited to Tom Wang/Shutterstock.com

achieve ethical goals and make ethical choices. This can be viewed as challenging the status quo or putting a stop to current practices in the workplace (Fig. 9.1).

Although moral courage is needed in everyday tasks, those who speak up and out against wrongdoing may come to mind, when we consider exemplary character strength. People who demonstrate moral courage may lead others to fight for what's right, just and fair. Case in point, I was recently reminded of (Fig. 9.2) Lech Wałęsa's courageous fight to achieve labor rights in Poland. Known for his trade-union organizing and human-rights activism this legendary organizational leader shared insights with management scholars at the *European Academy of Management Annual Conference* (Warsaw, Poland, June 17, 2015). The former President of Poland and Laureate of the Nobel Peace Prize emphatically underscored the importance of moral values serving as the basis for management decision making. As the leader of *Solidarność*, Wałęsa insists that establishing a successful global economy calls for basing its existence upon universal values; that is, if it is to be productive, peaceful and lasting.

When studying moral courage, scholars often look at those who rise up against injustice as the focal point for inquiry (Miceli and Near 1984; Near and Miceli 1995; Nielsen 1989; Treviño and Victor 1992). Indeed, acts of valor like speaking truth to power, coalition building in the face of adversity and whistleblowing require moral courage (Grant 2002). However, it is also important to explore and consider moral courage as an everyday practical capability (Walton 1986), one that managers apply proactively (rather than reactively) to their regular activities. Such an approach to understanding everyday courage is essential if we hope to cultivate its application in routine work performance (Worline et al. 2002).

Fig. 9.2 Lech Wałęsa
addresses management
scholars. Image credited to
Leslie E. Sekerka, EURAM
annual conference, Warsaw,
Poland (2015)

To better understand what factors contribute to managers' ability to respond to ethical challenges, we needed to learn what helps them move toward a moral response and to sustain the will to behave ethically when facing external and internal influences. To address this concern, my colleagues and I launched a research and education program with the United States Navy, working to educate managers and develop tools for management development. The "Ethics in Action Program" was a formative stepping stone in guiding scholars and practitioners to a more proactive approach to organizational ethics, intended to foster moral strength as a management practice. An important objective of our work was, and continues to be, the advancement of an organizational ethics framework that integrates compliance- and value-based approaches.

Ethical Challenges at Work

The very concept of management emerged within the military, influencing the development of factory processes, and ultimately creating what we now refer to as public administration (Giddens 1981). While today's military and civilian organizations may differ somewhat in structure and culture, leadership is a common element. In the military, managers at every level are trained to consider leadership as part of their daily management responsibilities. This is often true in civilian organizations as well, but the military requires it. The traditional career track for military managers is to progress along a very structured leadership pipeline, which eventually extends to assuming an operational command.

From the first day of training, military managers (officers) are required to develop traits and behaviors for effective leadership to progress from performing a task-based job to managing others who perform these tasks (Bartone et al. 2007). The culture of the military places additional emphasis on continuous character development, complementing personal expertise, more so than many non-military organizations (Ulmer 2005; United States Navy core values http://www.navy.mil/navydata/navy_legacy_hr.asp?id=193). Military managers typically see themselves as being ethical, an essential starting point for learning more about how people think and reason when contemplating moral actions (Sekerka, Bagozzi et al. 2011, Sekerka, McCarthy et al. 2011).

Our training and research efforts were sponsored by the United States Naval Supply Corps, a department of the armed forces made up of approximately 3,500 officers who provide operational logistics and business management support to the Navy and their joint force operations. The "Ethics in Action Program" was an initiative targeted at middle management, with a goal to better understand what supports a manager's ability to engage in moral action in the course of conducting their daily tasks. As front-line supervisors, the leader-managers we studied face demanding challenges that cross hierarchical boundaries. Middle management is a unique layer within an organization. Individuals in this role must deal with concerns, issues, and dilemmas that involve people who are both junior and senior to them (Jick and Rosegrant 1993). In this position, these men and women observe the behavior of leaders and subordinates and, combined with their personal experience, hone management skill sets as they strive to progress professionally.

We began the study[1] using a modified version of the classic critical incident interview technique (Flanagan 1982). A group of managers engaged in the program were asked to recall an ethical issue, a specific event in which they faced a difficult situation at work, one that challenged their ability to proceed with moral action. After recalling the event, they were guided to add details, prompted by the following questions:

- What was the ethical challenge?
- At the time, what were you thinking and feeling?
- At the time, what supported or curtailed your ability to engage in moral action?
- What about senior management supported or curtailed your taking action?

One-on-one interviews produced 98 different scenarios, with incidents categorized and themed, resulting in three general areas of concern:

(1) Rule-bending to accomplish a task (29.3 %);
(2) Rule-bending to accommodate a senior officer's request (13.1 %); and
(3) Inappropriate use of funds or missing funds/resources (13.1 %)

---

[1]Elements of this research originally appeared in Sekerka, McCarthy et al. (2011).

Ethical Dilemma Types	Percentage
Rule-bending to accomplish a task	29.3
Rule-bending to accommodate senior management request	13.1
Inappropriate use of funds or missing funds/resources	13.1
Sexual activity	10.0
Stealing	8.1
Cheating/lying	8.1
Harassment	7.1
Drug or alcohol abuse	6.1
Payoffs, bribery, or inducements	5.1
	100.0

Fig. 9.3 Ethical dilemma types. Figure adapted from Sekerka, McCarthy et al. (2011)

Figures 9.3 and 9.4 outline the ethical dilemma types and descriptive accounts, examples, of the information that the managers shared.

From this initial inquiry, we learned that our manager participants responded to their ethical challenges in varying ways. Most people revealed a host of details related to their circumstances, providing insights around what fuels or curtails the desire to respond to an ethical challenge with character strength. Unexpectedly, we found that 42 % of the challenges were situations related to rule-bending. This suggests that when hierarchically driven organizations become heavily laden with rules, policies, and procedures, managers experience ethical challenges as they try to navigate compliance alongside their performance expectations.

With pressure to get the job done, meet target goals, and please superiors, ethics viewed as "the rules" can end up competing against the desire to be efficient, effective, and successful. Caught in a bind, some managers find themselves in situations that involve a great deal of tension. Many struggle with sorting out their competing values as they strive to be effective managers, team players, and responsible leaders. In such cases, managers often manufactured justifications and rationalizations to support a work-around or a rule-bending activity that helped them to achieve their performance goals. The term "rule-bending" as opposed to "rule-breaking" is often used as a way of dealing with this conflict.

While ethical action is an assumed aspect of management duties, there is also a high value placed on readiness, mission accomplishment, "zero-defect" operations, and having a "can-do" approach toward leadership commands (Sekerka et al. 2005). With the proliferation of rules, occasions may arise where rules and goals conflict, especially when compliance and orders are not congruent. Competing values may generate internal strife (Cameron and Quinn 2006), requiring professional courage in forming moral judgment and the intention to act. But no matter how difficult this may be, organizations rely upon managers to activate operational strategies that enable them to achieve their goals with moral strength. This can be especially

Type of Ethical Dilemma	Descriptive Explanation
Rule-bending	Work ethics and organizational duties compete for priority, with real or perceived pressure to go outside the confines of rules, regulations, or stated policies to achieve performance goals or supervisory demands. Referred to as rule-bending (as opposed to rule-breaking), a person moves to achieve a perceived justifiable goal (which may be directed by a higher level of authority), not adhering to the rules. For example, a manager was asked to use monies left over in one account (appropriated) to procure something else. While motives were framed as waste prevention and to prevent future budgetary reductions, the action was in violation of stated policies.
Stealing, lying, and cheating	A person is aware of money/property being inappropriately taken or used for personal gain. Goes beyond minor office supply theft, but about lying (collecting pay for time not worked) and stealing valuable property (for personal use or resale). Examples describe the challenge of knowing "at what point" to report other employees on their "use" of property (i.e., the line between misuse and stealing). Cheating emerges in broad ways, including employees sleeping on the job, time card fraud, taking unauthorized flex-time, cutting corners on contract specifications, and expense report padding.
Sexual activity	Intimidation, office liaisons, and viewing pornography in the workplace. Other examples, specifically in military settings, still reflect perceived concerns about homosexuality becoming deleterious to camaraderie and mission accomplishment.
Drugs and alcohol	Often described as "valued workers" coming to work hung over and smelling of alcohol. Uncertainty about what "crosses the line" in terms of impacting the ability to perform effectively, wanting to help someone, and knowing when to report the issue (especially when the person is your boss).
Bribery and corruption	The use of funds to accomplish a related performance goal, typically emerging in cross-cultural business interactions, where different social and work norms conflict or compete for supremacy. Examples range from small sums paid to get through customs quickly, to large amounts for building permits and unloading shipments in foreign ports of call.
Harassment	Involves intimidation, discrimination, and/or bullying behaviors. Includes inappropriate staring, use of crude language, or rude comments and verbal abuse. Present across gender combinations, with female bullying becoming more prevalent.

Fig. 9.4 Descriptive summaries for ethical dilemmas. Figure adapted from Sekerka, Bagozzi et al. (2011), Sekerka, McCarthy et al. (2011)

challenging for managers who face pressures to establish (Fig. 9.5) camaraderie and be team players, while also being responsible for bolstering morale within multiple hierarchical power structures.

Fig. 9.5 Military duty presents ethical dilemmas, where values compete for supremacy. Image courtesy of the Naval Postgraduate School

Features of Professional Moral Courage

Furthering this empirical research, additional analyses was conducted to explicate the term professional moral courage (PMC). The data gathered via the critical incident interviews were qualitatively analyzed to determine what best describes managers' behavior associated with moral strength. In general, the results portrayed managers who chose to proceed with moral action when facing an ethical challenge in possession of similar themes. Managers with PMC have learned how to deal with (put aside and/or draw upon) their fears or doubts, to help establish a more durable form of the will to proceed (with moral action) (Charlton 1988; Gosling 1990). Our efforts led to the identification of five core themes that were then distilled and ultimately validated, thereby representing the construct of PMC, stated as:

1. Moral Agency
2. Multiple Values
3. Endures Threat
4. Supersedes Compliance
5. Moral Goal

To better understand each element of PMC, let us now consider the specific meaning of each theme, with specific examples drawn from the research itself.

1. Moral Agency
Moral agency reflects a predisposition toward moral behavior and persistence of the will to engage. The use of your will implies the exertion of personal influence to achieve a goal. This theme reflects your individual initiative to consciously affect or

influence something through your actions or behavior. For those who choose to proceed with right action when facing an ethical challenge, moral agency is typically present. There is no surprise that managing with moral strength, PMC begins with wanting to be moral and having the desire to demonstrate this value with action. Moral agency is represented by an ongoing striving to do the right thing; not just with the stated circumstance, but continually and consistently in a person's everyday work life.

Kohlberg (1969) explained how moral reasoning is shaped by different levels of personal moral development. But even amongst the higher levels, moral agency is still challenging when decisions incorporate fiduciary responsibilities coupled with other organizational and personal interests. In management, having an ability to respond to a challenge with moral strength is a reflection of the person's broader assumption of moral responsibility. Because being responsible involves the potential for blame as well as praise, managers need a commitment to moral agency to sustain their willingness and resolve to proceed with moral action when deterrence may seem more attractive (or acting is problematic).

Managers who are moral responders are primed for engagement and show a consistency in striving toward right action or to achieve a moral good. These managers describe their immediate involvement and are ready to address the issue upon awareness. This does not mean immediate action, but it indicates a quick assumption of responsibility to manage ethical or moral matters. The capacity of responsibility and ownership of duty to act demonstrates a readiness to pursue moral decision-making as a matter of course. This suggests that these managers may be more likely to perceive ethical issues (than those who do not possess moral agency). Because managers with PMC view themselves as moral agents, they do not spend time trying to determine whether or not they should engage—they assume they will—then "get on with it." In taking ownership of the challenge automatically, seemingly as a matter of proper course, little time and energy is expended upon deciding whether or not to engage, as they move swiftly to resolve the matter.

In one scenario, a manager was being pressured to give away government property to a visiting dignitary. In this case, the manager viewed his reliability in right action as a part of his commitment to the organization and an element of his consistency as a trusted leader:

> The commitment is to lead by example and to learn all you can about a situation, and be consistent, and just really provide leadership from sunup to sundown. But it is a commitment...I wasn't about to break that trust. And that covenant. And the word covenant... meaning an agreement between two parties. I wasn't about to break that trust making an artificial scenario OK just because people wanted it for a PR ploy...my subordinates knew that I'd stand up for them, and I'd stand up for what was right.

The core elements of PMC include a stable pursuit of principled action. Managers seem to have made a personal commitment to themselves that they are moral agents and ethical leaders. This theme reflects an ability to be primed for engagement, possessing an automatic readiness to address the ethical challenge and a presumption of moral agency. Moral agency is represented by the following statements: *I am the type of person who is unfailing when it comes to doing the right thing at work*; *When I do my job I regularly take additional measures to ensure my actions reduce harms to others*; and *My work associates would describe me as someone who is always working to achieve ethical performance, making every effort to be honorable in all of my actions.*

2. Multiple values

Multiple values is the second theme, reflecting the importance of what defines "right" action (Davis and Frederick 1984). Sometimes referred to as values, principles are used to help people determine what is the ethical thing to do with regards to the goodness or badness of a judgment and/or response action. Individuals who proceed with right action will strive to consider what is good for others and what actions might help to support humanity, in the long run (Sekerka and Bagozzi 2006). This requires an internal decision and resolve to conform to the standards of right behavior as guided by character and conscience, influenced both by implicit and explicit criteria.

And yet, people are often guided to make judgments based on their personal convictions of what is considered right from their own perspectives. In examining the judgments made by managers with PMC, they appear to be informed by multiple value sets, including personal as well as professional and organizational values. Rather than acting only on physical evidence, perceived consequences, or in response to pressures, managers with PMC also apply a broad internal ethic to support their will to achieve moral good. Importantly, those who exercise moral strength work to align their personal, professional, and organizational principles of right and wrong as they strive to determine what to do (Carlson et al. 2002). In this effort, managers with PMC depend upon their cognitive and emotional schemas (Abelson 1981; Gioia and Poole 1984), which contribute to the development of internal scripts for their various roles. These scripts then help to support the application and use of principles and/or values ascribed to various value-identities (Gecas 2000) (Fig. 9.6).

Fig. 9.6 Undergraduates discuss their values and listen to a lecture on moral courage. Image credited to Leslie E. Sekerka

Managers who proceed with a moral response demonstrate an ability to draw upon value sets, such as those associated with their role as a manager, and their identity as a subordinate, friend, team member, husband (wife), father (mother), or son (daughter). In the process of proceeding toward right action, they often encounter social norms or pressures to conform, which may go against some of their value-identities. Moreover, some of their own internal scripts may conflict. Thus, managers who proceed with a moral response have the ability to sort out and determine value priorities and to hold firm to principles despite external pressures. For example, one manager describes how he felt pressured to do something against the rules in order to be regarded as a team player. He had to turn to his personal principles to determine what was right:

> That's what they were telling me up in the stateroom, and I understood that: you need to be a team player. And that's the truth, I need to be a team player, but NOT when there's an ethical situation of that nature on my mind. I'll be a team player as long as it doesn't compromise my integrity, and I have to purchase beyond what my ethical values can purchase....That means that I know in my mind that this was something that I should not be using those funds for.

Personal values can be complemented by professional and organizational values, extending one's value system (Rokeach 1977). Ethical codes are often superficially grafted onto a professional or organizational role without attending to their application (Potts and Matuszewski 2004). But managers who respond to ethical challenges with PMC adopt a variety of values as ascribed by multiple identities. While managers may be expected to incorporate professional and personal values into their decision-making rubric, those with PMC show a particular ability to petition a variety of value sets, and to combine and reconcile them. Being able to use and apply multiple value sets, this second theme refers to the application of principles from different perspectives.

Taken together, this theme reflects an ability to draw on multiple value sets in moral decision-making and to effectively sort out and determine what needs to be exercised, holding firm to previously held beliefs despite external pressures or demands. It is represented by the following statements: *I am the type of person who uses a guiding set of principles from the organization when I make ethical decisions on the job*; *No matter what, I consider how both organizational and personal values apply to the situation before making decisions*; and *When making decisions I often consider how my role in the organization and my upbringing must be applied to any final action.*

3. Endures threat

Endures threat, the third theme, reflects the notion that managers who face and address their ethical challenges experience perceived and real dangers, and must possess strength to overcome them. Those facing an ethical concern will likely face some level of threat, which is often accompanied by trepidation. Those with PMC endure this threat with self-determination. In facing an ethical challenge, a person's position, identity, and/or character may be put at risk. This can jeopardize a manager's status along with acceptance among peer groups and the broader organizational community. In some cases, stepping up to address an ethical challenge can put one's livelihood on the line. While ethical challenges do not typically require physical bravery, to the extent that PMC poses a threat to self, facing them often requires moral bravery. Moral responders are aware that their position, identity, or character may be at risk; however they deal with this by managing their negative emotions and the anxiety or doubt that comes with the territory. Interestingly, managers often acknowledge that their initial response may *not* be to take action. Yet, consciously or unconsciously, they apply self-regulation that helps them proceed despite a potential reluctance to do so.

The reality is, for most managers, PMC is unlikely to be an instinctive or natural automatic response. Based on its difficulty, it requires deliberate practice. To sustain the effort, standing up to an ethical challenge, managers need to be aware that their initial response may in fact not be the desire to act. In other words, people with PMC do not necessarily feel like "stepping up to the plate" (hence the importance of the first theme, forming a preestablished commitment to moral agency). To garner the requisite desire, they learn to look to some other aspect of their moral identity for the motivation to act (Whitbourne 1986). For example, saying to themselves, "This is what my father would expect of me," "This is what good leaders do," "I want my daughter to know her mother is worthy of my respect," or "This is how my friend Rick or Jennifer would go about addressing this situation" (i.e., trusted colleagues) (hence the importance of the second theme, drawing upon multiple value sets).

Moral strength is not saved up, preserved for that big or special ethical event. Consistency of morality is essential to human flourishing (Miller 2005). As Solomon suggests, moral courage is consistently doing what one knows one ought to do (1998). This mantra is often augmented by internal affirmations like, "even if I don't want to," "no matter what," or "regardless of what happens." As individuals work to address their daily tasks, they must build fortitude through habits that support responsibility, moral endurance, and reliability. It is a routine effort to maintain and fortify ethical thoughts and actions. Over time, practice can become embraced as a more durable value or trait, making ethical responses feel more natural and automatic. Therefore, when the difficult ethical challenge emerges, there have been pre-rehearsed efforts to be ethical, which can then give the manager a "running start" at being ethical, even in the face of threat.

The crucial nature of continual practice is underscored when facing ethical challenges. At some point the situation may require character strength. People can be challenged by circumstances where they have to defy convention or authority. Learning how to speak truth to power (O'Toole 2008), requires an ability to persist, in spite of one's fear (Rachman 1990). This can be particularly important in hierarchical organizations, where power may be exerted in ways that curtail empowerment (via control and limited inclusion). Principles of duty in some organizations include adherence to upper-level leadership. One manager described this difficulty as:

...it was kind of like a no-man's land. Until he'd (commanding officer) made that decision not to go out, it was kind of lonely. Yeah, definitely it's not a comfortable zone to be in. But going back to what I said about having a feeling that I was grounded in...I was on solid ground in the decision I made...by the same token, if it presented itself, I thought I could probably make a similar decision.

As ethical situations unfold, managers must endure and sustain their willingness to proceed, dealing with their negative and/or self-conscious emotions and the internal strife that may emerge. Managers with PMC have an ability to be "out on a limb," being alone with their decision or action, and holding firm in their resolve to do the right thing, even when it feels like they are on their own. As managers balance their desire to proceed with moral action with other competing instincts to survive (e.g., keep one's job), they have learned to bolster their motivations to proceed. It is likely that routine efforts to maintain this willingness to proceed comes from exercising self-regulation daily (see Chap. 10). In this way, moral responders continue to work on and build up their will to act, and thus making the trait more durable over time. Acting in the face of threat or fear can be particularly relevant in hierarchical organizations, where principles of duty include adherence to upper-level senior authority (Directors, Vice Presidents, Presidents, CFOs, CEOs, etc.).

As appropriately described by Rate et al. (2007), a person who exercises a moral response is unlikely to be fearless, but knows how to endure threat. Managers who proceed with a moral response seem to expect that their effort could "cost" them something (loss in status, social connections, etc.) and they accept this from the onset (again, the pre-commitment having been made to moral agency; the first theme). In general, managers with PMC appear to have previously determined that the value of being ethical outweighs a pending personal sacrifice (Hannah et al. 2007; Goud 2005). Along with enduring the fear of retaliation, one manager expressed that the dread of alienation is present when reporting unethical activities. He suggests that the perception of such a threat can, however, be overcome in a supportive organizational culture:

I think people will be more hesitant to report unethical situations for fear of, like I said, repercussions, or alienation. And so what I mean by command climate is that if your command, in the last example I gave, is very supportive on ethical issues, and in doing the right thing because it's the right thing all the time, I think you're going to find more people inclined to report unethical issues.

Taken together, endures threat, the third theme, is represented by the following statements: *When I encounter an ethical challenge I take it on with moral action, regardless of how it may negatively impact how others see me; When my job record may be affected negatively, I am still likely to get involved with an ethical challenge;* and *I am the type of person who is willing to bring an ethical issue forward.*

4. Supersedes compliance

Supersedes compliance describes the fourth theme, depicting how managers take a proactive ethical approach, going beyond avoidance of unethical behavior to achieve moral action. Regulation theory (Higgins 1998, 2000) has been used to

Fig. 9.7 Legal mandates are
a moral minimum,
professional moral courage
supersedes compliance. Image
courtesy of FreeImage.com

show how individual and organizational regulation orientations can be identified
(Sekerka and Zolin 2005). As applied to moral behavior, a prevention focus works
to safeguard against failure, to ensure safety, and to address duty and responsibilities to maintain order and stability.

While this approach is essential to establish norms, create order, and to exert
control to prevent unethical behavior in organizational settings, it is unlikely to help
you achieve moral courage in daily task actions. A proactive approach or promotion
focus, one that incorporates moral aspirations in goal pursuit, may help support the
will to engage toward values-driven achievement that advances moral good. One
manager's account reflects how perceptions of impropriety are of concern, thinking
about how things might look to others. This concern is combined with an aspirational goal to be a steward of the public's trust (as a government employee). He is
cautious, wanting to play it safe, staying above the moral line:

> I looked at the spirit of the rules and regulations in my position as a steward of the public
> trust…and in a larger atmosphere, where the contract was coming due for renegotiation,
> and putting all the pieces together. Again, it was a stretch…could this have all been totally
> innocent? Absolutely. But in that specific point in time, I weighed the balance of
> appearance of impropriety versus hey, let's just play it safe.

The ethical character of an organization is shaped by the people who work there.
In metaphorical terms the organization is sometimes referred to as the "barrel,"
providing a context or container for workplace behavior (Treviño and Youngblood
1990). But it is also the character of the "apples" in that barrel, in particular,
management, who have a compelling influence on the ethical health of day-to-day
operations and in shaping the barrel itself (its ethical stability). Research conducted
by the Ethics Resource Center reflects that a staggering number of employees still
observe misconduct at work (45 %) and a disconcerting number of employees
report feeling pressure to compromise their ethical standards to achieve their performance goals (13 %) (ERC 2012). Regulations intended to bolster organizational
ethics have had some success. Yet efforts to go beyond compliance are needed, as
pointed out by a review team who examined the impact of the Federal Sentencing

Guidelines, since the legislation's inception twenty years ago.[2] Key areas for organizational ethics clearly remain at issue, specifically with regards to how compliance programs fall short. A "check-the-box" approach remains the norm. However, we know that "going through the motions" does not create a culture of moral strength (ERC 2012).

Recommendations entail directives imposed by the Department of Justice and Congress (among other entities), (Fig. 9.7) but the review also strongly advises that the private sector do more than adhere to legislative requirements, directing leaders to impose greater diligence toward the *spirit* of the standards, not just a surface approach via box-checking activities. The report suggests this begins by "defining the mission of a company as comprising both strong financial performance and a strong commitment to integrity...boards of directors and senior executives should demand compliance/ethics programs that are effective in preventing and detecting misconduct and help build ethical and law-abiding cultures" (p. 13, 2012). By implication, this underscores the need for managers to raise the bar for their own ethical best practices.

Slowly but surely, managers, practitioners, and scholars alike are realizing that compliance-driven approaches can help people become aware of the rules, but they do not cultivate, support, or build the competency necessary for moral strength (Morales-Sánchez and Cabello-Medina 2013). People can fall short of the moral baseline when ethics relies upon regulation alone. It has become clearer why management must develop workplace environments that complement compliance with moral strength. Managers with PMC establish a healthier and more robust form of workplace ethics, going beyond compliance.

As expressed by one manager, he describes how he took action in accordance with regulations, even though his actions went against social norms, in addressing a senior officer engaged in an extramarital affair:

> Lead by example. Compliance with Navy regulations. Obviously, stopping this inappropriate behavior...it could have been an example for the rest of the ship that we will not tolerate this type of behavior...and perhaps it did break their relationship up and maybe I saved some people's marriages.

Interestingly, we also see a keen understanding among managers with PMC that both the spirit and letter of the law have relevant value. As one manager reflects on his own thought process, he looked to the rules, but also to the basis of their intent, in concert with his own principles. Also recognizing that perceptions of impropriety matter, this manager describes how he had to challenge authority :

> Look at the situation, look at the spirit of the rules and regulations. In my position as a steward of the public trust, what is the spirit of the entire thing look like? I wasn't doubting the commanding officer's ethics and morals. This wasn't a personal attack, this was the appearance of impropriety...I made that point to him (commanding officer) when I presented my case.

---

[2]For more information see http://www.ussc.gov/Guidelines/.

Fig. 9.8 Moral strength requires critical refection. Image credited to Gajus/Shutterstock.com

Managers who proceed with a moral response to an ethical challenge maintain a proactive approach to workplace ethics. Although it may seem proactive to strive to prevent unethical behavior, the focus is still on controlling the negative. Those who demonstrate PMC also exercise a promotion orientation, one that leverages moral aspiration. With this perspective, managers support their will to engage in values-driven achievement, while also attending to the intent (spirit) of the regulations designed to prevent wrongdoing. Moral responders incorporate concerns about compliance but also move to achieve their ethical ideals. These managers not only consider the rules, but reflect upon their purpose, going beyond compliance-based measures to consider what is right, just, and appropriate. This can take some extra time, which often requires patience, both with yourself and others (Comer and Sekerka 2014) (Fig. 9.8).

Taken together, this theme was represented by the following statements: *My coworkers would say that when I do my job I do more than follow the regulations, I do everything I can to ensure actions are morally sound*; *When I go about my daily tasks I make sure to comply with the rules, but also look to understand their intent, to ensure that this is being accomplished as well*; and *It is important that we go beyond the legal requirements, seeking to accomplish our tasks with ethical judgment and action.*

5. Moral goal

Moral goal represents the fifth and final theme to describe PMC. This addresses how making a decision to engage and establishing movement to accomplish the goal of action is driven by virtuous ends (Kateb 2004). Managers who engage in a moral response are driven by more than task accomplishment. They use virtues (e.g., prudence, honesty, and justice) throughout the decision-making process to achieve a moral goal. This involves the use of goal-setting strategies to achieve a solution that resolves the issue, while also being mindful of the broader or greater good. This typically involves a consideration of peers, subordinates, upper management, the organization, and some larger entity (e.g., the United States Constitution, taxpayers, or the environment).

Moral responders have goals that go beyond self-serving interests that influence the formation of their moral judgment. This desire to "do good" often extends the issue itself; that is, the manager views the challenge as part of a larger constellation of concerns. Moreover, managers with PMC seem to understand that how they respond *each* time, over time, is important, as this builds a profile of their ethicality (moral identity). We found that managers who proceed with right action via moral strength reflect intentions that show respect and consideration for others and the larger whole, which transcend self-interest. This suggests that the goal is based on a more substantive application of virtues in action.

One manager describes an ethical challenge of how to address his concern regarding the senior officer's apparent drinking problem. He explains his thought process in forming a plan for action:

> I was thinking about he could possibly put himself or others into danger, compromise safety...he might have an accident...hurt himself, hurt any people. I felt that I had to do something....(reporting the commanding officer) was obviously good leadership, lead(ing) by example, possibly it saved this individual's life, and other people. It brought the awareness that this does occur, and that there is a mechanism in place to report. I didn't do this for personal gain, I did it to help the individual. I felt that he did have an urgent problem, and maybe he didn't know how to get help...I think as they progressed through their Naval careers, maybe, when faced with a similar situation, would be able to possibly handle this, or not feel like there would be repercussions if they reported it.

Here, the manager tries to examine his motives to discern how he can best help the person in need (his boss). He checks his intentions and reasoning, as well as the longer-term issues at play. As outlined by this example and many others, managers who engage in PMC do so with right motives and deal with it as a goal-setting and - striving process. Their intentions are based on substantive virtues and moral goals. As with moral agency, the first theme, managers who are moral responders are primed for engagement and show a consistency in striving toward right action or to achieve a moral good. This also supports a feedback loop, as depicted in the ethical decision-making process (refer to Fig. 8.3), i.e., the manager wants to achieve a moral goal, which then supports ethical awareness, which is a feature of being a moral agent.

Managers with PMC move to address their moral goal by looking for the ethical elements of situations, even before ethical issues emerge. When problems do arise, they consider how others might view the situation. For example, people who proceed with moral action when facing an ethical challenge think about the big picture, concerns outside of their own immediate needs. This means toggling between personal values and respect for others, while also working to see the bigger picture. One manager describes how he envisioned the situation from outside the immediate circumstances, considering how it might appear to others:

I was relatively new on board. So who was I to say…? I sort of put that behind me and went forward. I kind of used a past incident in addition to the training that we received, to again ground myself to consider the appearance of impropriety, and yeah, that's enough. I needed to bring it (the ethical concern) up to the skipper. So I just sort of took it and processed it in my mind. And said, if anybody was external to the situation, that could see all the factors, what would they see?

The volition in this account appears to be part of a constant striving to do the right thing or to achieve moral good on a broader level. Managers with PMC are able to consider the past, present, and future, envisioning what potential actions might convey to others. Such determination is vital if the person is to sustain motivation toward ethical action as a goal.

When courage, as a voluntary act (Shelp 1984), is linked with morality (the Latin root *mor* meaning custom, habit, or practice), the importance of its routine nature is revealed. By making one's "will to proceed" a habit, it can potentially become a standard practice. As discussed previously, habituated deliberate practice of right action as a personal goal can eventually become more automatic. Taking this information together, addressing a moral goal is a theme expressed by these statements: *It is important for me to use prudential judgment in making decisions at work*; *I think about my motives when achieving the mission, to ensure they are based upon moral ends*; and *When engaged in action, I consider how virtuous (or sound) my motives are as I move to accomplish an ethical objective.*

Additional Insights

We used the five core themes that emerged from the qualitative analysis as the starting point for the development of a tool (scale) to measure professional moral courage (PMC). The next step was to draw from the existing literature to further develop these themes. Analyzing the prior scholarship on moral courage, ethical/moral decision-making, and virtue excellence in the workplace gave us the opportunity to add additional statements, offering more clarity and richness to the descriptive items (Sekerka et al. 2009).

Moral agency—specifically the kind needed by managers facing daily ethical challenges—is an effort which is not synonymous with rash or overconfident behavior in response to danger. Rather, it is a self-directed effort that works "toward the good" (Harris 2000) or "at what is right and moral" (Pury et al. 2007). Woodard and Pury (2007) suggest that courageous efforts have a purpose or a goal to do what one thinks is right or necessary. If the manager is motivated to do good, such behaviors are exemplified in a person's regular daily actions (Gioia and Poole 1984). In other words, the person models moral strength in their work routines. Harris (2000) suggests that practicing and modeling courageous behavior is important for the development of courage in organizations. Kidder (2005, p. 214) explicitly identifies "modeling and mentoring" as one of the modes of learning and teaching in his paradigm for moral courage (Fig. 9.9).

Fig. 9.9 A military officer affirms his commitment to moral agency in daily decisions. Image courtesy of the Naval Postgraduate School

In this same vein, PMC is not a resource that one occasionally draws on in a rare or difficult situation, but is a sustained effort that conveys an ongoing sense of seeking (Harris 2000). Kidder (2005, p. 172) emphasizes that our intuition can be improved through practice, so that the "spontaneity of our gut impulse [i.e., initial inclination to do what is right] grows increasingly sure-footed and reliable." In fact, "practice and persistence" constitute another aspect of this paradigm (p. 214). Taken together, the following statements describe moral agency: *Others can rely on me to exemplify moral behavior; I am determined to do the right thing*; and *Engaging in principled action is an ongoing pursuit for me*.

Managers must apply principles of right and wrong to determine what action is appropriate (Carlson et al. 2002). Hence, the determination of what is "right" must involve multiple values, but does this mean multiple personal values? Whose values are we referencing? Naturally, people draw upon their personal values endorsed by experiential learning. In fact, courageous actions actually move or work to affirm truths about one's self and one's own beliefs (Woodard and Pury 2007). However, the values of those around us must also be considered. While some values and the relative importance attached to them can vary across demographic and geographic boundaries (Kidder 2005), others, such as honesty, fairness, respect, responsibility, and compassion have universal appeal. And yet, the application of this shared belief may vary widely, according to cultural interpretations (Sekerka, Marar Yacobian et al. 2014, Sekerka, Godwin et al. 2014). Moreover, our role and the organization where we work can foster specific values associated with our profession and industry sector.

Clearly, ethical behavior can be inspired by a variety of value sets. But for values to be applied they must be grounded in one's view of morality (Higgins and Currie 2004). This suggests that an organization can promote PMC by reminding managers of their obligation as organizational members and management professionals, along with their responsibility to the larger community (Harris 2000). The above concerns are summarized by McBeath and Webb (2002), who state that recognizing virtue is not as simple as following a system of rules but rather involves a "grasping of the interplay between self, others, and environment." The literature added depth to our statements to describe multiple values, adding: *I draw on my personal values to help determine what is right*; *I draw on the values of those around me to help determine what is right*; and *I draw on my professional values to help determine what is right*.

Woodard and Pury's (2007) description of courageous behavior suggests that it is far more complex than a simple characterization of a response to a threat faced by an actor. That said, it is generally accepted that courageous people require hardiness and determination to achieve their goal (Woodard 2004). For example, a person may have to go against social norms or expectations (Woodard 2004) or face an element of social disapproval (Woodard and Pury 2007). This ability to endure despite fear (Rachman 1990) is particularly important in hierarchical organizations, where principles of duty include adherence to upper-level command. Another possibility, perhaps the most obvious challenge to moral courage, is that one may lose something essential, important, or desirable such as a job, esteem, or self-respect (if proceeding with moral strength). Kidder (2005) makes this point by posing the following question: "How many employees [in] global firms that have endured moral implosions ... had to choose between paying their bills and sounding the alarms [to their superiors]?" (p. 135). To augmenting the theme "endures threat" in facing and addressing an ethical challenge, we therefore added: *I hold my ground on moral matters even if there are opposing social pressures*; *I act morally even if it puts me in an uncomfortable position with my superiors*; and *I am not swayed from acting morally by fear and other negative feelings*.

While rules and regulations set forth by the manager's profession and organization serve as a guide for ethical behavior in task actions, a compliance-based approach to achieve a moral good or right action is not sufficient to inform PMC. Solomon (1998) argues that moral psychology is not limited to "bloodless [legal] concepts of obligation, duty, responsibility, and rights," while Higgins and Currie (2004) assert that organizations and their members must meet ethical obligations to clients, investors, and the community at large. McBeath and Webb (2002) argue that compliance may even create impediments in the path of moral decision-making, explaining that current trends present a more defensive decision-making strategy. People tend to adopt action tendencies that present minimal risk exposure, while still adhering to procedures.

As previously stated, PMC is viewed as a process of values and character strengths in action. The traits that support such behavior have the potential to be developed in most people. While Solomon (1998) does not frame courage as a character trait, he supports the notion of moral courage entailing concrete actions. Harris (2000) affirms this notion by similarly describing courage in the workplace as a path from thought to action. Kidder (2005) describes this thought-action in competency-like terms when he states that a person must "go out of his [or her] way to be responsible [and exhibit moral courage]," (p. 197) explaining that courage in the workplace calls us to "step firmly up to the decision-making process rather than duck responsibility" (p. 251). Taken together, this informs the basis for going beyond or superseding compliance, adding several other statements to this theme: *I proactively aspire to behave* morally; *For me, doing what is right is not the same as avoiding what is wrong; and I consider more than rules and regulations in deciding what is right.*

Principled performance includes an aspiration to achieve and the condition of virtuousness, as manifest by accomplishing some form of greater good (Bright et al. 2004). It is a form of unconditional regard that can generate heightened moral awareness. But what drives a person to want to engage in moral action? Perhaps it is based on some deep-rooted impulsion, described by Kidder (2005) as the firmness of a moral principle, one's duty, private convictions, a desire to reject evil conformity, to denounce injustice, or to defy immoral orders. Such desires are driven by virtuous motives, not self-serving ones. Even if personal desires creep in, when PMC is "exercised in conjunction with other virtues such as wisdom and justice" (Harris 2000), self-serving motives can be countered (Solomon 1998).

Woodard (2004) observes that courage requires more than acting despite a perception of vulnerability; it involves grace, nobility, credibility, sensibility, practicality, and meaningfulness. McBeath and Webb (2002) add that virtue is often linked to the phrase "doing the right thing" because those with PMC are likely to have a conscience about what they should do when constraints imposed by weaker values or reasons actually oppose or thwart the action informed by virtue. Taken together, these considerations inform the final elements, which address working to achieve a moral goal, stated as: *When I act morally, my motives are virtuous; I act morally because it is the right thing to do*; and *When I act morally, I do not need to be praised and recognized for it.*

A Definition and Scale

As a result of this scholarship, the definition of professional moral courage is marked by the presence of five elements:

1. **Moral Agency**: possesses a predisposition to be a moral agent;
2. **Multiple Values**: uses multiple value sets to determine moral action;
3. **Endures Threat**: faces danger or threat, yet pursues moral action;
4. **Supersedes Compliance**: applies rules but also goes beyond compliance to consider what is right, just, good and appropriate; and
5. **Moral Goal**: moves to complete tasks with the application of moral principles to achieve a moral outcome.

Drawing from the items derived from field research and fortified by the extant literature, we tested and validated each statement, ultimately forming a final scale. The instrument to measure professional moral courage (see Appendix), has been used in a variety of studies to better understand moral strength in organizational settings (Harbour and Kisfalvi 2014; Hannah et al. 2011).

Fig. 9.10 Similar to emergency responders, ethical agents know they will proceed with right action. First responders from St. John ambulance and local fire departments assist paramedics during an exercise near Thunder Bay, Ontario, Canada (November, 2008). Image courtesy of Frmatt

If we hope to reach the highest levels of organizational performance, we must understand the factors that foster people's abilities to respond to challenges with courage and to inspire others to broaden their capacity for moral agency (Woreline et al. 2002). For PMC to be developed as a managerial practice, the features of moral strength must be applied in daily routines, with top executives relinquishing control, risking the release of moral capacity and responsibility throughout the organization, at every level, trusting that when given a platform of ethical excellence, employees will choose to do the right thing when given the chance (Quinn and Spreitzer 1997).

To cultivate proactive organizational ethics, managers can expand their views to include moral courage as a professional goal. A framework for this approach depicts how managers need to go beyond the moral minimum to demonstrate moral strength (refer to Fig. 6.6). This calls for treating PMC in moral decision-making and action as a practical ideal. Organizations can influence management norms, which can ultimately affect how others will respond to ethical challenges in the workplace. While managers are responsible for developing their will to proceed and acting with moral strength, establishing contexts that encourage people to exercise their character strengths must be supported through education and training and performance reward systems. Having created a rich definition of the behavior, this research helped to determine what specific skills are associated with the capacity to address an ethical challenge with professional moral courage. These skills, also known as moral competencies, are tools for building moral strength. But before we discuss them in greater detail, it is important to consider the power of your potential —choosing to be your best self.

In the next chapter, we consider how your moral courage at work means being a moral agent, even before an ethical challenge or opportunity emerges. Like emergency responders, people and organizations need to determine their ethicality before an issue even emerges (Fig. 9.10). People need to decide if they are a person who engages in moral action, making a decision to be that type of person, even before an ethical event occurs. Relying upon an assumption that you will rise to the occasion and be ethical is a bit risky. If you do not build your moral strength, how do you know it will be there when you need it? In order to bolster your ability to proceed with right action, organizational members need to incorporate moral agency as an intrinsic feature of their professional identity. In so doing, they naturally alter the initial questions they ask themselves when facing an ethical challenge. Rather than getting stuck on the question, "Should I respond to this issue?" you ask, "What is the right thing to do in this circumstance?"

If you want to build moral muscle, so that when you face an ethical challenge you have an ability to withstand the negative forces that make it difficult to endure, you will need specific skills. What competencies or tools actually support the ability to engage in professional moral courage? A more focused examination of these skills, referred to as personal governance, can be learned, honed, and edified. Through regular use of the moral competencies, most people can develop moral strength.

Takeaway Points

1. Some organizations inadvertently support rule-bending behavior, especially when policies conflict with the ability to achieve performance goals.
2. People with professional moral courage work at being ethical—it takes practice.
3. Professional moral courage consists of moral agency, use of multiple values sets, ability to endure threat to self, going beyond compliance, and possessing and sustaining a moral goal.

Reflection Questions

Fill out the PMC scale (save your score). When you get to the end of this book, wait a week and then fill it out again (without looking at your original answers). Why do you think your score stayed the same, went up or down? How do you plan to build your moral muscle?

Appendix

Professional Moral Courage Scale[a]						
Never		Sometimes			Always	
1	2	3	4	5	6	7

Evaluate the statements as they pertain to you at work, from 1 (never true) to 7 (always true).

Theme 1

_____ 1. I am the type of person who is unfailing when it comes to doing the right thing at work.
_____ 2. When I do my job I regularly take additional measures to ensure my actions reduce harm to others.
_____ 3. My work associates would describe me as someone who is always working to achieve ethical performance, making every effort to be honorable in all my actions.

Theme 2

_____ 4. I am the type of person who uses a guiding set of principles from the organization when I make ethical decisions on the job.
_____ 5. No matter what, I consider how both my organization's values and my personal values apply to the situation before making decisions.
_____ 6. When making decisions, I often consider how values, based upon my role in the organization, my boss's ethical concerns (supervisor or leader), and upbringing are applied to any final action.

Theme 3

_____ 7. When I encounter an ethical challenge I take it on with moral action, regardless of how it may pose a negative impact on how others see me.
_____ 8. I hold my ground on moral matters, even if there are opposing social pressures.
_____ 9. I act morally even if it puts me in an uncomfortable position with my superiors.

Theme 4

_____ 10. My coworkers would say that when I do my job I do more than follow the regulations; I do everything I can to ensure my actions are morally sound.
_____ 11. When I go about my daily tasks I make sure to comply with the rules, but also look to understand their intent, to ensure that this is being accomplished as well.
_____ 12. It is important that I go beyond the legal requirements, seeking to accomplish tasks with ethical action as well as compliance.

Theme 5

_____ 13. It is important for me to use prudential judgment in making decisions at work.
_____ 14. I think about my motives when achieving the mission, to ensure they are based upon moral ends.
_____ 15. I act morally because it is the right thing to do.

Suggested scoring:

1) For each dimension: Add scores for each dimension (3 questions) and ÷ 3.
2) For overall PMC: Add the question scores (15 questions) and ÷ 15.

[a] The scale was adapted from Sekerka, Bagozzi and Charnigo 2009 and is registered with the American Psychological Association PsycTESTS as an empirically validated scale (Sekerka et al. 2011).

References

Abelson, R. P. (1981). Psychological status of the script concept. *American Psychologist, 36*, 715–729.

Aristotle [350BC]. (1999). *Nicomachean ethics*. T. Irwin (Trans.) Indianapolis, IN: Hackett Publishing Co.

Bartone, P. T., Snook, S. A., Forsyth, G. B., Lewis, P., & Bullis, R. C. (2007). Psychological development and leader performance of military officer cadets. *The Leadership Quarterly, 18*, 490–504.

Bright, D. S., Cameron, K., & Caza, A. (2004). Exploring the relationships between organizational virtuousness and performance. *American Behavioral Scientist, 46*, 766–790.

Cameron, K. S., & Quinn, R. E. (2006). *Diagnosing and changing organizational culture: Based upon the competing values framework.* San Francisco, CA: Jossey-Bass.

Carlson, D. S., Kacmar, K. M., & Wadsworth, L. L. (2002). The impact of moral intensity dimensions on ethical decision making: Assessing the relevance of orientation. *Journal of Managerial Issues, 14*(1), 15–31.

Cavanaugh, G. F., & Moberg, D. J. (1999). The virtue of courage within the organization. In M. L. Pava & P. Primeaus (Eds.), *Research in ethical issues in organizations, 1* (pp. 1–25). Greenwich, CT: JAI Press.

Charlton, W. (1988). *Weakness of will.* Oxford: Basil Blackwell.

Comer, D., & Sekerka, L. E. (2014). Taking time for patience: Recognizing, respecting, and reclaiming an undervalued virtue. *Journal of Management Development, 33*(1), 6–23.

Davis, M. A., & Frederick, W. C. (1984). *Business and society: Management, public policy, ethics* (5th ed.). New York: McGraw-Hill.

Ethics Resource Center. (2012). *The federal sentencing guidelines for organizations at twenty years.* Arlington, VA: ERC.

Flanagan, J. C. (1982). The critical incident technique. *Psychological Bulletin, 4*, 327–358.

Gecas, V. (2000). Value identities, self-motives, and social movements. In S. Stryker, T. J. Owens, & R. W. White (Eds.), *Self, identity, and social movements* (pp. 93–109). Minneapolis, MN: University of Minnesota Press.

Giddens, A. (1981). A Contemporary Critique of Historical Materialism. *Social and Politic Theory from Polity Press 1.* Berkeley, CA: University of California Press.

Grant, C. L. (2002). Whistleblowers: Saints of secular culture. *Journal of Business Ethics, 39*(4), 391–400.

Gosling, J. C. B. (1990). *Weakness of will (The problems of philosophy).* London: Routledge.

Goud, N. H. (2005). Courage: Its nature and development. *Journal of Humanistic Counseling, Education, and Development, 44*, 102–116.

Hannah, S. T., Avolio, B. J., & Walumbwa, F. O. (2011). Relationships between authentic leadership, moral courage, and ethical and pro-social behaviors. *Business Ethics Quarterly, 21* (4), 555–578.

Hannah, S. T., Sweeney, P. J., & Lester, P. B. (2007). Toward a courageous mindset: The subjective act and experience of courage. *The Journal of Positive Psychology, 2*(2), 129–135.

Harbour, M., & Kisfalvi, V. (2014). In the eye of the beholder: An exploration of managerial courage. *Journal of Business Ethics, 119*, 493–515.

Harris, H. (2000). *Courage as a management virtue.* Paper presented at the Association for Practical and Professional Ethics, 9th Annual Meeting, (Arlington, VA).

Harris, H. (1999). Courage as a management virtue. *Business & Professional Ethics Journal, 18* (3/4), 27–46.

Hesselbein, F. (2005). The leaders we need. *Leader to Leader, 35*, 4–6.

Higgins, E. T. (1998). Promotion and prevention: Regulatory focus as a motivational principle. In M. P. Zanna (Ed.), *Advances in experimental psychology, 30* (pp. 1–46). San Diego, CA: Academic Press.

Higgins, E. T. (2000). Making a good decision: Value from fit. *American Psychologist, 55*(11), 1217–1230.

Higgins, J. M., & Currie, D. M. (2004). It's time to rebalance the scorecard. *Business and Society Review, 109*(3), 297–310.

Jick, T. D., & Rosegrant, S. (1993). Three in the middle: The experience of making change at Micro Switch. *Harvard Online,.* doi:10.1225/491022.

Kateb, G. (2004). Courage as a virtue. *Social Research, 71*, 39–72.

Kidder, R. M. (2005). *Moral courage.* New York: HarperCollins.

Kohlberg, L. (1969). Stage and sequence: The cognitive development approach to socialization, In D. Goslin (Ed.), *Handbook of socialization theory and research*: 347–480. Chicago: Rand McNally.

Miller, R. (2005). *Moral courage: Definition and development*. Washington, DC: Ethics.

Morales-Sánchez, R., & Cabello-Medina, C. (2013). The role of four universal moral competencies in ethical decision-making. *Journal of Business Ethics, 116*(4), 717–734.

McBeath, G., & Webb, S. A. (2002). Virtue ethics and social work: Being lucky, realistic, and not doing one's duty. *British Journal of Social Work, 32*, 1015–1036.

Miceli, M. P., & Near, J. P. (1984). The relationships among beliefs, organizational position, and whistle-blowing status: A discriminant analysis. *Academy of Management Journal, 27*(4), 687–806.

Near, J. P., & Miceli, M. P. (1995). Effective whistle-blowing. *Academy of Management Review, 20*(3), 679–709.

Nielsen, R. P. (1989). Changing unethical organizational behavior. *Academy of Management Executive, 3*(2), 123–131.

O'Toole, J. (2008). Speaking truth to power. In Warren Bennis, Daniel Goleman, & James O'Toole (Eds.), *Transparency: How leaders create a culture of candor* (pp. 45–92). San Francisco, CA: Jossey-Bass.

Pears, D. (2004). The anatomy of courage. *Social Research, 71*(1), 1–12.

Peterson, C., & Seligman, M. E. P. (2004). *Character strengths and virtues: A classification and handbook*. Washington, D. C.: American Psychological Association.

Potts, S. O., & Matuszewski, I. L. (2004). Ethics and corporate governance. *Corporate Governance, 12*(2), 177.

Pury, C. L. S., Kowalski, R. M., & Spearman, J. (2007). Distinctions between general and personal courage. *Journal of Positive Psychology, 2*, 99–114.

Quinn, R. E., & Spreitzer, G. M. (1997). The road to empowerment: Seven questions every leader should consider. *Organizational Dynamics*, Autumn, 37–49.

Rachman, S. J. (1990). *Fear and courage* (2nd ed.). New York: W. H. Freeman and Company.

Rate, C. R., Clarke, J. A., Lindsay, D. R., & Sternberg, R. J. (2007). Implicit theories of courage. *Journal of Positive Psychology, 2*, 80–98.

Rokeach, M. (1977). *The nature of human values*. New York: McGraw-Hill.

Sekerka, L. E., & Bagozzi, R. P. (2006). Moral courage in the workplace: Self-regulation as the cornerstone to virtuous action. In A. Delle Fave (Ed.), *Dimensions of well-being: Research and Intervention*: 226–240. Milano, Italy: FrancoAngeli.

Sekerka, L. E., & Bagozzi, R. P. (2007). Moral courage in the workplace: Moving to and from the desire and decision to act. *Business Ethics: A European Review, 16*, 132–149.

Sekerka, L. E., Bagozzi, R. P., & Charnigo, R. (2009). Facing ethical challenges in the workplace: Conceptualizing and measuring professional moral courage. *Journal of Business Ethics, 89*(4), 565–579.

Sekerka, L. E., Bagozzi, R. P., & Charnigo, R. (2011). Professional moral courage scale (revised form, 3/21/11). *PsycTESTS*. Washington, D.C.: American Psychological Association.

Sekerka, L. E., Marar Yacobian, M., & Stimel, D. (2014). Business ethics in a transnational economy: Embracing the tribal-collectivist perspective. *Global Business & Economics Anthology*.

Sekerka, L. E., Godwin, L., & Charnigo, R. (2014). Cultivating curious managers: Motivating moral awareness through balanced experiential inquiry. *Journal of Management Development*.

Sekerka, L. E., McCarthy, J. D., & Bagozzi, R. (2011). Developing the capacity for professional moral courage: Facing daily ethical challenges in today's military workplace. In *Moral courage in organizations: Doing the right thing at work: 130–141*, ed. D. Comer, and G. Vega. M. E. Sharpe: Armonk, NY.

Sekerka, L. E., & Zolin, R. (2005). Proactive versus reactive approaches to ethical dilemmas: Battling moral mediocrity with professional courage. *Business & Professional Ethics Journal, 24*(4).

Sekerka, L. E., Zolin, R. & Simon, C. (2005). Change now because I say so! Specialized management identity and coercive rapid transformation. *Technical Reports* #NPS-GSBPP-05–003, Naval Postgraduate School, Monterey, CA.

Shelp, E. E. (1984). Courage: A neglected virtue in the patient-physician relationship. *Social Science and Medicine, 18*(4), 351–360.

Solomon, R. C. (1998). The moral psychology of business: Care and compassion in the corporation. *Business Ethics Quarterly, 8*(3), 515–534.

Srivastva, S., & Cooperrider, D. L. (Eds.). (1998). *Organizational wisdom and executive courage* (1st ed.). San Francisco, CA: The New Lexington Press.

Steenhaut, S., & Van Kenhove, P. (2006). The mediating role of anticipated guilt in consumers ethical decision-making. *Journal of Business Ethics, 69*, 269–288.

Treviño, L. K., & Victor, B. (1992). Peer reporting of unethical behavior: A social context perspective. *Academy of Management Journal, 35*(1), 38–65.

Treviño, L. K., & Youngblood, S. A. (1990). Bad apples in bad barrels: A causal analysis of ethical decision-making behavior. *Journal of Applied Psychology, 75*(4), 378–386.

Ulmer, W. F. (2005). Comparing military and business leaders. *Leadership in Action, 1*, 18–19.

Verschoor, C. C. (2003). Eight ethical traits of healthy organization. *Strategic Finance, 85*(3), 20–30.

Walton, D. N. (1986). *Courage: A Philosophical Investigation.* Berkeley, CA: University of California Press.

Whitbourne, S. K. (1986). *The me I know: A study of adult identity.* New York: Springer-Verlag.

Wilcox, T. (2012). Human resource management in a compartmentalized world: Whither moral agency. *Journal of Business Ethics, 111*(1), 85–96.

Woodard, C. R. (2004). Hardiness and the concept of courage. *Consulting Psychology Journal: Practice and Research, 56*, 173–185.

Woodard, C. R., & Pury, C. L. S. (2007). The construct of courage: Categorization and measurement. Consulting Psychology Journal, 59(2), 135–147.

Watson, G., Freeman, R. E., & Parmar, B. (2008). Connected moral agency in organizational ethics. *Journal of Business Ethics, 81*(2), 323–341.

Worline, M. C., Wrzesniewski, A., & Rafaeli, A. (2002). Courage and work: Breaking routines to improve performance. In R. Lord, R. Klimoski, & R. Kanfer (Eds.), *Emotions in the Workplace: Understanding the structure and role of emotions in organizational behavior San Francisco.* CA: Jossey-Bass.

Chapter 10
Moral Competencies

Fig. 10.1 Bus
shape the
human
Fra
200

Professional moral courage is not a one-time task. It is represented by an ongoing commitment to being ethical. Ethicality is not something saved up for special occasions, parsed out for certain problems, or applied when it's convenient or others are watching. Ethics is a personal decision with regards to how you go about conducting yourself—in all areas of your life. You cannot save your ethical self for when challenges and dilemmas present themselves. Management ethics is not something you can check off a list or "pick up" in an annual online training class. To sustain a path on the moral high ground, it is essential to practice being your best ethical self in your everyday task actions. This entails seeing ethics as a sustained goal, motivated by personal desire. Being morally responsible in the workplace means we choose to take ownership of shaping the world we want to live in, each and every day (Fig. 10.1).

As individuals, we are a microcosm of the planet. We all reflect and shape human existence. The strengths, conflicts, and tensions we carry within us, or demonstrate outwardly, reflect our past, influence who we are today, and serve to direct the course of our collective future. Continuing to seek awareness, balance, and well-being supports your ongoing development and strengthens an ability to be ethically and morally responsible when working with others. It seems curious that most ethical decision-making models begin with recognizing the issue. The irony is that if you wait until a problem is identified, you are usually in a reaction mode, responding to a realized concern. Do you wait for the ethical issue to emerge? Or, do you look for the ethical elements of the circumstance, striving to pre-empt or address ethical issues, *before* an ethical problem emerges? Senge (1990) points out this inherent issue at every level of analyses. He describes the need for systems thinking, recognizing that when we react to issues we get stuck in creating solutions that are merely short-term fixes in the here and now. But because we are not altering the originating system that created the issues, actions to correct apparent problems offer no real and lasting change. When the problems reoccur, we wonder why. This "band-aid" approach to life, as people or organizations, never evokes deep development.

© Springer International Publishing Switzerland 2016
L. E. Sekerka, *Ethics is a Daily Deal*, DOI 10.1007/978-3-319-18090-8_10

Certainly, it is important to respond to an ethical challenge when it appears. But why is ethical decision-making framed as a response to an issue that has already happened? You might say, "I am just trying to do the right thing, working to fix this unethical situation." That's fine. But if we are actually experiencing a problem, we need to consider the system that produced or caused it in the first place. It is important to discern what contributes to the manifestation of ethical issues, not just make them "go away." Moreover, it is important to look at what role we play in creating the existing circumstances, the crucible that created or enabled the issue to form and fester. If we profess to live our values, ownership of moral responsibility suggests we have to look more deeply into what produces the ethical issues, unethical behaviors, or curtails our desire to perform management duties with professional moral courage.

Being a systems thinker means getting out of a perpetual reactionary cycle and creating a more integrated approach to how you go about understanding and making decisions (Senge 2008). The word integrity comes from the Latin term *integer*, implying that ethicality is associated with the whole—the complete picture (Oxford English Dictionary 2013). Applying systems thinking to ethics is about looking at the big picture. Ethical thinking with a systems approach implies you are not afraid to examine how your own actions may be a contributing factor to the very issues you are attempting to resolve. Systems thinking is a continuous exploration to unearth what contributes to ethical weakness and moral courage. A willingness to examine and assume responsibility for the implications of your actions calls for a steadfast commitment to challenge your current assumptions and perceptions. To do this, you need tools that support your moral competency (Fig. 10.2).

Building Moral Strength

To be ethical at work is about creating an integrated process for building and sustaining a routine of making informed responsible choices. If we are to engage in such an effort before problems arise, a commitment to self-awareness is essential.

Fig. 10.2 Moral
competencies are the tools
needed for moral
development. Image credited
to Maxx-Studio/Shutterstock.
com

It means looking for and examining the ethical elements in all of our actions, not just when a problem takes center stage. This calls for the development of moral strength, understanding that we are in a constant state of learning and becoming. Others' inability, unwillingness, or moral blindness when it comes to being ethical increases the burden of moral responsibility on everyone else. Therefore, it is essential that employees identify and work on specific practices, skills that can help them engage in daily work life in a way that supports an ability to create a world we want to live in, be a part of, and pass on to future generations.

Thanks to many spiritual leaders, aspirational insights encourage us, helping us to embrace the notion that every person can make a difference. We have the power to effect positive change and can use our energy to make the world sustainable for all living things. But such guidance can lack specific means for application and appear incongruent with the harsh realities of everyday strategic business operations. Being the change you want to see in the world may seem like a conclusive end point, rather than a revised action plan.[1] You may ask, "While I may have a pocket full of passion and good intent, what exactly does moral development look like? What exactly am I supposed to do?" Broad-scale sweeping positivity, processes that encourage appreciative thinking, can sometimes fall short of implementation. Ideal visions may lack pragmatic applicability. Tackling the "Now what?" of transformation in business ethics begins with a truthful look at the self.

Sometimes our society seems to work against the assumption of personal responsibility and being honest. In the West, we can easily become distracted and enticed by our ubiquitous infusion of technology, consumerism, and the subtle lure

---

[1]This statement paraphrases elements of Mahatma Gandhi's quote, "If we could change ourselves, the tendencies in the world would also change. As a man changes his own nature, so does the attitude of the world change towards him....We need not wait to see what others do" (see http://www. compassionatespirit.com/wpblog/2012/08/14/be-the-change-where-did-this-saying-come-from/).

of entitlement. Taking time for quiet reflection and discernment, coming to recognize how our daily choices reflect our ethical identity, may fall to those who make such practices their calling, or to people who have an inner faith that drives their development. Perhaps a more realistic path forward for adult moral development in the workplace, one that is both pragmatic and actionable, is a competency-based approach.

Prior research in adult development focuses on the use of competency-based skills as the tools for management practice. Learning skills that support a particular behavior has become commonplace in managerial training, in both academic and organizational settings (Sekerka 2009). Given decades of research conducted by McClelland (1973), Boyatzis (1982), and other management scholars, there are a number of empirically-driven studies supporting the use of this approach for adult learning and development (Kolb 1984). A competency is a term used to describe a skill that supports economic, intellectual, and human value (Boyatzis 1996). Competencies are abilities, typically a set of related but varied behaviors organized around an underlying intent (Boyatzis 2009; McClelland 1985). As skill sets, competencies are characteristics, resources, or abilities used to achieve effective and even superior job performance (Boyatzis 1982; Manz 1986; Klemp 1980). As personal abilities, job competencies relate to specific and desired behavioral actions associated with accomplishing certain tasks.

What kinds of skills support an ability to demonstrate professional moral courage? As we considered, having a willingness to be ethical to "do the right thing" is a critical starting point. This requires a sustained mindfulness to look for, perceive, and address the ethical elements and issues that emerge in daily life. The willingness and ability to be ethical requires personal maintenance, an ongoing capacity-building effort to be ready for ethical action. To build this type of moral competence, people need practice using specific tools.

As with exercising for good health and performance, people strive to build their strength and endurance. To effectively perform any particular skill, you need to use it to enhance your ability. You cannot expect to be effective at being ethical unless the skills that back the behavior are honed. The ability to proceed with right action is supported by specific skill sets of personal governance referred to as moral competencies. Consider these competencies as the workout regimen for your ethical identity. They are tools, in the sense that they provide a conduit or platform to exercise your moral strength. In looking at how managers face their ethical challenges, we discovered that ethical acts, namely those that reflect moral strength, are associated with specific intentions and behaviors (Sekerka et al. 2011). These particular behaviors, framed as skills, serve as the foundation for a person's ethicality, enabling them to manage everyday decisions with responsibility and address ethical issues with professional moral courage.

To advance your ethical *response-ability*, it is essential that you understand, practice, and utilize particular skills associated with moral strength. Empirical research has been conducted to distill the key behavioral skills that support a person's ability to effectively respond to an ethical challenge with professional moral courage (see Chap. 9). Formally stated, they are referred to as: emotional signaling, reflective pause, self-regulation, and moral preparation. Rather than saving your moral strength for an urgent matter, the idea is to utilize these moral competencies daily. As a workplace practice, the skills need to be applied to situations that emerge in your everyday routines. Framing moral competency as a practice reflects the notion that these abilities can be honed through regular use. In so doing, people can extend their capacity to apply them to challenging ethical concerns with greater ease, and potentially mitigate the propensity for ethical issues to emerge. Looking at the competencies one by one, prior research is used to explicate each skill, helping you to see them as tools for everyday management use.

Emotional Signaling

Scholars recognize that affect and cognition are so intertwined that it is often difficult to separate them. Emotions contain important signals that influence the cerebral process of moral decision-making. As such, emotional affect plays a critical role in motivating or hindering the choice to address an ethical challenge and to do so with rigor and durable commitment. Researchers have learned that the particular emotions managers most frequently experience when facing an ethical challenge are: worry, loneliness, fear, shock or surprise, and feelings of hurt or anger (Sekerka et al. 2011). The sensation of being hurt often stems from a sense of betrayal. This seems to occur when a person perceives that a friend, peer, or upper level management are behaving unethically or doing nothing to address an unethical issue when it becomes known to them.

For example, it is a great disappointment to learn that your boss has opened and read your personal mail. Not only are you angry that he engaged in an illegal act, but you are now faced with having to deal with the matter. Additionally, you are worried and irritated that he now has personal information about a job offer you have received at another firm. This is likely accompanied by sadness, as you realize that the bond of trust you had thought was there has been broken. Similarly, when we encounter people who alter, change, or embellish the facts, it can be both a stressful and frustrating experience. Once suspicions are raised, you have to determine what is the right action by getting more information and then determining if and how you might go about reporting or addressing the offense.

As you think about the matter, your values, social norms, and a host of thoughts and feelings may come flooding in, as you work to discern what might be the right thing to do. You can readily understand why a common experience among those who demonstrate professional moral courage is an initial agitation and/or a sense of uncertainty or even helplessness. It is easy to become overwhelmed. And it is even easier to look away, minimize, and to find excuses for not taking action. For example, when facing an ethical issue many people claim it's not their job to report an unethical activity. Rationalizations include, "I don't want to be a snitch," "It's not that big of deal," or "Everyone is doing it." In the case of those who display moral courage at work, their affective reaction is often accompanied by a feeling of personal harm (being let down) and some level of discomfort or distress. When negative emotions are experienced by moral agents, they are not ignored, repressed, or sublimated. Rather, those with moral strength recognize and use this affective information, allowing it to serve as an emotional cue—a signal—that they are being called to duty.

Despite the negative feelings that often accompany an ethical issue, moral agents seem to be enabled by their emotional awareness rather than being blocked or thwarted by it. It appears that the capacity of being aware of one's emotions, but not overwhelmed by them, gives people a cue to navigate and better manage their circumstances. Rather than quelling or turning away from negative emotions, trying to reduce them, morally courageous managers experience them as important signals for their sustained commitment to the matter at hand. Once such signals are recognized, people with professional moral courage learn to effectively draw from this input, directing the negativity toward a more deeply felt, sustained intention to proceed with right action. Such openness to one's feelings enables certain people to proceed with their decision-making efforts with more informed awareness, honoring their visceral reactions to the situation at hand.

Some people, what I refer to as the "matter-of-fact" group, seemingly more experienced moral agents, describe how they always strive to live above the moral line, not close to it. They treat incoming negative affect as standard fare, not the anomaly. They are prepared for it and rather than reacting surprised, they expect it, as if it goes with the territory of being an ethical agent. Because they assume that dealing with negative emotions is part of the package deal, they address and deal with them, and move to get on with their next steps in formulating their response. These managers seem more irritated than angry, feeling inconvenienced by unethical people and ethical challenges often created by human weakness (namely selfishness and greed). Other managers seem to experience the negative feelings on a deeper, more personal level. It's almost as if they are disappointed in humanity itself, downhearted that someone they looked up to or respected is not the person they had thought or imagined.

One manager described how he became aware of his emotions and then managed them, "I felt hurt. My heart was beating fast. I went to go eat, to relax my mind. About 2 h later I called my clerk in and said, 'Hey, let's go through it again.'" In this case, the manager was concerned about accounting fraud. He went on to explain that by recognizing and letting his feelings play out, he was better equipped to move forward. Examples such as this one portend that moral managers do not view their emotions as overwhelming powerful distractions, nor do they suppress them. Instead, emotions are prompts to spark concern and/or greater attention to a situation, serving as cues to inform the thought-action process. Thus, the skill of emotional signaling is important in supporting professional moral courage, helping to facilitate informed decision-making. When attentions to one's emotions segue into a reflective pause, a time-out is then typically used to process and understand these feelings. In so doing, individuals are better equipped to proceed more effectively on the path to moral action.

Fig. 10.3 Take time for
reflection. Image credited to
Robnroll/Shutterstock.com

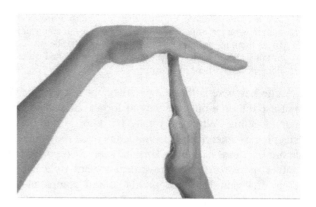

Reflective Pause

The use of a reflective pause as part of one's strategy in ethical decision-making
represents an ability, regardless of time constraints, to purposively self-impose a
time-out for reflection (Fig. 10.3). During this break, managers examine possible
avenues for their next steps, often weighing the pros and cons of the situation or
thinking about the implications of their potential actions over time. For example,
they may think about situations that occurred in the past and compare them to the
present circumstances. Or, perhaps they may think about the present and attempt to
forecast what the future might look like if they engage in a particular action or
choose to do otherwise. Reflective time-outs often display prudential judgment.
Prudence is a virtue of vigilance and helps to integrate other core virtues (Pieper
1966; Keenan 1995). It is useful because it helps to ensure justice, fortitude, and
temperance in the here-and-now, and to anticipate how and when other virtues can
be applied subsequently.

Reflection is useful in determining the appropriate application of intellectual and
practical wisdom, important for proceeding effectively in moral judgment processes
(McBeath and Webb 2002). It provides an opportunity to explore elements of moral
awareness, helping a person see what the issues are, what is at stake, what is most
important, and what needs to be done (Sternberg et al. 2000). Discernment
(Beauchamp and Childress 1994), thoughtfulness (Bennett 1998), mindfulness
(Langer and Moldoveanu 2000), and practical wisdom (Fowers and Tjeltveit 2003)
often require time.

Toggling between short- and long-term repercussions of various scenarios
appears to be an important element of professional moral courage that often
manifests during self-imposed reflection periods. It is as though the reflective pause
helps people discern options, then garner and build informed momentum toward
moral action. Individuals use this period to consider the options and their associated
outcomes, as they work to gather additional information about the rules and other
particulars regarding the situation at hand. One participant explained how a
time-out helped him move forward:

It was more reflecting on the situation. I guess some of the things in the past that started weighing on my mind was a sense of fairness—reading and following the rules. That's what I was thinking primarily about. Because of what he was doing, and what I had done. I had to think of it in terms of the present, because if I had waited too long, it would have been a done deal, and hard to undo.

The key here is that the person came back to the situation. In so doing, they do not use the time-out as a way to forget about the matter or to rationalize their way out of acting. While they may be doing a completely unrelated activity (eating, sleeping, or exercising), within a day or so they take the next step in moving toward assuming responsibility. This may be to report the matter, seek out counsel, or gather more facts. But movement toward right action continues to progress after their time-out. Research on the moral competencies has helped us to see that professional moral courage is bolstered through reflection as people use it to collect their thoughts, generate options, and seek support during the initial stages of their decision-making effort. Taking the time to reflect often alters, overrides, or postpones some initial reactions while also targeting responses for appropriate timing. When applied as a daily habit this reflection skill may actually serve as a portal for all the personal governance practices, but it is especially important for self-regulation.

Self-regulation

As described thus far, initial reactions to ethical challenges require the use of emotional signaling and reflection. But to habitually pursue right action and to manage and address tough moral decisions, individuals must balance their reactions, knowing how to manage responsibilities alongside of their personal desires. Regardless of the industry or type of organization, managers have a variety of goals to achieve; hence, they must be adept at balancing the pursuit of task accomplishment while also proceeding with ethical means. How people ethically set and achieve their goals must be tempered with decisions about when and how to tackle the ethical challenges that emerge. They must discern whether to postpone a response, or engage in immediate action. This ability to regulate one's initial reactions necessitates restraint coupled with an ability to prompt movement forward —despite perceptions that may impose negative impacts to self or others. It can be particularly difficult when peers or leaders are the ones engaged in questionable activities, or when asking others to engage in actions that challenge the status quo.

One manager described their leader's behavior as starting out with small improprieties (inappropriate phone use), but then events gradually escalated. Over time, this extended into taking special trips to engage in an extramarital affair:

I didn't realize how a situation like that would snowball. And by ignoring it a little bit early [I] emboldened him to do more and more. We [the officer and two other officers on board] each had a little piece of the puzzle...and we couldn't understand the whole picture, we just saw a piece of the picture. But once we shared what we knew and composed the picture, at that point the problem was so far down the road that it was unsalvageable.

Eventually, the manager realizes that his delayed response is contributing to the ethical issue:

I think in the future, once I get a piece of the picture, and learn to trust that little voice in my head that says, 'something doesn't smell right here' then I need to do something about it right away, because it gets worse with time. I think if I was faced with a situation again today, I would close the door, take off the rank, and I would have said, 'Knock it off.' But that's not easy to do, particularly if it's the first time you face a situation like that.

Self-regulation is an effective tool for personal governance. This moral competency is used to corral immediate impulses and then to manage emotions, using them to help fuel a move toward ethical action.

Many of the managers we have interviewed over the course of our research expressed that they should have acted sooner. They describe how their respect, appreciation, or care for someone, or sense of loyalty to those in charge served to inhibit action and/or their self-regulation (at least initially). Many who waited, however, saw in hindsight that this just exacerbated the problem:

[The Captain] was probably the most charismatic, dynamic, effective leader I've ever worked for, and he flushed it all away because of a character flaw, essentially...I saw how big that snowball got as it rolled downhill.

The application of self-regulation underscores how professional moral courage comes from within. It is an inner strength and internal compass that provides motivation and direction, often developed through personal struggle. Individuals must be willing to demonstrate moral fortitude even when those around them, including leaders and peers, do not. Such self-control has been regarded as "moral muscle"—an inner directive to alter one's immediate responses and to redirect them toward the good of others (Baumeister and Exline 1999).

In this light, psychologists have referred to control and regulation of one's affective reactions as the cornerstone of virtuous behavior. In rare cases some may apply this competency naturally, but there is enormous potential for further development of this capability in most people. Learning to quiet one's impulse to react or ignore the problem, then moving to reflect upon and manage one's immediate thoughts and feelings, can begin a course of personal development marked by habits of moral strength.

Moral Preparation

Finally, a commitment to right action is developed through a deep understanding of self, fueled by an ongoing thought process concerning how one would or would not act when faced with an ethical challenge in the future. That is, morally mature managers appear to think through the likely consequences, as they pertain to both themselves and others, before events even occur. This ongoing preparatory effort includes a variety of elements, including a consideration of when action should be taken, felt or perceived emotions, evaluation of circumstantial variables, and discernment of the needs of others in the moment and down the line. People who continue to be aware of how their emotions and situational factors can influence their reactions, have often learned how to choose to respond in ways that support "what an ethical person would do" as the scenario plays out and the situation variables continue to emerge.

Moral agents essentially commit to an ongoing effort of learning and development, sustaining a willingness and ability to question one's motives with rigorous self-honesty. This is commonly revealed by a heightened level of moral preparedness for ethical challenges, often demonstrated by a sustained vigilance to remain above "the moral line," staying above reproach at all times, even before any situational problems occur. For example, one manager said, "At what point do I draw the line and say you've now crossed? I know now it would be much earlier in the process." This manager realized he needed to draw the line sooner. People with professional moral courage have thought through positive and negative consequences of acting and/or not acting. They learn to recognize and manage their emotions, developing a conscious awareness of morality on a daily basis, even before ethical challenges emerge. It is a way of life that incorporates a rehearsal process, helping a person to prepare for a mindful response-action when problems do occur. By working to locate one's moral line above the rules and regulations, a misstep does not mean immediate infraction.

The competency of moral preparation is likely intertwined and potentially dependent upon the use and application of the other moral competencies. For example, emotional signaling, taking a reflective pause, and exercising self-regulation are typically precursors for an ability to proceed with right action. To integrate moral courage as a way of doing business, managers continually self-monitor and work to maintain an ongoing understanding of their intent. As such, moral agents look forward and backward, questioning themselves about their own motives. They look to ascertain lessons learned from current and past challenges, but also plan ahead about how to prohibit ethical issues from occurring. This includes striving to be more effective at dealing with such situations in the future, by considering where ethical risks may reside and working to eliminate the potential for their reoccurrence. Based on the insights provided by managers who were characterized by dealing with ethical issues with professional moral courage, moral competencies include a sustained preparation phase. This ongoing process requires self-awareness and sustained efforts toward personal introspection. In other words, a person continues to challenge themselves, seeks to learn from their experiences, to reflect on what happened, to garner takeaway lessons, and to seek out continuous improvement (Fig. 10.4).

In aggregate, as a suite of capabilities, these moral competencies are skills that can be further developed in most people. That said, it is important to recognize that the practices outlined herein can never be perfected. Because each person and every situation is different, responses to an ethical challenge, on any given day, are likely to vary. This underscores the importance of continually building the capacity for moral strength within the organization by providing ample opportunities for where moral competencies can be supported, encouraged, and further established. Perhaps most importantly, the competencies that support professional moral courage (emotional signaling, etc.) need to be viewed as part of successful performance. The management saying that "you are what you measure" is particularly salient in this light. If organizational leaders expect ethical performance, such an expectation implies that how you go about achieving your goals is as important as achieving the goals themselves. Incorporating training and performance metrics that hone and measure the moral competencies is a way to strengthen ethics in organizational settings (Sekerka 2009).

To build personal and organizational moral strength, practitioners can leverage what is currently done well (strengths), as well as areas where there is room for improvement (weaknesses). Today there is a marked shift in how scholars view and study people in organizational settings. A focus on the positive has created new knowledge about what it means to be well, thrive, and achieve success in work and daily life. This focus on strengths in business ethics has opened new vistas, ways to understand effective ethical decision-making and socially responsible actions in the workplace (Sekerka et al. 2014).

Given that engaging in professional moral courage can pose uncertainty, risk, and may be accompanied by negative emotions, an appreciative or purely positive approach is not well suited for ethical development. To help employees practice and exercise their moral competencies, practitioners have found that a balanced approach is effective (Sekerka and Godwin 2010). In the spirit of Aristotle himself, people need to be proactive about developing both their strengths and weaknesses. Adult learning calls for techniques that promote the cultivation of people's moral strength, as well as working to prevent ethical risk from emerging, and bringing harm to their organizational settings.

Fig. 10.4 A management team considers an ethical challenge in an executive ethics training session. Image courtesy of Naval Postgraduate School

Takeaway Points

1. Moral competencies are skills that most people can develop, enabling them to be effective moral agents and engage in professional moral courage when facing an ethical challenge.
2. People who are ethical are not super-heroes; rather, they commit to an ongoing effort of learning and development, questioning their own motives, and maintaining rigorous self-awareness and personal honesty.
3. The moral competencies include emotional signaling, reflective pause, self-regulation, and moral preparation.

Reflection Questions

Examine a recent ethical challenge that you incurred while at work. How did you use your moral competencies to pursue moral action? If you were unable to respond with moral strength, consider how you can practice your moral competencies. Tomorrow, look for ways to utilize and demonstrate each moral competency as you accomplish your objectives.

References

Baumeister, R. F., & Exline, J. J. (1999). Virtue, personality and social relations: Self-control as the moral muscle. *Journal of Personality, 67*, 1165–1194.

Beauchamp, T. L., & Childress, J. F. (1994). *Principles of biomedical ethics* (4th ed.). New York: Oxford University Press.

Bennett, J. B. (1998). *Collegial professionalism: The academy, individualism and the common good*. Phoenix, AZ: American Council on Education and Oryx Press.

Boyatzis, R. E. (1982). *The competent manager: A model for effective performance*. New York: John Wiley & Sons.

Boyatzis, R. E. (1996). Consequences and rejuvenation of competency-based human resource and organization development. In R. W. Woodman & W. A. Pasmore (Eds.), *Research in organizational change and development, 9* (pp. 101–122). Greenwich, CN: JAI Press.

Boyatzis, R. E. (2009). Competencies as a behavioral approach to emotional intelligence. *Journal of Management Development, 28*(9), 749–770.

Fowers, B. J., & Tjeltveit, A. C. (2003). Virtue obscured and retrieved: Character, community, and practices in behavioral science. *American Behavioral Scientist, 47*(4), 387–394.

Keenan, J. F. (1995). Proposing cardinal virtues. *Theological Studies, 56*(4), 709.

Klemp, G. O. Jr. (Ed.). (1980). *The assessment of occupational competence*. Washington, D.C.; National Institute of Education.

Kolb, D. A. (1984). *Experiential learning: Experience as the source of learning and development*. Englewood Cliffs, NJ: Prentice-Hall.

Langer, E. J., & Moldoveanu, M. (2000). The construct of mindfulness. *Journal of Social Issues, 56*(1), 129–139.

Manz, C. C. (1986). Self-leadership: Toward an expanded theory of self-influence processes in organizations. *Academy of Management Review, 11*(3), 585–601.

McBeath, G., & Webb, S. A. (2002). Virtue ethics and social work: Begin lucky, realistic, and not doing ones duty. *British Journal of Social Work, 32*(8), 1015–1036.

McCelland, D. C. (1973). Testing for competence rather than "intelligence". *American Psychologist, 28*, 1–14.

McCelland, D. C. (1985). *Human motivation.* Glenview, IL: Scott, Foresman & Co.

Oxford English Dictionary (2013). Retrieved December 19, 2013, from http://www.oed.com/.

Pieper, T. (1966). *The four cardinal virtues.* Notre Dame, IN: University of Notre Dame Press.

Sekerka, L. E. (2009). Organizational ethics education and training: A review of best practices and their application. *International Journal of Training and Development, 13*(2), 77–95.

Sekerka, L. E., Comer, D., & Godwin, L. (2014). Positive Organizational Ethics: Cultivating and Sustaining Moral Performance. *Journal of Business Ethics, 119*(4), 435–444.

Sekerka, L. E., & Godwin, L. (2010). Strengthening professional moral courage: A balanced approach to ethics training. *Training & Management Development Methods, 24*(5), 63–74.

Sekerka, L. E., Bagozzi, R. P., & Charnigo, R. (2009). Facing ethical challenges in the workplace: Conceptualizing and measuring professional moral courage. *Journal of Business Ethics, 89*(4), 565–579.

Sekerka, L. E., McCarthy, J. D., & Bagozzi, R. (2011). Developing the capacity for professional moral courage: Facing daily ethical challenges in today's military workplace. In D. Comer & G. Vega (Eds.), *Moral courage in organizations: Doing the right thing at work: 130-141.* M.E. Sharpe: Armonk, NY.

Senge, P. M. (1990). *The fifth discipline: The art and practice of the learning organization.* New York: Doubleday.

Senge, P. M. (2008). *The necessary revolution.* New York: Doubleday.

Sternberg, R. J., Forsythe, G. B., Hedlund, J., Horvaith, J. A., Wagner, R. K., Williams, W. M., et al. (2000). *Practical intelligences in everyday life.* New York Cambridge University Press.

Chapter 11
Ethics Education and Training

In the pluralistic world of business, the creation and use of professional standards of practice is a common approach to addressing ethics. A set of guidelines is formally accepted by a particular group of practitioners and the law. Some fields, like accounting, have developed ethics programs specifically linked to professional standards for their various needs (Matherne et al. 2006). When professional standards of practice set forth ethical guidelines (Cressey and Moore 1983), expectations are explicit (Brown and Duguid 1998). However, occupational socialization can influence how people respond to issues that violate or test these standards and ethical guidelines (Smith and Rogers 2000). Hence, the degree of reliance on and use of organizational codes of behavior varies significantly.

As described by Matherne and his colleagues, management is a field that lags in terms of standards of practice and adherence to codified ethical codes (2006). Priorities and objectives at the core of business ethics and ethical decision-making are unclear. In part, this may be due to an ongoing disagreement about the underlying management philosophy. The debate continues with regards to corporate service to shareholders versus broader stakeholders (e.g., Davis et al. 1997; Sundaram and Inkpen 2004). There simply is not, and is not likely to be, a universal consensus to resolve these competing interests. As a result, there is no agreed-on standard to codify; thus, a pluralistic approach grounded in ethical principles to process competing interests and perspectives is necessary.

Ethical standards are socially constructed norms that develop in the absence of codes of ethics or licensing requirements. In disciplines where there is little or no codification, there is an especially strong need to link education with standards that exist within the specific community of practice. Recognizing that standards exist, understanding they are based on ethical principles, and identifying ways to discover and apply them is essential for development of moral responsibility in a field like business management. Given that the usefulness of professional standards relies upon ethics education and training, it is important to understand how to conduct effective adult ethics education in workplace settings.

The technique *Balanced Experiential Inquiry* originally appeared in Sekerka and Godwin (2010).

© Springer International Publishing Switzerland 2016
L. E. Sekerka, *Ethics is a Daily Deal*, DOI 10.1007/978-3-319-18090-8_11

The ability to be ethical in management infers that the moral competencies that support right action are like muscles: they need to be toned. Moral strength is not something that can ever be perfected; rather, it is developed and maintained through regular use. Moral competency must be kept in shape through exercise, coupled with self-awareness, introspection, and staying open to learning. In order for managers to build ethical capacity and sustain a willingness to proceed with moral action, values and skills need to work in concert. If organizational leaders want to see ethics as a vibrant element within their operational environment, ethics education and training programs need to support personal development of employees and their managers.

We Only Hire Ethical People

Management needs to ensure that ethical awareness and action has become an expected and endorsed feature of their everyday work life. Being ethical is viewed as a featured element of one's duty as an employee. In most training programs, skills are studied, worked, honed, and exercised. Unfortunately, the ethics education and training in many organizational settings is a matter of absorbing content on policy, rules, and rote material, followed by multiple choice quizzes. Much of this training is conducted in an online setting, one hardly conducive to social interaction.

Current training programs for ethics in organizations are largely static. The idea of teaching people how to create a work environment that supports ongoing learning and development, working to build moral strength, is all too rare (Sekerka 2009). While understanding what is necessary for compliance helps to secure a moral minimum, targeting a baseline standard suggests that the goal is to stay out of trouble. Such an approach rarely incorporates moral strength as a performance objective. Compliance programs convey rules and regulations and highlight reporting channels and requirements. Such efforts are of course complemented by the organization's ethics code. Together, these elements may underscore the need to be ethical, but do little to build employees' moral competency to act that way.

An assumption that merely providing information (content) will ensure ethical behavior is risky—at best. This presumes that simply describing what people should do automatically enables them to act accordingly. While a deontological approach helps to ensure that rules are known and that it is the employee's duty to adhere to them, actually knowing how to recognize and attend to ethical challenges presumes a great deal of personal awareness and character strength. People also need environments (context) that foster ethical reflection, dialogue, and action. Needed are additional activities that nurture organizational process norms to develop ethical thinking in support of personal accountability and moral development. A greater focus on context implies that supervisors and managers need to bring forward ethical issues in staff meetings, become aware of and responsible for areas of ethical risk, and link ethical practice to goals and personal performance.

By emphasizing ethical competency, employees will come to see ethics as a self-directed practice rather than a path to forced compliance.

Table 11.1 outlines the strengths and challenges of organizational ethics training programs in workplace settings, based on the content and context of their organizational best practices. While content is where the preponderance of emphasis is placed in most organizational ethics training, context is just as important (Sekerka 2009). If employees are expected to comply with regulations and exercise values in their daily tasks, processes that promote dialogue, identify ethical risks, and link ethics with performance are an essential extension of the rote material. If moral strength is an expected element of work routines, training programs must provide employees an opportunity to exercise their moral muscles to build moral strength in community with others.

Table 11.1 Strengths and challenges in organizational ethics education and training

Content	Context
Strengths	
• Address key compliance requirements, such as reporting channels and whistleblower protection • Focus on prevention of unethical behavior and promotion of values • Describe and define ethics as applicable to daily tasks • Use relevant issues that target problem areas • Use of online delivery reaches all employees, typically upon hire and then biannually	• Reporting mechanisms are in place • Code of Conduct ethics policy is easily accessible, typically through a website that also provides supplemental question/answer section • Code of Conduct is available in multiple languages and typically signed by all employees
Challenges	
• Online delivery promotes awareness but does not encourage reflection, practice, and dialogue. While outcomes associated with face-to-face delivery are desired, time, interest, and resources restrict applications to special groups or when problems arise • Training efforts can become siloes (e.g., legal, human resources, sales/marketing departments), detracting from ethics integration and a competency development approach • Organizations assume employees will exercise values in resolving ethical challenges: "We only hire ethical people." • Ethics training for vendors, suppliers, and partners is nonexistent • Employees are not petitioned for their personal stories or for insights on cases or issues to be used in training	• Lack a sustained ethics message in corporate communications (e.g., publications, events, announcements, and leadership messages) • Employees are not included in the process of ethics program efforts, training, and Code of Conduct development • Ethical risk assessment tools are rarely applied and, when they are, are not linked to workplace routines and performance metrics • Managers do not explicitly assume responsibility for handling areas of ethical risk (a reaction orientation dominates: focused attention on problems after they emerge) • Ethical issues are not routinely addressed at staff meetings • The link between ethics and performance goals is often vague—if present • Focus is on training rather than education; the goal is to disseminate information rather than to foster personal and organizational development

Figure adapted from Sekerka (2009)

Working with ethics training program leaders, research shows that these people often believe that, "Our employees already know how to be ethical." And, that "If our people do not know how to be ethical it is not the company's responsibility to teach them how to behave appropriately." An ethics officer explained, "You cannot teach ethics or morals to adults. People either learn ethical thinking as children—or they do not." It is interesting that these people often feel quite certain their company will sustain its ethicality because, "We only hire ethical people."

Given these beliefs and attitudes, it seems all the more important to recognize that organizational contexts can inadvertently create and support social norms that unwittingly encourage unethical decision-making and/or wrongdoing. Even if you could ensure that ethical people are hired, certain environments or situations can weaken a person's ethical resolve.

If ethics training programs are to be effective, they must help managers learn and practice skills that support ethical decision-making and action, and create a learning environment that attends to their own learning style. Further examination into the structure of education and training in organizations closely mirrors the coursework model used in formal higher-educational settings. This pedagogical model is highly content-focused (i.e., learning specific ethical frameworks, theories, and policies) and instructor-driven (i.e., the instructor presents content for students to memorize or master).

Insights from adult learning theory suggest that this method is not the most effective for working managers (Fig. 11.1). Knowles, a predominant adult learning theorist, argued that these types of approaches have developed from traditional

Fig. 11.1 Executive ethics education. Image credited to the Naval Postgraduate School

pedagogy; the term literally translates as the "art and science of helping children learn" (1968; 1973, p. 42). The pedagogy of adult education is a contradiction in terms. Most adults, including professionals, have been taught as if they were children (Knowles 1973, p. 42). Educators have worked to advance the concept of andragogy, which Knowles defined as the "art and science of helping adults learn" (1980, p. 43). While the premise and practice of adult learning theory is vast, its core assumptions underlying andragogy help create a framework from which administrators can begin to build more effective ethics education and training programs. Summarizing the work of Knowles, Merriam (2001) defines the adult learner as a person who:

(1) has an independent self-concept and who can direct his or her own learning,
(2) has accumulated a reservoir of life experiences that is a rich resource for learning,
(3) has learning needs closely related to changing social roles,
(4) is problem-centered and interested in immediate application of knowledge, and
(5) is motivated to learn by internal rather than external factors (p. 5).

Brookfield (1996, p. 377) said, "the belief that adult teaching should be grounded in adults' experiences, and that these experiences represent a valuable resource, is currently cited as crucial by adult educators of every conceivable ideological hue." This concept echoes even to the earliest work on adult education, that as stated by Lindeman, "experience is the adult learner's living textbook" (1926, p. 7). Since this early work, the value and use of experiential methods have become well-established (Sanyal 2000) with the idea that personal involvement leads to retaining information for longer periods (Calloway-Graham 2004; Hemmasi and Graf 1992). Kolb's work on experiential learning theory has become the dominant framework guiding much of the educational practices for today's adult learners. The theory proposes that "knowledge is created through the transformation of experience" (Kolb 1984, p. 41). While many discussions on experiential learning focus only on the experience portion of the theory, Kolb's model suggests that learning actually takes place through a four-step process called the experiential learning cycle. The steps in this cycle include having a concrete experience, reflecting on that experience, conceptualizing abstractly about the experience, and actively experimenting with a new behavior.

Kolb and his colleagues have explored how experiential learning unfolds through conversation (Fig 11.2), describing how the "tension between individuality" (life as an individual process) and "relationality" (life as an experience of connection with others) are intersubjective processes (2002, p. 60). Baker et al. (2005) detail the concept of "conversational learning" as "an experiential learning process through which people construct meaning together from their experiences" (p. 426). Laditka and Houck (2006) have shown how experiential approaches in teaching ethics are particularly effective, stimulating interest and understanding. When group discourse is fostered as a part of this process through conversational learning, participants engage in shared sense-making as people explore their

Fig. 11.2 Millennials engage in adult moral development activities. Images credited to Leslie E. Sekerka

experiences with others (Weick 1995). Other studies that examine best practices in ethics education and training in organizational settings support the importance of collective learning spaces, revealing that employees benefit from face-to-face learning groups (Sekerka 2009). As people explore what is important to them regarding workplace ethics, they are in a better position to examine what contributes to their thinking and behavior, as well as uncover assumptions and tacit knowledge regarding business ethics.

Importance of Balance

Balanced Experiential Inquiry (BEI) is an example of a training technique that provides managers with an opportunity to actively practice their moral competencies that support professional moral courage (Sekerka et al. 2011). The experiential and inquiry-based aspects of the process are central to the effort and are set forth in this chapter. This process features the notion of "balance," a concept promoted throughout the exercise. As an ethics training process, BEI provides a holistic learning experience that brings balance to a variety of tensions. To meet the learning needs of adults, employees work together to establish equilibrium between tensions. Tensions often stem from prior experiences that present conflicting positive versus negative memories, felt versus anticipated emotions, personal or organizational strengths versus weakness, individual conscience versus peer pressure, and individual versus collective moral identity.

The activity itself is a balance of two interwoven core change management techniques: diagnostic (deficit-based) and appreciative inquiry (strength-based). The process invites participants to share their stories, honoring both positive and negative aspects of their ethical issues, and to think about factors that support and impede their ability to proceed with ethical action. The idea for a hybrid process stems from empirical research reflecting how uniquely useful outcomes emerge from the initial phases of both strength- and deficit-based approaches (Sekerka et al. 2006). Traditional gap analysis that targets weaknesses, problems, or deficits has been shown to help unify employees around a common problem to resolve important issues (Sekerka, Zolin et al. 2009). Problem-focusing tends to highlight the negative, which may thwart a desire to proceed when it comes to facing and enduring a perceived threat, as is often the case in workplace ethics.

Ethical challenges are rarely experienced as positive encounters. But when people adopt a problem-based approach it runs the risk of shortchanging their potential knowledge acquisition, which stems from a sole exploration of weakness and/or negative encounters. A process that only focuses on eliciting negative examples also runs the risk of demotivating participants. Moral action necessitates the ability to overcome barriers and deal with negative emotions, while also building on past learnings and successes. Studies have shown that a focus on strengths can be particularly useful in broadening and building organizational capacity and to help prepare employees for learning, growth, and change (Sekerka and Fredrickson 2007). My colleagues and I have found that a hybrid approach to ethical inquiry, one that leverages both positive and negative experiential knowledge, helps individuals explore what they and their organizations do best, and also where issues reside that require corrective action (Sekerka et al. 2012). A balanced type of discovery effort helps organizational members build strength from weakness, as well as strength from strength (Cooperrider and Sekerka 2006, Sekerka et al. 2006).

Using hybrid strength- and deficit-based processes, *Balanced Experiential Inquiry* unites employees around their ethics experiences, drawing from employees' successes and challenges as they relate to salient ethical concerns. This establishes a platform for participation and engagement, prompting reflection and discovery into what builds moral strength. Employees gain an understanding of how barriers block moral action and learn how to overcome them, in part, by drawing on their current moral strengths—especially moral preparation, the moral muscle requiring continual affirmation of realizing one's own willingness to face ethical challenges. Ethical decisions require balancing rationality, emotions, and morality with situational factors and external demands of the situation. In pursuing both positive and negative experiences, along with personal assets and weaknesses, the process helps employees explicitly work on stabilizing tensions produced by such dichotomies. Educators suggest that talking about emotions in the context of others helps people appreciate similarities and differences (Sánchez 2008), and highlights the relevance of social self-conscious and moral emotions. Emotional expression helps people get used to the idea of recognizing the emotional element of decision-making and the relevance of honoring feelings as a useful tool.

The issues that emerge are realistic to the organization because the content is provided directly from the employees. Unlike traditional ethics education and training programs that use generic or third-party cases for discussion, *Balanced Experiential Inquiry* uses personal stories, which helps strike a balance between individual reflection and collective dialogue. While creating an atmosphere for conversational learning through group discussion, participants also begin with personal introspection. As the process unfolds, it allows for both individual reflection and collective meaning-making, which are important elements in the learning cycle.

Finally, BEI also invites participants to seek balance between their individual conscience (what they think is right) and collective peer feedback from the group reaction and dialogue. This tension elevates the need to establish equilibrium, motivating participants to explore the nature of their individual moral identity as compared to the collective moral identity of the group and organization. The principles of adult learning and insights from experiential learning theory suggest that ethics education and training be designed to recognize the unique needs of employees. Like other experiential learning activities, BEI addresses the needs of adult learners while helping them build moral muscle, working to increase a capacity for professional moral courage in the workplace (Sekerka, Bagozzi et al. 2009).

Balanced Experiential Inquiry

Balanced Experiential Inquiry is a dedicated ethics education and training session where organizational members exercise their moral muscles on real ethical challenges from work experiences. The technique has been used by others in a variety of organizations, predominantly with government employees and military service personnel at the junior, middle, and senior management level (Sekerka and Godwin 2010; Sekerka et al. 2012). It is a dedicated workshop session where individuals apply their moral competencies toward understanding and unpacking their own ethical challenges from past or current organizational experiences. Although a trainer facilitates the process, BEI is not trainer-centered; rather, it focuses on identifying and using salient examples of participants' ethical dilemmas as the learning content.

The process of BEI is not a prepackaged or lecture-based activity. Each session is tailored to the unique experiences of the employee participants. There are specific steps in the process, but instructors must remain flexible, using situations relevant to the employees in the organizational setting. When employees engage in BEI, they are guided to better understand professional moral courage and to practice using the moral muscles that help facilitate it (Sekerka, Bagozzi et al. 2009). Inquiry, reflection, and dialogue are used to help employees discover how they can build their own moral strength and to see how their efforts can help shape the ethical culture of their organization. Table 11.2 summarizes the steps for conducting a BEI session, as well as which moral muscle each step exercises and the adult learning principles considered. The steps are now described in detail.

Table 11.2 Relating the Balanced Experiential Inquiry (BEI) process to moral competencies and adult learning principles

BEI step	Competency exercised	Adult learning principle considered	Phase in the experiential learning cycle
1. Identify ethical scenario	Moral preparation; reflective pause	Builds on personal life experience; allows for self-directed learning	Concrete experience
2. Examine strengths and barriers	Emotional signaling; reflective Pause; self-regulation	Allows for a problem-solving focus; allows for a strength-based focus	Reflection and abstract conceptualization about experience
3. Report-outs and group discussion	Emotional signaling; reflective pause; self-regulation; moral preparation	Allows for immediate application of knowledge	Conceptualization about experiences and beginning to experiment with new behaviors

Figure adapted from Sekerka et al. (2012)

Step 1

Identify an ethical scenario. At the outset of a *Balanced Experiential Inquiry* session, employees are asked to individually write down a brief description of an ethical challenge that they have faced in the workplace and what they were thinking and feeling at the time (similar to the critical incident interview technique) (Flanagan 1982). Participants are guided to consider situations that may have been difficult (hard to act), problematic (uncertain), or set forth a dilemma (no one correct answer). The following instructions are read aloud:

> Think back to a time when you faced an ethical challenge while at work. An example might be a situation where there is a conflict between doing what you think you should do and what the organization, boss, or peer norms suggest. This might involve a conflict between your own values and the organization's goals. The situation may have made it difficult for you to act, to know what to do, or to determine how to resolve the issue. As you think back about your experiences that you have encountered while on the job, this is a time when you may have been unsure how to act or did not know what to do. The situation was likely undesirable, based upon the risks you perceived. The experience presented a moral issue and, at the time, none of the options seemed particularly favorable.

People are then given time to reflect, consider their ideas, and take notes about personal experiences with their own personal ethical challenges at work. Group members are asked to address the following questions during this period:

- What was the ethical issue and what did you do?
- What were you thinking and feeling at the time?

This step is used to commence moral preparation. Every session begins with the solicitation of ethical challenges participants have encountered, prompting self-directed learning based upon life experience, a core tenet of adult learning theory.

Employees are asked to consider their past feelings, decisions, and actions (or inaction). In so doing they begin to discern their own moral agency. Situations often present conflicting or competing values, and participants generally seek verification to establish what they should have done (i.e., identify the potential right action(s) in the situation). While the facilitator works to validate and affirm their experiences, they remain nonjudgmental about what is (or is not) an ethical challenge or what is (or is not) a "right" decision or response. The scenarios vary, but often include stories that involve rule-bending; stealing, lying, and/or cheating; sexual activity; drug/alcohol problems; bribery/corruption; and harassment (Sekerka et al. 2014; see Appendix for examples). Regardless of whether or not the scenario resulted in a moral action, every case presents a learning opportunity to exercise participants' moral muscles. Central to the muscle of moral preparation, Step 1 invites participants to consider, examine, and begin to look honestly at their willingness to engage in moral action.

Step 2

Examining strengths and barriers with a partner. Participants are then asked to form pairs to share their story with a partner. This starts an ethics dialogue and encourages conversational learning among employees, which, according to Baker et al. (2005), is a fundamental element of "meaning-making that in turn guides and informs behavior that creates new concrete experiences for reflection" (p. 423). As the group members work in their dyads, the facilitator visits each pair to see how they are doing and to determine some of the key issues for this organization. Supportive probes are provided to pairs less comfortable with this initial engagement, affirming their effort and helping them to launch their dialogue.

After the exchange of scenarios and experiences, the pair is asked to determine what supported (or curtailed) any ability to proceed with moral action in the reported circumstance. Participants are reminded that this may be an internal or external characteristic of their process or the situation itself. This step is designed to emphasize an action orientation, considering specifically what promotes or blocks moral action. Additional time is provided to address the following questions in the dyads:

- What supported (or curtailed) your ability to respond with moral action?
- What about the organization or management supported (or curtailed) your ability to address this situation effectively?

This step helps participants exercise their moral muscles of reflective pause, emotional signaling, and self-regulation. Additionally, it takes into consideration the adult learning principle of focusing on real-life issues with a problem-solving approach.

Step 3

Report-outs and group discussion. This final step continues to elevate the experiential focus and conversational learning nature of the activity, bringing people together through collective storytelling about personal issues. The facilitator asks for volunteers to present situations in community (to the larger group). In describing their stories, participants connect to others, establishing shared value around the desire to "do the right thing." Most people have never discussed their ethical issues with anyone and, if they have, rarely with a group of organizational members. While everyone has an instinct to avoid public scrutiny, the desire to remain silent is superseded by the opportunity to discover and learn.

Many people share because they seek affirmation for their actions, want ideas for solutions, or consider their situation as a learning resource for the group. Rarely do participants present a scenario where they see themselves as moral exemplars. Rather, participants often select situations that they see as unfinished episodes (i.e., some aspect of the event or their response is still unresolved) or that surprised them. The choice to impose a self-directed time-out and consider their story before sharing it publicly exercises the moral muscle of reflective pause. Self-regulation also gets a workout as participants manage their feelings and desires, allowing themselves to become vulnerable to public scrutiny for the sake of learning and personal development.

Participants empathize with their colleagues as they report their dilemmas, ask one another questions, and determine key knowledge from their shared challenges. Often they collectively presuppose what they might do differently in the future, or even how they might change organizational policies and practices to better support ethical performance. Barriers to moral action emerge over the course of the session, typically revealing how narrow self-focused concern is a deterrent for professional moral courage. People often move to blame some person, place, or thing that is out of their control (i.e., nothing they can say or do will make it "right"). This is used as a learning point to affirm the need for personal responsibility and moral preparation as a part of one's identity.

As participants work together to deconstruct the situation and identify what promotes or curtails their willingness to engage in moral action, the facilitator tracks and diagrams this information on a whiteboard or flip chart at the front of the room. Here the facilitator notes the specific situations deemed problematic, what emotions were experienced, what happened, and where moral muscles were exercised (or could have been) in the specific encounter. Depending on the length of time allotted for the workshop (typically between 2 and 3 h), four to five scenarios are examined with additional probes set forth during the exchange, such as:

- How will you overcome these challenges?
- How will you sustain your own moral strength, as a model to others?

In addition to helping participants exercise moral muscles, this step also honors the adult learning principles to allow immediate application of knowledge to work-related issues they will soon face.

Facilitating Self-directed Learning

The process is not designed to determine what the "right" action should be, but how one learns to manage the emotions, thoughts, motives, evaluations, and intentions in the decision to engage (or not engage) in moral action. Although the process of *Balanced Experiential Inquiry* is self-directed and rooted in the content raised by participants, it is important to recognize that the facilitation is not passive. Rather, a BEI facilitator has an important and active role to play in the session while adhering to the principles of adult learning outlined above. For example, in some workshops members know one another; in others they do not. Therefore, to create a safe space the facilitator establishes a Socratic dialogue, promoting ongoing reflective questions back to the group to let them review and deconstruct the scenario, potentially reframing but without imposing judgment. In some cases, a decision to take no action may be an appropriate moral response.

The facilitator consistently guides the discussion by elevating the positive aspects of the stories. Combined with affirmations, this helps establish trust for openness as participants engage in reflection and dialogue. The facilitator becomes a pseudo-role model for practicing the technique, demonstrating how to share insights, pose concerns, and challenge employee peers to examine situations in varying ways. In so doing, participants develop a shared sense of ownership for the issues presented and conduct an ethics dialogue in an open forum-type setting. The facilitator should "check in" with each participant, ensuring that they have discussion time, if so desired. Without pressure to share, each person should be encouraged to participate in some fashion. Equity is established by having everyone engage in some way. If some remain aloof, quiet, or removed, the facilitator should try to include them by simply asking their opinion on a matter or inviting their involvement in procedural duties without inducing pressure.

Throughout the process, the facilitator prompts the group to examine both the strengths and weaknesses of each case, at the individual, group, and organizational levels. The facilitator continually points out what moral muscles were demonstrated in the story being shared, how and when they are used in the session, and how ethical challenges serve as a platform to strengthen them in the future. As employees openly describe their issues to others, they begin to experience a sense of vulnerability. The process can be anxiety-provoking as people become open to criticism in front of others and the tensions originally present in the circumstance are recalled (Fig. 11.3).

Participants can immediately begin to exercise their moral muscles and experience emotions, both positive and negative, that mirror the experience of facing an ethical challenge with professional moral courage. They have to manage their

Fig. 11.3 Informal prompts encourage ongoing reflection to a group of adult learners. Image credited to Monkey Business Images/Shutterstock.com

thoughts and feelings in the moment. Sometimes participants are timid about offering their stories and remain quiet for much of the session. Others are more emboldened, expressing enthusiasm to share their encounter as if they finally have an opportunity to get help. Most are curious and want feedback. As the conversation unfolds, however, increased stress is likely, as decisions and actions are challenged. This can emerge as nervousness or even anger. Again, such negative emotions are similar to what is experienced at the onset of facing an ethical challenge.

It is the role of the facilitator to continually remind participants that they are now actually practicing what it feels like to engage in professional moral courage, assuring them that this is an appropriate, managed, and safe process. It is essential that the facilitator supports the group in this effort, affirming that the process is about inviting emotional signaling and self-regulation in a group context, which is key for ongoing moral preparation. After conducting several workshops, facilitators build a repertoire of stories. Anonymous vignettes from other sessions can be used to: (a) highlight any missing points (e.g., ensuring emphasis on self-regulation), (b) alleviate tension in the room by generating humor from external examples, and (c) emphasize how workshops take-aways can be used for personal and organizational improvement. The notion of personal responsibility is underscored throughout the process, and employees leave with an experience that affirms how moral muscles need exercise to be strengthened.

Shaping the Future

As companies work to strengthen ethics in organizational settings, their education and training programs need to go beyond the "cookie-cutter" modules that myopically focus on drilling compliance with specific policies. If moral strength is desired, organizations need to shift to a more developmental format, one that helps employees extend their current abilities and exercise the requisite skill sets needed to deploy ethical action. This means employees' moral muscles are developed and toned, becoming a part of managers' repertoire of competencies practiced in their everyday business decisions. To build and strengthen the skills that support professional moral courage, individuals need to understand their current capabilities and extend them.

Through use of activities like *Balanced Experiential Inquiry*, employees can bring their concerns forward in a safe environment and learn how they can address ethics in cooperation with others. Such practices give people an opportunity to share their thoughts and feelings in community, which lends credibility to ethical performance and simultaneously exercises people's moral muscles in a group context. Organizational members can benefit from exercising their moral competencies in community, because they must be used in situations where social pressures are piqued. Exercising one's moral muscles in the presence of others can also help people learn how to draw upon others' strengths as a resource to further support movement toward right action. Finally, people can practice how to stand up to and buffer opposing forces: influences that may deter sustaining a commitment to achieve a moral action.

Balanced Experiential Inquiry is but one process to encourage adult moral development. Other techniques should be considered, as there is certainly no one right way to achieve moral strength. For example, theoretical research outlines how personal reflection on one's best self, focusing on character strengths, prompts awareness of a person's virtuous self (Roberts et al. 2005a, b; Spreitzer et al. 2009). Roberts and her colleagues describe how feedback on how we have made a memorable impact on the lives of others can produce a wave of positive emotion (e.g., gratitude, pride). This affirming experience supports a virtuous view of self, potentially elevating the saliency of moral strength, which, in turn, may support the desire and fortitude to proceed with future ethical actions.

This type of ethical development training in organizational settings encourages other scholars, practitioners, and educators to edify existing theory. It is important to help organizational members recast Rest's (1986) linear model, expanding it to reflect a more systemic process, seeing ethical thinking and action as an ongoing process, rather than a finite effort. Seeing ethical decision-making and subsequent behavior as a continual cycle, can foster self-renewal and learning from one's efforts. Once a decision has been made and action taken, embracing moral preparation as ongoing endeavor can help bolster the endorsement of ethics as an ongoing duty.

Rest's seminal work sets forth an argument that moral awareness is a necessary first step toward moral action. His well-known four-component model of moral decision-making suggests that an individual must begin with moral awareness (Step 1) before he or she is able to make a moral judgment (Step 2). This is followed by the further establishment of their moral intent, forming the determination and will to address the moral concern as an important element in the decision-making trajectory (Step 3), and then ultimately engaging in a moral action (Step 4). Just as the process of *Balanced Experiential Inquiry* begins and ends with strengthening moral preparation, similarly the concept of moral development may ultimately be reconceptualized as an upward spiral of increasing awareness and ongoing moral growth.

Building on the concept of moral preparation, engaging in a moral act is not meant to be a final and conclusive effort. Rather, it is a prelude for ongoing improvement. For example, upon completion of an ethical act, engaging in post hoc reflection can be useful. Learning from the experience one might also strive to where systemic change is needed (at the personal and organizational levels). An attitude of ongoing discovery can affirm and bolster sustained moral intent, increasing ethical vigilance that sets the stage for future acts of professional moral courage. Insights from Fredrickson and Joiner's work (2002) show how upward spirals of broadening and building capacity can be triggered by positive emotions. By implication, successfully engaging in a moral act can fuel additional moral action. As individuals learn to use their moral muscles and successfully navigate ethical situations, positive experiences can be used to gain strength, which in turn helps them prepare for their next challenge (Fig. 11.4).

Fig. 11.4 Positive organizational ethics takes a commitment to ongoing learning and development. Image courtesy of FreeImage.com

The capacity for positive ethics in organizations can be built and strengthened by attending to content and context. But for leaders to be committed to addressing both compliance and competency aspects of ethics education and training, developmental processes must be woven into the organization's ongoing learning agenda. No matter what you call it, other processes that promote individual and group reflection, dialogue, and personal and organizational ethical development, like BEI, may also be useful and effective (e.g., Giving Voice to Values, http://www.babson.edu/Academics/teaching-research/gvv/Pages/curriculum.aspx). The critical point is that development happens daily, over time, with practice and peer and management support. When ethics becomes relegated to a once-a-year annual training initiative, the notion of growth and development is unlikely to ever get off the ground. If employees are expected to go beyond the moral minimum, moral strength needs to be inculcated into the meaning of work itself. Facilitated inquiry into salient ethical challenges, as offered by *Balanced Experiential Inquiry*, is a starting point for discovery into what supports individual and collective moral courage in every business profession.

It should be mentioned that there is a vast difference between ethics training that emphasizes values and development, versus coercively focusing on compliance-based ethics. Research by Stansbury and Barry (2006) highlights several potential drawbacks of ethics programs, including the specter of indoctrination, a politicization of ethics, and an atrophy of competence. Their work is a cautionary warning that when ethics programs rely upon coercive control, they may undermine their own effectiveness at prohibiting misbehavior.

An Inside Job

Ironically, business and educational systems often fail to encourage the ongoing and developmental nature of habituated ethics into our daily lives. Ethics is often taught via case study, with issues that require problematic resolution. A sole reliance on the case method doesn't exercise one's ability to be ethically aware, because the issue is handed to you. Especially disconcerting is that the issue set forth may never have occurred if someone thought about the ethical elements of the circumstances in advance. Broaching ethics in this manner never gets out ahead of the problem. Inadvertently we tend to communicate that we value ethics when it emerges as a solution to a problem, rather than as a way of living. If we want to put value back into our values, really live them, we need to do more than wait for issues to emerge. While reactions are sometimes necessary, it is essential to teach decision-makers how to embrace ethics—*before* trouble unfolds.

As a leading scholar in moral psychology, Haidt says we need to understand why people behave unethically, even when they think they are virtuous (2014). He describes this problem metaphorically, as if the inner conscious is like a rider on the back of an unconscious elephant (2006) (Fig. 11.5). The rider is deliberate reasoning, the part of us that learns facts and formulates arguments. The elephant is the

Fig. 11.5 Learning to ride
your inner elephant. *Mahout
on an elephant*, gouache on
paper, Murshidabad, India
(18th century); image credited
to the V&A collection, is in
the public domain

other 99 % of what goes on in our minds, the automatic process elements like intuition, emotion and habit. In a mature adult, the rider and elephant work together to sort out competing values and inner conflicts. In the event of an ethical issue, the rational right and wrong of the rider just isn't powerful enough to steer the mammoth, the power of our unconscious. Citing Ovid's poem Metamorphoses, Haidt says we most likely: "see the right way and approve it, but alas...follow the wrong." Think about it, if you had a disagreement with an elephant, who would likely win?

Haidt says ethics classes are typically aimed at teaching the rider, aimed at training the logical part of our thought processes. Regardless of how much you know about moral philosophies, decision-making models, and case exemplars, if you are tempted to engage in an ethical activity at work, your conscious reasoning is unlikely to be strong enough to control your inner elephant. Pointing to research studies conducted by Ariely, Gino and Mazar, Haidt says this reality is actually made worse by the fact that our riders are often willing accomplices in the rationalization of taking the elephant's unethical path. These scholars have also found that people will cheat if they think they can get more money, but they typically only cheat up to the point at which they can find excuses and justifications that maintain a belief in their own virtue. Creative people actually cheat more than others, because they are better at finding self-serving justifications. Taking this information together, we need to teach our inner riders to be more aware, and to create structure, discipline and supervision for the wild elephant.

Haidt also notes that motivated cognition research outlines how our reasoning abilities evolved not to help us find truth, but to help us influence others. That's why you might be horrible at solving a simple logic problem, but you're incredibly resourceful when you are working to achieve your performance goals. Taking this info together, and in keeping with Haidt's metaphor, the elephant makes the decisions on which way to go and the rider justifies the action in case you get into trouble. In summarizing his concerns, he says you cannot make anything stick in ethics education and training, unless you're working to educate the elephant.

To support this notion, business schools also need to represent the ethical cultures we hope to see in the workplace; that is, environments where professionalism and trust are valued, and count for something. To advance this notion, what about making a percentage of the grade based on a peer determination of a student's level of professionalism in class? Evidence of character might be used as a basis for selection and retention in entrance requirements. Like the workplace, policies on cheating need to be consistent, rigorous, and imposed across the board: *you cheat, you're out*. Working with student leaders, academic institutions need to define school-wide norms of professional behavior, which apply to everyone (students, faculty, and the administration). Regardless of how effective these measures may be, in certain circumstances we know that social forces can influence and supersede that use of core values.

To improve ethical behavior in business, we've got to alter the path, change where our elephant can go. This means incorporating insights from social psychology, helping the next generation of leaders to learn how to construct guardrails and re-route paths away from slippery ethical slopes. Perhaps more importantly, it means learning how to design ethical organizations as a functional and healthy sustainable system. Haidt says an ethical culture isn't just about "nudging" individuals to stay clear of bad and to push them to do good. Rather, it requires a mindful and strategic effort to shape an ethical organizational culture and craft internal processes to protect and edify that culture. This means ethics is woven right into the fabric of organizational design—it's not just an afterthought.

In the past decade we have seen a demonstrative shift, with educators working to better prepare business students for their role in organizations as one that incorporates ethics. We have a surge in topics that cover stakeholder-driven corporate social responsibility (CSR) and conscious capitalism. Sometimes referred to as a triple bottom line approach to business enterprise, CSR assumes that firms consider the impact of their operations on people and the planet in route to making a profit. Rather than a sole focus on establishing returns for shareholders, *how* income is generated becomes relevant. The challenge of sustainable enterprise continues to press scholars for theories and empirical research to show how moral responsibility can be effective in the context of capitalism. Some managers look at what is going on around them and do not believe they can compete with one arm tied behind their back. When business ethics is driven by cost-cutting measures or imposed regulation, it may not be based upon a moral motive. How ethics is operationalized provides the platform for how people go about doing their work. Thus, moral development that is transferable to daily operations requires a real and lasting internal commitment by the firm's leadership, with both short- and long-term business ethics strategy.[1]

Beyond the organization's approach to ethics in business, moral development is vastly personal. Ethics is an inside job. Insights about this "inside" effort stem from the psychology of ethical decision-making (Bazerman and Trenbrunsal 2011) and moral identity (Aquino and Reed 2002). Examining and reflection upon who you are and how your values may or may not be represented in your decisions and actions, demonstrate personal choices. These choices, over time, shape your character, further endorsing your strengths, but also potentially accentuating areas of personal weakness (Rokeach 1973). Your identity is essentially a portfolio of the decisions you have made and the actions they influenced.

Rarely do managers take time to inventory the authenticity of the choices, seeing that they match personal and organizational values (Taylor 1991). An entryway for adult moral development is to consider to what degree our decisions reflect the values we say we hold. Ethicists describe moral growth as a process of becoming more adept and fluid with one's moral functioning (Hardy and Carlo 2005). Important to this effort is the integration of self-governed internal cognitive and emotional systems (Colby and Damon 1992, 1993; Lapsley and Narvaez 2004). By implication, this suggests that everyone will benefit from working at how to become more ethically responsible as a matter of choice.

Most people say that "family comes first" and work tirelessly to care for and support those they love. Family is at the core of our human social structure, a basic element of our survival. And yet, people who show deep care and compassion for their loved ones can also be completely unethical in their day-to-day routines (Fig 11.6). Amoral characters like Tony Soprano on the well-known HBO series, *The Sopranos*, claimed to be "doing everything for them"—his family. While this is a fictitious example, management at BP and AIG might similarly describe their motivations for involvement in unethical disasters as being driven by a desire to make money for their families or efforts to protect or advance the firm's mission. One might ask, "Does a passion to care for loved ones legitimize decisions that are not in the best interest of others?" Perhaps self-serving motives are at bay, motivated by an underlying desire to get ahead and establish power. Consider your root motives when you make strategic decisions, asking yourself, "Who am I doing this for and why?" Some people have a hard time being honest with themselves, losing sight of their real motives behind their actions. After determining the true reason and purpose, consider if you fairly appropriate quality, decency, respect, and well-being to others. Do you limit access, benefits, or rewards to only those within your immediate family, circle, or special group?

---

[1]Additional information can be found at: http://www.ethicalsystems.org/content/jonathan-haidt.

Fig. 11.6 With the Sopranos, it's supposedly "family first". Image credited to the Everett Collection/Shutterstock.com. Robert Iler, James Gandolfini and Jamie-Lynn Sigler of The Sopranos, New York, 9/5/2002

Our desires, whether they are for money, power, achievement, or otherwise, fuel our actions. In business, ethical identity is expressed in where and how we direct our time and energy. What we truly want shapes our goals, which in turn, influence the decisions we make and the actions we take. If ethical action is to emerge in the workplace, people at every level of the organization need to value the idea of being ethical in all of their activities, not just when it is convenient or has to do with meeting the demands of a specific policy, rule, or condition. To be ethical, you've got to want it on a sustained basis in all areas of your life. This shows up in the small decisions and actions you engage in daily. Do you take the time to park legally or just grab any spot and then justify your actions? Do you read the company policy or just check the box saying you did? Do you lie to buy time? Being responsible to your ethical self is not something you can turn on and off as a matter of convenience. Being honest with yourself and others is a way of life.

Everyone has innate character strengths. Whether it is a proclivity to play a certain sport or instrument, communicate ideas, curiously pursue discovery, or to enhance or build camaraderie on a team, we all have unique gifts. You may possess an ethical sensibility, a profound and acute commitment to using your core values, such as being diligent, staying committed or assuming responsibility without external demands. But to be a person of moral strength requires a concerted and ongoing effort. Being ethical is not something you arrive at, at some point in time, as a result of completing a process. Nor is being ethical based on mastering one specific ability. It is a suite of competencies, such as self-regulation, that are cultivated over time and require consistent use to be maintained. Because one's physical and mental states, along with circumstances, are varied and ever-changing, so too can our ethical competency waver. Based on who you are, the people you are with, and the circumstances and context, you have the propensity to respond in varying ways. Thus, your propensity to be ethical in any given situation can be different on any given day. In short, just because you were ethical yesterday, does not necessarily mean you will be ethical today.

As an adult, you can still learn to play the piano or study a foreign language. Altering your diet or adding exercise to your daily regime is doable. While such efforts require a mindful focus to keep up the effort, continuing to make a commitment to new behaviors, you can learn, grow and change with a decision to do so. New actions require sustained motivation to achieve daily or weekly goals over time. Similarly, people can advance their penchant for being ethical. But it takes effort, practice, and looking for the opportunity to exercise your moral competency. Having skills but not using them is like having learned Spanish in grade school but not speaking it since.

If you do not use our ability it is likely to be extremely limited or perhaps lost altogether. Certainly habituation of ethicality can become somewhat automatic over time. But with varying states and changing circumstances, learning how to maintain deliberate attention to your ethical self is central in sustaining ethical durability. Like any other talent, if you want to be truly excellent at something, it requires ongoing practice. Many assume that as we age, the experiences we encounter contribute to our character strength. This may be so. But it is no guarantee of moral maturity or continuity of ethical behavior. If you have a desire to be ethical, it is important to recognize that ongoing adult moral development is not only possible: it is vital to durable corporate social responsibility (CSR) performance in business.

To look at your ethical identity more closely you must begin by honestly understanding your starting point, "Who am I?" If you have decided that you have a desire to be ethical you must also make a decision that you are willing to work at it. Moral competency development will serve as the bridge toward helping you proceed with these goals. Building moral competency takes work. Like achieving any goal, including the desire to be ethical, you have to put in time and effort. When we hear the term "work," we envision labor and exertion. While it does not have to be drudgery, it requires focused determination. Therefore, to become your best ethical self, truly developing your character, you need to value your potential ethical identity. Given that this particular endeavor is about becoming a better person, learning to activate goodness from within, what could be more fascinating? The assumption is that your character is relevant and meaningful to you.

While the motivation to care about your personal development may vary over time, all you need is a modicum of interest to get started. If you want to take this challenge on and help lead others to do the same, you have an interesting adventure in store. At any moment, you can choose to become your best. It is up to you. Being ethical is an inside job.

Takeaway Points

1. Ethics education can leverage pedagogical insight from experiential learning theory.
2. Balanced Experiential Inquiry (BEI) is a technique used to cultivate adult moral development in the workplace.
3. Organizational ethics education and training program needs to link ethical compliance with employees' professional development.

Reflection Questions

Identify a particularly thorny ethical challenge you face at work. What thoughts and feelings come up for you around addressing the issue with professional moral courage? What can you do to pursue ethical action, despite the potential for negative blow-back? Do you have a strategy for using your emotions (positive and negative) as energy toward "doing the right thing?".

References

Aquino, K., & Reed, A. (2002). The self-importance of moral identity. *Journal of Personality and Social Psychology, 83*, 1423–1441.

Baker, A., Jensen, P., & Kolb, D. (2005). Conversation as experiential learning. *Management Learning, 36*(4), 411–427.

Bazerman, M. H., & Trenbrunsal, A. E. (2011). *Blind spots: Why we fail to do what's right and what to do about it.* Princeton, NJ: Princeton University Press.

Brookfield, S. (1996). Adult learning: An overview. In A. Tuinjman (Ed.), *International encyclopedia of education.* Princeton, NJ: Princeton University Press.

Brown, J. S., & Duguid, P. (1998). Organizational knowledge. *California Management Review, 40*(3), 90–111.

Calloway-Graham, D. (2004). The art of teaching and learning. *The Social Science Journal, 41*(4), 689–694.

Colby, A., & Damon, W. (1992). *Some do care: Contemporary lives of moral commitment.* New York: The Free Press.

Colby, A., & Damon, W. (1993). The uniting of self and morality in the development of extraordinary moral commitment. In G. G. Noam & T. E. Wren (Eds.), *The moral self* (pp. 149–174). Cambridge, MA: MIT Press.

Cooperrider, D. L., & Sekerka, L. E. (2006). Toward a theory of positive organizational change. In Joan V. Gallos (Ed.), *Organization Development: A Jossey-Bass Reader: 223-238.* San Francisco, CA: John Wiley & Sons.

Cressey, D. R., & Moore, C. A. (1983). Managerial values and corporate codes of ethics. *California Management Review, 25*(4), 53–77.

Davis, J. H., Schoorman, F. D., & Donaldson, L. (1997). Toward a stewardship theory of management. *Academy of Management Review, 22*(1), 20–47.

Flanagan, J. C. (1982). The critical incident technique. *Psychological Bulletin, 4*, 327–358.

Fredrickson, B., & Joiner, T. (2002). Positive emotions trigger upward spirals toward emotional well-being. *American Psychological Society, 13*(2), 172.

Haidt, J. (2006). *The happiness hypothesis: finding modern truth in ancient wisdom.* New York: Basic Books.

Haidt, J. (2014). Can you teach businessmen to be ethical? *The Washington Post.* http://www. washingtonpost.com/blogs/on-leadership/wp/2014/01/13/can-you-teach-businessmen-to-be-ethical/. Accessed on July 7, 2015.

Hardy, S. A., & Carlo, G. (2005). Identity as a source of moral motivation. *Human Development, 48,* 232–256.

Hemmasi, M., & Graf, L. A. (1992). Managerial skills acquisition: A case for using business policy simulations. *Simulation & Gaming, 23*(3), 298.

Knowles, M. S. (1968). Andragogy, not pedagogy. *Adult Leadership, 16*(10), 350–352.

Knowles, M. S. (1973). *The adult learner: A neglected species.* Houston: Gulf Publishing.

Knowles, M. S. (1980). *The modern practice of adult education: from pedagogy to androgogy* (2nd ed.). New York: Cambridge Books.

Kolb, D. A. (1984). *Experiential learning: Experience as the source of learning and development* (2nd ed.). Englewood Cliffs, NJ: Prentice-Hall.

Kolb, D. A., Baker, A. C., & Jensen, P. J. (2002). Conversation as experiential learning. In Ann C. Baker, Patricia J. Jensen, & David A. Kolb (Eds.), *Conversational learning: An experiential approach to knowledge creation* (pp. 51–66). Westport, CT: Quorum Books.

Laditka, S. B., & Houck, M. M. (2006). Student-developed case studies: An Experiential approach for teaching ethics in management. *Journal of Business Ethics, 64,* 157–167.

Lapsley, D. K., & Narvaez, D. (2004). A social-cognitive approach to the moral personality. In D. K. Lapsley & D. Narvaez (Eds.), *Moral development, self, and identity* (pp. 51–66). Mahwah, NJ: Erlbaum.

Lindeman, E. C. L. (1926). *The meaning of adult education.* New York: New Republic.

Matherne, B. P., Gove, S., Forlani, V., & Janney, J. J. (2006). "Walk the talk": Developing personal ethical agency through a business partnership program. *Journal of Management Education, 30*(1), 106–134.

Merriam, S. (2001). Andragogy and self-directed learning: Pillars of adult learning theory. *New Directions for Adult and Continuing Education, 89,* 1–13.

Rest, J. R. (1986). The major component of morality. In W. M. Kurtines & J. L. Gerwitz (Eds.), *Morality, moral behavior, and moral development* (pp. 24–38). New York: Wiley.

Rokeach, M. (1973). *The nature of human values.* New York: McGraw-Hill.

Roberts, L. M., Dutton, J., Spreitzer, G., Heaphy, E., & Quinn, R. (2005a). Composing the reflected best self: Building pathways for becoming extraordinary in work organizations. *Academy of Management Review, 30*(4), 712–736.

Roberts, L. M., Spreitzer, G., Dutton, J., Quinn, R., Heaphy, E., & Barker, B. (2005b). How to Play to your Strengths. *Harvard Business Review, 83*(1), 75–80.

Sanyal, R. N. (2000). An experiential approach to teaching ethics in international business. *Teaching Business Ethics, 4,* 137–149.

Sánchez, R. M. (2008). *Education Digest, 73*(7), 53–56.

Sekerka, L. E. (2009). Organizational ethics education and training: A review of best practices and their application. *International Journal of Training and Development, 13*(2), 77–95.

Sekerka, L. E., & Fredrickson, B. L. (2007). Creating transformative cooperation through positive emotions. In S. K. Piderit, R. E. Fry, & D. L. Cooperrider (Eds.), *A handbook of transformative cooperation: new designs and dynamics* (pp. 151–169). Stanford, CA: University Press.

Sekerka, L., & Godwin, L. (2007). Strengthening professional moral courage: A balanced approach to ethics training. *Training & Management Development Methods, 24*(5), 63–74.

Sekerka, L. E., Brumbaugh, A., Rosa, J., & Cooperrider, D. (2006). Comparing appreciative inquiry to a diagnostic technique in organizational change: The moderating effects of gender. *International Journal of Organization Theory and Behavior, 9*(4), 449–489.

Sekerka, L. E., Bagozzi, R. P., & Charnigo, R. (2009). Facing ethical challenges in the workplace: Conceptualizing and Measuring professional moral courage. *Journal of Business Ethics, 89*(4), 565–579.

Sekerka, L. E., Zolin, R., & Goosby Smith, J. (2009). Careful what you ask for: how inquiry strategy influences readiness mode. *Organizational Management Journal, 6*, 106–122.

Sekerka, L. E., McCarthy, J. D., & Bagozzi, R. (2011). Developing the capacity for professional moral courage: Facing daily ethical challenges in today's military workplace. In D. Comer & G. Vega (Eds.), *Moral courage in organizations: Doing the right thing at work* (pp. 130–141). Armonk, NY: M.E. Sharpe.

Sekerka, L. E., Godwin, L., & Charnigo, R. (2012). Use of balanced experiential inquiry to build ethical strength in the workplace. *Special Issue on Experiential Learning for the Journal of Management Development, 30*(3), 275–286.

Sekerka, L. E., Godwin, L., & Charnigo, R. (2014). Cultivating curious managers: Motivating moral awareness through balanced experiential inquiry. *Journal of Management Development.*

Shannon, J. R., & Berl, R. L. (1997). Are we teaching ethics in marketing? A survey of student attitudes and perceptions. *Journal of Business Ethics, 16*(10), 34–42.

Smith, A., & Rogers, V. (2000). Ethics-related responses to specific situation vignettes: Evidence of gender-based differences and occupational socialization. *Journal of Business Ethics, 28*, 73–86.

Spreitzer, G. M., Stephens, J. P., & Sweetman, D. (2009). The reflected best self field experiment with adolescent leaders: Exploring the psychological resources associated with feedback source and Valence. *Journal of Positive Psychology, 4*(5), 331–348.

Stansbury, J., & Barry, B. (2006). Ethics programs and the paradox of control. *Business Ethics Quarterly, 17*(2), 239–262.

Sundaram, A. K., & Inkpen, A. C. (2004). The corporate objective revisited. *Organization Science, 15*(3), 350–363.

Taylor, C. (1991). *The ethics of authenticity.* Boston: Harvard University Press.

Weick, K. E. (1995). *Sensemaking in organizations.* Thousand Oaks, CA: Sage.

Chapter 12
Self-directed Moral Development

Ethical development is a necessary prerequisite, if good character is to become a matter of practical life. Of course, your ethicality begins in childhood and emerges with observation, learning, time, and experience. The etymological ancestor of the word ethics, *ethike*, is a compound formed from the words *ethos* and *techne*. It literally means "the art or skill necessary to produce a showing of characteristic manner or spirit," complemented by a "bonding attitude" or "sense of comportment toward others." Interestingly, the notion of competency to act in a particular manner and to work well with others is at the very heart of the original term.

Aristotle explained that none of our moral virtues or character strengths arise by nature. He goes on to say that nothing contrary to nature can emerge from habit. For instance, a stone that falls cannot be habituated to go upward, not even if one tries to train it by throwing it up ten thousand times. He argued that nothing in nature that behaves in one way can be trained to behave in another. If one stops here, we might think Aristotle is suggesting that human nature cannot be altered. But reading further, the subtlety of his insight is revealed. He goes on to say that neither by nature, nor contrary to it, do the virtues arise within us. Rather, we adapt to receive them, and then we perfect them through our habits of use (NE1103a19-25).

As you think about your own nature, consider your capacity for personal growth. Are you willing to develop the necessary skills to be more ethical? Perhaps one of the most exciting revelations about being human is that we have a choice in how we steer our thoughts and behaviors. That means we can actually choose how our nature is manifest. But what is considered to be our nature by others can be perceived, experienced, or interpreted differently. Although we have little or no control with regards to how others see us, we can direct the course of who we are, who we want to be, and who we want to become.

Over time, many of us develop patterns, habits that are incorporated into our daily actions repeatedly. Rather than maintaining a conscious mindfulness of why we act in a certain way, we can become defined by unattended familiar thoughts and behaviors. Many adults fall into the comfort or ease of their own automaticity. It is easy to lose sight of the fact that there are opportunities for new ways of thinking and being throughout our day. As humans, we have an ongoing capacity to learn

© Springer International Publishing Switzerland 2016

L. E. Sekerka, *Ethics is a Daily Deal*, DOI 10.1007/978-3-319-18090-8_12

and change. But to tap into this capacity, we must *choose* to do so, making a conscious decision to stay open to new ideas and being willing to work at applying them.

Adults Can Change

One definition of learning is a relatively permanent change in behavior that occurs as a result of interacting with one's environment (Rathus 2008). Learning does not create a fixed or rigid modification in a person. Rather, it is a deliberate and sustained effort to alter natural tendencies or inclinations and to create new ways of responding. Therefore, to own the learning, it takes practice, use, and regular application. Thinking that just because you heard it, like and want this learning to be a part of your life, and apply it occasionally, doesn't mean it's yours. This is particularly the case with ethics.

Being ethical implies you have learned how to be honest with yourself about who you really are. This entails looking at your own behavior, inclinations and practices, and striving to do better on an ongoing basis. If you ignore or deceive yourself, how can you improve? While having integrity suggests adherence to moral principles and soundness of moral character, it also is about continuing to become whole or complete (Oxford English Dictionary 2013). A person with integrity works to sustain ethical congruency in all their affairs. It is essential that people continually strive to ensure that the values they say they hold are demonstrated in their daily choices and actions. Thus, the ethical soundness within a person's identity is a lifelong aspiration and daily chore. Your integrity is developed through conscious awareness, ongoing efforts to put your best ethical self forward. Because character is vulnerable to temptations and sometimes blind to automatic responses that can become engrained over time, we all need to take stock of our own behavior, to look within, committing to self-directed reflection, discovery, and improvement.

As we have considered, learning right and wrong as a child, we are exposed to the beliefs of others about what is good, right, and honest. Most of us are taught explicitly through instruction as well as implicitly through observation. We learn what to value, and the worth or relative importance of particular beliefs. Equality, honesty, justice, faithfulness, commitment, and other values are, over time, folded into our identity. This menagerie of values fuses, forming our adult ethical self. But the expectation of who we think we are may not match who we have become. The good news is that the capacity for human development remains available to us throughout our entire lives. Adults can change. But to do so requires a decision and a sustained commitment to address the change as a desired goal. This requires planning and practice.

The application of identity theory to understanding adult development is a means to encourage cognitive and behavioral modification toward desired new behaviors. But resistance has always been a barrier to personal growth. Indeed, the combination of past behaviors and psychological resistance tend to fortify the struggle against individual change. Breakwell's seminal work in identity formation (1986) outlines how a threat to self-identity is a major factor in resistance to change, even more so than a person's past actions (Murtagh et al. 2012). Ironically, seeing yourself a certain way, even if your actions do not support this perception, is hard to alter. Regardless of whether or not the behavioral change is a positive one, resistance is still palpable and can thwart movement to effect behaviors that we know to be beneficial.

Take, for example, a person who wants to quit smoking. Aside from the addictive elements of a nicotine habit, people crave smoking in association with other activities. There is a ritualistic feature of smoking, say, with a cup of coffee, taking a break, after a meal, or simply connecting with others. A broader interpretation of self-identity, in terms of both current and aspired behavior, provides us with a clearer understanding of how or when we might be willing and able to change our own behavior. Growing evidence suggests that the influence of self-identity on behavior can be a prevailing form of personal agency, fueling a desire to change and to sustain that change.

Creating an identity for a quitting-self is particularly important in forming an intention to quit. Likewise, envisioning both a quitting- and smoking-self are important for the process of cessation and in developing new habits. In studying people who are trying to quit smoking, van den Putte and his colleagues (2009) found that the ability to cultivate a quitting-self can attenuate the negative effects experienced during smoking cessation. In building a revised self-identity, seeing yourself as a non-smoker, you can better manage desires hurled by your smoking-self. For example, your quitting-self (the non-smoker identity) now thinks about taking a break in a new way (e.g., helping someone, calling a friend, engaging in something you enjoy, taking exercise), rather than going out for a smoke (Fig. 12.1).

By implication, this suggests that creating a perception of your best ethical self (moral or virtuous) may be an important factor in helping you move from a current state of ethicality to one with greater fortitude. The analogy illustrates the importance and ability to envision a best ethical self, even if there is no precedent for this identity. In the case of learning to exercise your values, perceiving this identity in advance of an action may help you proceed with moral action, providing intrinsic motivational support. In self-directed change efforts, some refer to this process as "acting your way into new thinking". By "acting as if," you begin to establish new behaviors, creating a bridge between the prior self and the revised (improved) self. In time, you establish precedents for exercising character strength. And, by experiencing and feeling what it is like to do the right thing, the pride and sense of accomplishment that often accompanies moral action can help endorse the change. Creating a new precedent for how you see yourself takes willingness to apply sustained attention to the effort, which requires work.

Identity is not only crafted by what we have done, our action tendencies, but it is also the basis for our development, continuing to be shaped and confirmed by our everyday behaviors. A systemic loop remains a self- reinforcing process unless or

Fig. 12.1 Changing behavior is difficult, but not impossible. Image courtesy of FreeImage.com

until your action tendencies are trumped, altered, or modified. The desire for change can result from a profound event. For example, you do not follow organizational procedures and get into trouble (are reprimanded, demoted, or fired). It is often very difficult to want to change behaviors unless there is a pending threat or we have no choice but to do so. And yet, when it comes to being ethical, recognizing that you may not be living up to your core values may provide the impetus to reconcile this hypocrisy.

The old adage "you cannot teach an old dog new tricks" is inaccurate. It forecasts the challenge, as this is not easy. Although our brain circuitry is laid out by the time we're an adult, most of us have cognitive dexterity—the power, ability, and capacity to change. Schelgel et al. (2012) writes in the *Journal of Cognitive Neuroscience*, we now know that the human brain continues to change—for the better—as we age. That is, so long as the individual continues to engage in learning. While most people equate gray matter with the brain and its higher functions, such as sensation and perception, it is the white matter (about half of the brain's volume), that acts as the brain's communications network. The gray matter, with its densely packed nerve cell bodies, does the thinking, computing, and decision-making. You might recall Agatha Christie's Belgian detective, Hercule Poirot, who referred to his "little gray cells"' (pointing to the side of his head), to solve the particular mystery at hand (Fig. 12.2). In addition to gray matter, scientists have recently started to look at the white matter, referring to it as the brain's network cabling system. Research to better understand this element of cognition has led to a novel field of inquiry, showing how the brain stays plastic throughout life.

The findings of this research show that adults are quite capable of change (i.e., imposing structural modifications to the brain). This presents implications for the development of new models of learning. Scientists have recently demonstrated that significant changes are occurring in the brain when adults learn, noting that the actual structure undergoes modification. "This flies in the face of traditional views

Fig. 12.2 Agatha Christie's Poirot uses his "little grey cells" to solve a mystery. Image credited to APT/WXXI public broadcasting council at http://interactive.wxxi.org/highlights/2011/06/agatha-christies-poirot-yellow-iris-wxxi-tv

that all structural development happens in infancy, early in childhood," Schlegel said. Now that we have tools enabling us to actually visualize cognitive development, we are discovering that in many cases the brain can be just as malleable in adulthood as compared to when you were a child or an adolescent (2012). This research affirms that most people have the capacity to develop, build and exercise new habits, and alter their brain circuitry. However, such developmental efforts require sustained awareness to choose to redirect your initial thoughts (e.g., to cheat or cut corners) toward a new course of action (e.g., to uphold policy). People can, over time, engrain new paths to such a degree that they eventually become revised automatic responses. The habituation of new cognitions and ethical behavior is indeed possible.

Be Your Own Role Model

Given the ability for cognitive and behavioral dexterity, you can learn to be your own role model. Taking a two-pronged approach, cognitive behavioral techniques outline how you can use both thought and action in this regard. You may not see yourself as a person with moral strength. However, if you begin to engage in actions that demonstrate virtue (your best ethical self), you essentially role-play your way into a revised identity, fostering a new way of being. The habituation of character is often portrayed as a rather mechanical process that precedes the reflective and moral development that emerges in adulthood. Some scholars challenge this view, arguing that habituation is primarily a form of critical practice dependent on capacities of choice, perception, and deliberation (Sherman 1991), influenced by cognitive, emotional, an spiritual growth.

It seems nonsensical that we are all children and then, suddenly, at some particular age, we are now fully-formed reflective adults. The reality is that as we grow up, over our lifetime, we gradually and incrementally engage with the world and become reflective adults, by choice. As one person writing to David Brooks in *The New York Times* described it, "Spiritual and emotional growth happens in microscopic increments" (June 5, 2015). But we may or may not be morally mindful on any given day, even if we generally possess the capacity to reflect and improve. Circumstances, context, and/or other physical or psychological stressors can debilitate or bolster our ability and willingness to engage in self-reflective thought and action. Given this variation and malleability we have to attend to how we're doing. Do you check on yourself frequently, considering where you have done well or poorly? On the former, reigning in your ego, seeking out humility, and determining how you might do even better. On the latter, consider who you may have harmed, apologize, seek out how to do better, and make reparations for mistakes.

Responsibility is about creating an internal process for building and sustaining a habit of ethical awareness and the desire and willingness to do the right thing. This effort begins with a decision to maintain your self-awareness and the willingness to be ethical, even before an issue emerges. This translates into paying attention to how, where, and when you can assume the responsibility for doing good and avoiding unethical missteps. Such efforts require looking for and attending to the ethical elements of a situation—before taking action.

To do this, one has to be mindful of the present and recognize that one's ethicality can improve or regress. There are people who do not possess ethical awareness or the desire to be ethical. This may stem from a lack of education, poor parenting, or abusive circumstances. Or it may be driven from anger, fear, apathy, or a sense of entitlement. It is likely driven by a host of variables, stemming from the person's environment, their personality, and the choices they make. When social consensus for being ethical is not supported, a commitment to being your best ethical self becomes all the more important and perhaps more difficult. But most people have the ability to improve their ethicality, if they choose to do so.

There is motivational power—for good or for bad—within our moral identity (Reynolds and Cerinac 2007). Sponsoring, looking for, or applying moral strength, rather than merely responding to an unethical situation, keeps you at the forefront of ethicality. Do you scout and look for the ethical features within your simple day-to-day actions? This is not as hard as it may seem. Consider these additional probes to spark your reflective introspection:

- Do you manage time so as not to keep others waiting?
- Do you keep your commitments so as not to impose undue burden on others?
- Do you work to serve your needs or are you interested in being empathetic to the situational needs of others?
- Are you so driven to get what you want that you do not seek out ways to help those around you?
- Do you look for and examine where ethical weakness may emerge, in yourself and in your organization, striving to address the potential for ethical risk?

Fig. 12.3 Ursula Burns, CEO of Xerox, the first African–American woman to head a fortune 500 company. Image is in the public domain

Looking for where you can apply your values, in advance of any problem, takes you out of a cyclical and systemic reaction modality.

The assumption is, of course, that people want to be ethical. While this may not be true for everyone, it is possible for most of us to not only be ethical, but to also rise above our existing station in life and enhance our ethical capabilities as well. Ursula Burns, for example, was raised by her single mother in a housing project. Through perseverance she became the first African-American woman to be the head of a Fortune 500 Company, now the CEO of Xerox (Fig. 12.3). Howard Schultz grew up in poverty, yet went on to discover a coffee shop called Starbucks. Because business leaders, athletes, and popular public figures tend to receive media attention for dramatic success, it affirms our association between position, money, and fame and achieving greatness. While some people experience oppressive circumstances in early life, some rise above them to become ethical role models (MSN Money 2009). Perhaps more relevant and to the point is that we observe the millions of unsung heroes who dedicate their lives to service work, reaching out to others in need of care, recovery, support, or safe haven on a daily basis. But take heed: doing well and doing good tends to melt together, and we may fall prey to believing in people who are morally fallible, just like everyone else.

Bringing a global tidal wave of interest to both cycling and cancer recovery, Armstrong was classified as having won the Tour de France—a record seven consecutive times between 1999 and 2005. Subsequently, the United States Anti-Doping Agency (USADA 2012) presented its findings to the Union Cycliste Internationale (UCI), which disqualified Armstrong from those races for doping offenses, and then banned him from competitive cycling for life. Despite having denied drug use throughout his career, in January 2013, Armstrong finally admitted to doping in a television interview conducted by Oprah Winfrey.

In September of that same year, he was asked by UCI's new president, Brian Cookson, to testify about his doping. Armstrong refused to do so, until and unless he got a complete amnesty, which Cookson said would be highly unlikely. Given the profound good that Armstrong was able to achieve through his Livestrong Foundation, it is both a shame and great loss that he did not align his character strength of compassion with ethical performance in his sport. According to Slate (Lapowsky 2014), the once high-flying charity (raising some $500 million over the years to help 2.5 million patients, caretakers, and survivors) was effective at helping people receive access to services such as fertility preservation, clinical-trial matching, and providing healthcare insurance assistance.

As Armstrong's credibility eroded, the loss of some of the charity's biggest sponsors soon followed, including Nike and RadioShack. Revenue fell to $38.1 million in 2012, from $46.8 million the previous year, and continues to plummet. In 2014, 13 of Livestrong's 100 employees resigned. Lance Armstrong's profound positive contributions to help others and his global advocacy for cancer care and recovery still continue (Fig. 12.4). They have, however, been inordinately curtailed because he failed to model ethical performance.

While people often serve as important role models to others, looking up to any one person as a pillar of strength has inherent risks. Everyone, even the shining examples of fortitude, has vulnerabilities, character defects, and can be subject to moral lapses. No doubt, Joe Paterno, or "JoePa" as he was called at Pennsylvania

Fig. 12.4 Sports heroes/philanthropists fall from grace. Image credited to Frederic Legrand/COMEO/Shutterstock.com. Paris, France, July 26, 2010, Lance Armstrong on the Champs Elysees after the last race in the Tour de France competition

Fig. 12.5 A life-time of wins, comes a legacy of moral failure and loss. Image credited to Richard Paul Kane/Shutterstock.com. Penn state coach Joe Paterno addresses the media at Beaver Stadium April 24, 2010 in University Park, PA; Penn state coach Joe Paterno looks down during a loss to Illinois at Beaver Stadium October 9, 2010 in University Park, PA

State, is a sad example of this harsh reality (Fig. 12.5). A hero to thousands of young men and women as their winning football coach, Paterno was also considered a leader within his community and across the state. Regrettably, he may be remembered more for his association with the Jerry Sandusky scandal rather than his strength of character and winning record. Sadly, his lack of moral fortitude has altered his legacy, now inextricably wound up with the child sex abuse scandal at Penn State.

The investigation on the scandal, conducted by Louis Freeh and his colleagues, concluded that Paterno concealed facts relating to Sandusky's sexual abuse of young boys (2012). Although Paterno was one of the most winning college coaches of all time, the NCAA vacated all of Penn State's wins from 1998 through 2011 as part of the court ordered restitution, eliminating 111 of the games Paterno coached and won, dropping him from the record books. We have all witnessed a rapid succession of people falling from grace over the years. This horrific case and its long-term outcomes highlight how people cannot take their eye off the ethics "ball." It also shows how a life-time of success can be destroyed by ignoring the moral elements of ethical decision-making.

Whether your champion was (or is) Jo Paterno, Lance Armstrong, Barry Bonds, Pete Rose or "INSERT NAME HERE," the takeaway lessons from observing the moral failure of others is rarely the supposition that we need to assume more responsibility in our own lives. A sense of externality—*we* are not the problem or the issue—is usually applied. Perhaps a more disturbing point is that we might all begin to lower our expectations for one another. Every time there is a moral lapse that goes public, we have the propensity to relax our ethical outlook.

What if examples of moral failure actually served as a catalyst for building greater moral fortitude in society? Given our current mindset, however, bad news tends to stir public interest, represented by shock, awe and disappointment. We talk about it, and try to discern who is responsible or at fault for the problem. But then we go on with our day. Any concern for morality tends to dissipate because most of us rarely take any action. The fallen hero is the problem/issue, not me/us. The concern for the lack of moral strength and the presence of moral decay never seems to last as an ongoing concern. Nor do we look to see how we might contribute to the problem. Do we use these stories as a lens, a preview to see how we too may be engaged in similar behaviors, letting our desires for money, power, sex or a sense of belonging get the better of us?

There is an inordinate amount of money generated in the sports entertainment industry. Coupled with the perception of the goodness in winning and enjoying competition, we embed a pressure to do so, i.e., win the game, gain market share, boost ratings, increase profits, etc. With such pressures comes added temptation to cheat, cut corners, and/or deliberately break the rules. Sadly, this is now all too frequent material for front page news headlines. It seems as though cheating has become a moving target and the bar for expected ethicality keeps getting lower (not higher). As fans, we are left wondering, what does it even mean to be a good sport?

Take for example the story of the New England Tom Brady, the poster boy of American sports and perhaps pro football's biggest star. He was initially suspended for four regular-season games without pay, found to be deliberately and secretively violating N.F.L. rules (Fig. 12.6). The league also fined the Patriots $1 million and took away two prized future draft picks, saying that both the team and Brady schemed to improperly deflate footballs in the A.F.C. championship game last season on the way to securing New England's fourth Super Bowl victory.

Fig. 12.6 Ethics as a daily deal is how you go about achieving your goals. Image credited to Mike Liu/Shutterstock.com. New England Patriot's Tom Brady handing off to Corey Dillon

As reported in *The New York* Times and *The Washington Post*, deflated footballs were apparently knowingly used in the game, in order to gain an easier grip in the cold and wet conditions (January, 2015). The investigation's findings were disputed, given they suggest a "probability" of unethical wrongdoing, but were lean on proof. Investigators felt that the game in question was not the first and only occasion when this type of activity occurred, with evidence referring to the deflation of footballs before the 2014 season. A judge eventually erased Brady's suspension, but the harm was already done to his reputation, casting doubt on his character and causing some degree of humiliation.

While the investigation determined Brady was most likely aware that team equipment staff members deflated footballs, the Federal District Court judge focused on the narrower question of whether the collective bargaining agreement between the N.F.L. and the players' union gave Goodell the authority to carry out the suspension, and whether Brady was treated fairly during his attempt to overturn the punishment (Belson 2015). The judge did not focus on whether or not Brady had tampered with the game balls, nor did he question the outcome of the game or final Superbowl victory (45–7 Patriots' win). As of October 26, 2015, a 61 page appeal has been filed by the N.F.L, opposing the decision. Goodell stated that the appeal has nothing to do with Patriots' quarterback; rather with the commissioner's power negotiated in the 2011 Collective Bargaining Agreement (Breech 2015).

Both individual players and athletic organizations like the N.F.L. appear to be a crucible for unethical mayhem. This ongoing scandal comes just months after an embarrassing 2014 season in which several prominent players were arrested in connection with domestic abuse and/or child abuse and suspended by the league. While the N.F.L purports to uphold ethical standards, whatever it is doing to promote and ensure fair play and honorable behavior among its members has obviously not been very effective. With Brady being named the most valuable player of the Super Bowl and the Patriots' still holding their win, there is something markedly incongruent, regarding espoused versus lived ethicality in sports.

Regardless of the cause for unethical actions—a sense of hubris, uniqueness or entitlement—through inability, unwillingness, or moral blindness, human beings continue to be fallible. There is no ethical perfection, a point in which we have finally arrived at full moral development. We are all eligible for varying degrees of ethical strength or failure, as people, situations, and contexts emerge, and as physical, mental, emotional and spiritual conditions are managed or ignored. Therefore people—heroes, mentors, friends, colleagues, leaders, or stars can disappoint us.

That's surely the case, with information recently come to light, regarding Bill Cosby's "calculated pursuit of young women, using fame, drugs and deceit" to gain sexual favors (Bowley and Ember 2015) (Fig. 12.7). In court documents obtained by *The New York Times*, the well known entertainer admitted to these actions over 4 days of intense questioning 10 years ago. Cosby describes and defends his

Fig. 12.7 The respect for Bill
Cosby has been shattered.
Image is in the public domain

actions, in a deposition for a lawsuit filed by a young woman who accused him of drugging and molesting her. The reporters on the story explain:

> Even as Mr. Cosby denied he was a sexual predator who assaulted many women, he presented himself in the deposition as an unapologetic, cavalier playboy, someone who used a combination of fame, apparent concern and powerful sedatives in a calculated pursuit of young women — a profile at odds with the popular image he so long enjoyed, that of father figure and public moralist.

Rather than reducing our expectations, however, incidents from downfallen heroes can be reframed as reasons to embolden our own sense of personal responsibility. To be sure, we must all strive to pay attention to our own behavior. And do so with rigorous honesty. This may feel like an unfair burden. After all, you might think, "It's not me on the front page!" But immoral acts represent our own propensity for moral failure; as such, they can become opportunities to help build the kind of society you want to live in, the one you want to pass on to future generations.

The challenge is to inspire your inner core to become your own role model. There is virtue within all of us. Your character strengths await your decision to leverage them, tapping the best of what resides within you. Do you work to build your virtues, striving to see how elements of your core character strengths might be applied to everyday situations or tasks at hand? Is your ego in check? Do you put all your faith in others or strive to be your own role model?

Freedom to Choose

In choosing to improve your best ethical self, there are many ways in which you can broaden and build your moral strength. Despite varied DNA and life experiences, different traits and coming from diverse cultures, belief systems, and societies, one thing we have in common is that people like to have a choice about how they live their lives. Everyone wants the right to freely select how they see things and the freedom to act accordingly. We do not all have this luxury. For those of us in the West, most of us have the ability to exercise our will freely. But we often lose sight of the fact that how we frame our experiences is also a choice. Our brain works by categorizing and creating typologies. To make sense of situations we reference the past and create shortcuts for understanding. These heuristics help us move forward with quicker response-actions. Using "rules of thumb" we quickly make sense of things, form decisions, and get tasks completed. We often leverage these typologies unconsciously, to correlate, make associations, and project causality.

For example, when driving, if I observe the speed limit I won't get a ticket. If I go faster, I will get there sooner and there will be a parking space. If I go too fast, I might not be able to react to a problem on the roadway and might cause unintended harm to others. We build up a repertoire of thought-action strategies using heuristics. While I'm not necessarily thinking about these specifically when I press the gas to go 70 mph in a 65 mph zone, I'm aware of the aforementioned potential implications of my choice to do this. Sometimes these frameworks are accurate, but they often need updating or revision; some may no longer even be valid. We are often unaware of our own biases, assumptions, associations, and stereotyping. For those who come from a more individualistic-centered culture like the United States, we might be offended by categorizations. Many of us like our uniqueness; independence helps to define our American spirit. We also expect the freedom to choose for ourselves and do not like to be told how and what to think. In short, Americans tend to value choice.

Given our desire to have our own way, from burgers to vacations (and everything in between), to cooperate in business we must learn to respect others' views, appreciating their perspectives, and honoring one another's beliefs. This requires tolerance, recognizing that other people's views have value, even if we do not fully understand them. Striving to learn where our shared values reside is a leverage point for getting along and working together. In business, this means we collectively work to embrace an underlying understanding that we will play fair i.e., go by the rules. Herein resides a core problem—people will cheat. Life is not fair because some individuals cheat, giving them an unfair advantage to "win" and prosper. So how can we maintain a desire to do the right thing and be ethical in business when those around us are getting ahead by stepping outside the boundaries, going against the rules, and not abiding by the norm of fair play? It takes a durable commitment to be ethical, if you aspire to "do well and do good" (see Ozcelik et al. 2008). In the short-term cheaters may prosper—in the long-term—ethicality in business enterprise pays off.

What does this commitment to ethics look like in our day-to-day organizational activities? When you move to "do the right thing" do you allow for discovery? Do you consider how your actions may potentially impact others? Do you think about the potential unintended consequences of your actions? Do you use limited resources to achieve your goals, without considering the impact of this use on others? Everything you do has reverberations and implications. Some actions are like the rings you see in a pond after tossing in a stone. They dissipate quickly and are only noticeable immediately after the action. Others actions may have long-term consequences. What you do is experienced and interpreted by others, with repercussions that may be immediate or emerge over time. Do you consider the implications of your actions? Do you think about how your job can influence others? Even when leaders espouse to be doing what seems to be just or even good, like creating jobs, collecting data, or making a quality product, do they consider how their business goals may impinge upon others' ability to make decisions for themselves? Do you engage in activities that are framed as "for the greater good," but are executed in such a manner that they may inadvertently impact others in a negative way? Does your behavior create long-term repercussions for other living beings on the planet?

Wear Your Character

Everything we buy has a heritage; it comes from somewhere. If we link this to our ethical identity, it is important to consider that we display our values in all of our consumer choices. For example, what was the process that created an article you last purchased? If that were visible to others, would you be proud to wear and display that information? When you put something on, are you marketing something that adds to or detracts from society? As hundreds of students walk across campus quads today, the Nike "swoosh" mark is clearly visible on much of their apparel (Fig. 12.8). How many people take the time to realize that the logos they wear not only make a fashion statement, they tell us what you value?

When I ask my students about their perceptions of manufacturers like Nike, they often extol the virtues of the product line. The image and brand are, quite literally, adored by the millennial generation. With free gear regularly being handed out to the young athletes by Nike, why wouldn't they love it? And yet, these young adults rarely seem to care about how the shirts, shoes, and hats they are wearing are made. The case reveals how these shirts, shoes, socks, hats, and other items are often made by someone half their age, working long hours, and at a pay rate well below what they would consider a livable wage (with geographic and economic differences accounted for). Activists targeted Nike because of the ubiquitous nature of their brand. But manufacturing within the garment industry throughout the world remains beset with substandard conditions and practices. Some argue that the creation of employment opportunities for those in need help those who are hungry and have nothing. As such, even substandard wages and conditions work to serve

Fig. 12.8 Nike factory store.
Image is in the public domain

the greater good. Proportionately, the "good" is greater than any harm being done. Others claim that this is simply a cost-saving measure and a tactic to avoid constraints imposed by Western and internationally supported regulatory demands that protect people against abuse and harm (Wokutch 2001; Kristof 2009).

The argument that "something is better than nothing" fails to consider that labor practices may provide opportunity for some measure of modest gain but, over time, create a form of indentured servitude (Powell and Skarbek 2004). After studying supply chain ethics and the broad-scale issues that emerge from this Nike case, I ask my students how they feel about the firm now, having learned more about the practices in the apparel industry. Most of them remain entranced by the brand, based on the many years of marketing dollars spent to convince them that they need Nike to win. Many of my students swear by the brand's link to their own performance, and want to remain loyal to it, regardless of what happens "behind the scenes." Interestingly, most of the students also admit that their stance is selfish. Few students come to realize that what we buy and wear is not just a product or

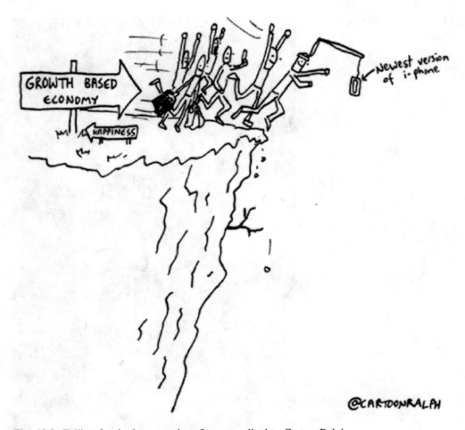

Fig. 12.9 Falling for the latest product. Image credited to CartoonRalph

service: it says something about what we value. In turn, what we buy is an extension of who we are: consumer choices reflect our values.

Startling, and leaving educators of business ethics with a real challenge, is the realization that for many Millennials, products like Apple and Nike are so inextricably linked with their identity that they cannot disentangle themselves from these brands (Fig. 12.9). In dialogue with these young people about care for people and the planet in route to profit, I've been told that, "There just aren't enough pictures and messages that help us believe that it's a real problem." So, is the solution to invest as many media dollars into selling ethics as we do for I-Phones and athletic gear? Occasionally, you'll see an ad from The Foundation for a Better Life (via the *Pass It On* initiative). However, extolling the virtues of living a values-based living is not the norm in advertising.[1] We often hear values

---

[1]See http://www.values.com/.

communicated from major American corporations (e.g., trust, integrity, care). But are they real or just window dressing?

Wal-Mart, Exxon Mobile, Apple, and General Motors were among the top ten revenue-earning firms in the United States in 2013 (CNN Money 2014). Do these companies go beyond compliance as they pursue making huge profits? Do these firms consistently demonstrate values that reflect social responsibility? While they position integrity, honesty, and/or care among their value statements, given that every one of these firms has made recent headlines with a major ethical issue, there is reason to doubt their authenticity (e.g., Wal-Mart Mexico scandal, Exxon Mobile's misleading environmental advertising, Apple and Foxconn, GMs handling of the switch defect, etc.). What price are we willing to pay—potentially at the expense of our ethical core—for a growth-based economy?

Ignoring how firms go about creating and delivering the goods you buy is to consume with blinders on. What you wear—for that matter, everything you buy—is an extension of your identity. These everyday decisions reflect your choices and offer up a statement about who you are in the world. Headlines note that Nike comes out the real winner at the Olympics and Super Bowl, regardless of who claims the prize, medal, or ring. As the outfitter for American athletes, such exposure helps to solidify the brand in the hearts and minds of millions of young sports enthusiasts all over the planet. Nike is associated with skill, winning, and ultimate success. Our notion of success is often defined by those who market to us the most effectively.

Alas, many of our hard earned dollars are spent on products that consider the common good in route to meeting our wants and needs. A lot of our money is spent on products that will supposedly help make us feel better and look good, fulfilling short-term gratifications based upon perceptions that are continually fed to us by the titans of industry. The marketing machine runs 24/7, stoked with messages that compel us to buy products that presumably give us comfort, joy, talent, and a sense of self.

Some firms, like H&M and Primark, are beginning to invest in safer conditions for workers and to ensure that a living wage is paid. Privately held companies like Bechtel, along with a host of publically traded firms, like AMD, Flextronics, Gap, Inc., Google, NetApp, Symantec, Yahoo!, and VISA are making an overt effort to reach out to the next generation of business managers, elevating the importance of ethical performance. Organizational ethics can impose additional costs in time, energy and funding, calling for sustained resource commitments (e.g., employee training and development). Although an ethical strategy requires some investment, it pays off in reputational credit and customer commitment over time. The relenting demands for profit, particularly when shareholder investors expect increased earnings each quarter, reveals how capitalist goals are often wired to produce short-term gains. Who will pay for the ethical performance we want to see? The answer resides within the relationships between firms, suppliers, customers and other stakeholders.

The illusion of ultra-cheap clothing for consumers has been achieved by cutting corners on the rights of other living beings, i.e., the right to perform one's job in safe conditions and being paid a fair wage. Shoppers may choose to ignore the reality of what is behind the merchandise they buy. They can act without shame, remorse, or guilt, because too few of our social norms ignite the moral emotions often necessary for mindful consumerism (reacting with pride or disgust toward ethically/unethically-produced goods or services, respectively). *Why?* Humans have a propensity to be selfish and narcissistic. And the reality is that people are often persuaded by the onslaught of marketing dollars pushed our way, striving to create demand, by affirming how a particular line of clothing (or other product) helps to define us. Our identity is often shaped—who we want to become—by advertising. Marketing can create an image of what sellers want us to perceive as important, worthwhile, or popular. We are told that appearances matter and brands provide us with a particular look that can give us that sense of self and that feeling of belonging to a group, community or a desirable connection.

What's particularly curious is that we pay to be marketed to. The cost of advertising is baked into the cost of goods sold. Worth noting is that we now pay for ads in ways that used to be free. It is essentially impossible to watch television today without cable. As such, we pay for the privilege of being marketed to every time we watch a program. We pay more and more money to have other people tell us what we need to buy, in order to be perceived as a trendy, successful and/or affluent individual or team player. Companies dictate to us what should be deemed relevant, which influence social norms and values, imposing upon us what we should consider relevant, of value, or worth pursuing.

Businesses sustain brand loyalty for unethical goods by executing management strategies that work to ensure consumers do not see the consequences of their purchasing decisions. We all, however, in one way or another, pay a toll for this blind-sighted ignorance. Eventually, someone has to pay for the lack of ethics in our society. In discussing the potential costs imposed by social responsibility in business, an editor at the Ethical Corporation, Mallen Baker says, "If customers are so used to low prices that they won't accept the change—well, whose fault is that?" (Baker 2013). Consumers will hopefully wake up to the fact that they have to take responsibility for their actions. Buying ethically sound products is like taking out a little bit of insurance, insurance in your children's—mankind's—future. When we learn to produce and purchase goods and services in a way that reflects equity and respect, both for people and the planet we inhabit, we will have earned the right to be proud of our evolutionary development as a society, culture, and as a species in largess.

When people take less ownership of exercising their character strengths and virtues, they run the risk of moral decline. In the West, we have come to expect the privilege of free choice. But to maintain this freedom, we need to be engaged, alert, aware, and assume responsibility for the ethical elements within our daily decisions. Do you consciously stay engaged, rigorously working to safeguard that you act in a morally responsible manner? Having the freedom and privilege to conduct business in an open capitalistic market assumes that there is an associated duty to engage in commerce in a socially responsible manner (Watkins 2003). In a free market society, with power and wealth comes an even greater responsibility to be ethical. As an employee, manager, and/or leader are you self-directing your personal, professional, and organizational development in this light? How do you continually work to achieve your personal and organizational goals in an ethical and moral manner?

Ethics Is a Daily Deal

As we come to a close, let's take a moment to reflect on what has been presented. While the entire book can be summed up by simply saying: "Just do the right thing!", if it were that easy we would be talking about something else. The fact of the matter is that being ethical is not always easy. Being ethical at work takes work. This effort pays well and in many forms, but not necessarily immediately. It requires a commitment to exercise your moral strength, even when you may not be certain of a particular return. The irony is that to have moral strength in business, you have to live your values—not just when it is convenient—but all day every day. To own and develop your ethical identity requires taking the bull by the horns and owing responsibility for your decisions and actions.

To understand business ethics on a practical level, the first three chapters considered how each person is the starting point. What you care about, how you direct and assert your power, and what you do on a daily basis depicts your identity. Waking up and paying attention to your truth, genuinely taking an honest look at yourself, noting how we are all vulnerable to our own self-deceptions is essential to personal growth. Taking your self-awareness forward, I outlined the ethical decision-making process, pointing out where the lack of knowing how to sustain a desire to be ethical can potentially knock you off the moral path. To ensure that your commitment to ethics is sustained, building moral strength is about professional moral courage. Courage in the workplace is supported by specific skills sets —moral competencies—that can be developed in most people. Suggestions for how to effectively build moral strength in the workplace is an important aspect of organizational life. Ethics education and training is not just about compliance and how to prevent or avoid unethical issues. Rather, adult moral development is about helping people to see how their experiences can foster ongoing learning (Fig. 12.10). When individuals begin to exercise their character strengths in achieving their personal and professional goals, ethics becomes inculcated into how business is actually conducted.

Throughout the book we considered how your ethical character is reflected by the choices you make each day. These decisions, regardless of whether they are deliberate, well thought out determinations, or simply automatic reactions to circumstances, influence our behavioral responses. Everyday actions mold our character over time. Given we all face a variety of issues, challenges, and changing circumstances in our organizational lives, there is a steady stream of opportunity to be more or less ethical and moral on a regular basis. We may choose to turn away, or just ignore the potential to exercise our best self. Some of us may follow the rules, policies, and codes that align our decisions and actions with legal compliance.

Fig. 12.10 Students engage in experiential learning activities to study ethical consumerism. Image courtesy of Leslie E. Sekerka

The former is to shirk responsibility and the later is but a bare moral minimum. These same situations also present platforms for opportunity, where we can choose to work toward building our moral strength. If we say we have a desire to be ethical, we must build our moral muscle through ongoing practice. The concept of ethics as a "daily deal" is a way to remind us that we all start fresh, begin anew, and must recommit to being ethical and moral every day of our lives. This means taking charge of advancing your own moral development.

Integrating ethics into business performance indubitably creates a rift that must be addressed by each employee. There will never be a level playing field, as cheaters can make gains and life is rarely fair. Thus, metaphorically speaking, when the drive to succeed in business is combined with personal and organizational character strength, a rather paradoxical coupling emerges. In this marriage, one half of the partnership seeks to command a win, often pushing for gains that can be made as quickly as possible. The other half is mindful, considers others, adopts a longer-term perspective, and is, in some cases, motivated to do the right thing without the need for affirmation or measured gain (virtue as its own reward). Seeking a balance between these two forces is a cornerstone for business ethics, reflecting a shared effort to survive, engage, interact, and evolve as individuals and as organizations that reflect our humanity in community (Fig. 12.11).

As adults, we have rehearsed our biases and reinforced our preferences for years. Many of us, especially those in business, allow automaticity to run our lives without paying attention and applying deliberate care. We forget (or have decided not to) place value on an ongoing consideration of how the lack of ethics in our daily lives can contribute to our own moral decay. Like a slow process of erosion, this deficit

Fig. 12.11 Corporate leaders reach out to college students, emphasizing global ethics in business education. Image credited to Menlo College, with special thanks to Andy Hinton and Marie Wilson (Google and Symantec; respectively)

of attention toward exercising moral strength can reduce the dexterity of our moral character. Moreover, a lackadaisical regard for ethics in our business dealings can interfere with our desire and willingness to grow—to be better today than we were yesterday. Regardless of your starting point, adult change and development is possible. The choice is yours.

My hope is that from the points and examples brought forward in this book, I have challenged you to be more aware of your ethical identity. Taking this on means getting honest about how you apply and live the values you say you hold. Perhaps something within this text has reawakened your desire to be better than you are right now, sparking a willingness to examine your thoughts and actions on a more regular basis. To experience the best in life, we must start by examining and improving ourselves, continually striving to become the best person we were meant to be and become. *That's the daily deal.*

Takeaway Points

1. Adults can change through learning, growth, and development.
2. Identify role models, but recognize that people, even ethical ones, can fail. Strive to be your own role model.
3. Pay attention to your daily decisions, taking ownership for the ethical elements embedded within them.
4. Moral development requires having a desire to become your best self, then making a commitment to achieving growth through practice as a daily goal.
5. Being ethical is a moral minimum; moral strength means choosing to become your best self on a daily basis.

Reflection Questions

How do you enact your ethical identity in your daily task actions, both at work and at home? How are your character strengths demonstrated in all of the various roles you assume in life?

References

Aristotle [350BC]. (1999). *Nicomachean ethics.* T. Irwin (Trans.) Indianapolis, IN: Hackett Publishing Co.

Baker, M. (2013). *Gathering storm of shopper choice.* Retrieved February 4, 2014, from http://www.ethicalcorp.com.

Belson, K. (2015). *Judge Erases Tom Brady's Suspension; N.F.L. Says It Will Appeal. The New York Times.* Retrieved September 5, 2015 from http://www.nytimes.com/2015/09/04/sports/football/tom-brady-suspension-deflategate.html.

Breakwell, G. M. (1986). *Coping with threatened identities.* New York: Metheun.

Breech, J. (2015). Goodell: *NFL's Deflategate appeal has 'nothing to do' with Tom Brady, CBS Sports.* Retrieved on November 8, 2015, from http://www.cbssports.com/nfl/eye-on-football/25356719/goodell-nflsdeflategate-appeal-has-nothing-to-do-with-tom-brady

Brooks, D. (2015). The small, happy life, *The New York Times*. Retrieved June 5, 2015, from http://www.nytimes.com/2015/05/29/opinion/david-brooks-the-small-happy-life.html?WT.mc_ev=click&WT.mc_id=NYT-E-I-NYT-E-AT-060415-L13&nl=el&nlid=19197202.

Bowley, G., & Ember, S. (2015). Bill Cosby Deposition Reveals Calculated Pursuit of Young Women, Using Fame, Drugs and Deceit, *The New York Times*, Retrieved July 18, 2015, from https://mail.google.com/mail/u/0/?tab=wm#inbox/14ea3b8c2eb41795.

CNN Money. (2014). *Fortune 500*. Retrieved May 6, 2014, from http://money.cnn.com/magazines/fortune/fortune500/.

Freeh, L. J, Sporkin, S., & Sullivan, E. R. (2012). *Report of the special investigative counsel regarding the actions of the Pennsylvania State University related to the child sexual abuse committed by Gerald A. Sandusky*. Retrieved July 13, 2012, from http://www.freehsporkinsullivan.com/news/23.

Kristof, N. D. (2009). Where sweatshops are a dream, *The New York Times*. Retrieved February 1, 2014, from http://www.nytimes.com/2009/01/15/opinion/15kristof.html.

Lapowsky, I. (2014). Livestrong without Lance. *Slate* (Moneybox). Retrieved January 16, 2015, from http://www.slate.com/blogs/moneybox/2014/04/01/lance_armstrong_livestrong_how_the_charity_came_back_from_the_scandal.html.

MSN Money. (2009). *Rags to riches CEOs*. Retrieved March 26, 2014, from http://money.ca.msn.com/investing/gallery/gallery.aspx?cp-documentid=22633418&page=4.

Murtagh, N., Gatersleben, B., & Uzzell, D. (2012). Self-identity threat and resistance to change: Evidence from regular travel behaviour. *Journal of Environmental Psychology, 32*(4), 318–326.

Oxford English Dictionary (2013). Retrieved December 19, 2013, from http://www.oed.com/.

Ozcelik, H., Langton, N., & Aldrich, H. (2008). Doing well and doing good: The relationship between leadership practices that facilitate a positive emotional climate and organizational performance. *Journal of Managerial Psychology, 23*, 186–203.

Powell, B., & Skarbek, D. (2004). Sweatshops and third world living standards: Are the jobs worth the sweat? *Independent Institute Working Paper, 53*.

Rathus, S. A. (2008). *Psychology: Concepts and connections (brief version)* (8th ed.). Belmont, CA: Thomson Wadsworth.

Reynolds, S. J., & Ceranic, T. L. (2007). The effects of moral judgment and moral identity on moral behavior: An empirical examination of the moral individuals. *Journal of Applied Psychology, 92*(6), 1610–1624.

Schlegel, A. A., Rudelson, J. J., & Tse, P. U. (2012). White matter structure changes as adults learn a second language no access. *Journal of Cognitive Neuroscience, 24*(8), 1664–1670.

Sherman, N. (1991). *The fabric of character, Aristotle's theory of virtue*. New York: Oxford University Press.

USADA. (2012). Lance Armstrong receives lifetime ban and disqualification of competitive results for doping violations stemming from his involvement in the United States Postal Service pro-cycling team doping conspiracy. Retrieved January 16, 2015, from http://www.usada.org/lance-armstrong-receives-lifetime-ban-and-disqualification-of-competitive-results-for-doping-violations-stemming-from-his-involvement-in-the-united-states-postal-service-pro-cycling-team-doping-conspi/.

van den Putte, B., Yzer, M., Willemsen, M. C., & de Bruijn, G. (2009). The effects of smoking self-identity and quitting self-identity on attempts to quit smoking. *Health Psychology, 28*(5), 535–544.

Watkins, S. (2003). Ethical conflicts at Enron: Moral responsibility in corporate capitalism. *California Management Review, 45*(4), 6–19.

Wokutch, R. E. (2001). Nike and its critics: Beginning a dialogue. *Organization and Environment, 14*(2), 207–237.